Fodor's Family

NEW YORK CITY WITH KIDS

1st Edition

Where to Stay and Eat for All Budgets

Must-See Sights and Local Secrets

Ratings You Can Trust

Excerpted from *Fodor's New York City*

Fodor's Travel Publications New York, Toronto, London, Sydney, Auckland

www.fodors.com

FODOR'S FAMILY NEW YORK CITY WITH KIDS

Editor: Maria Teresa Hart
Writer: Meryl Pearlstein

Production Editor: Astrid deRidder
Editorial Contributors: Lynne Arany, Alexander Basek, Nina Callaway, Jay Cheshes, Michelle Delio, Michael de Zayas, Adam Kowit, Sandra Ramani, Jacqueline Terrebonne
Maps & Illustrations: David Lindroth, Mark Stroud, *cartographers*; Bob Blake and Rebecca Baer, *map editors;* William Wu, *information graphics*
Design: Fabrizio LaRocca, *creative director*; Guido Caroti, *art director*; Ann McBride, *designer*; Melanie Marin, *senior picture editor*
Cover Photo: top, Judie Long/age fotostock; bottom, Photodisc/Alamy
Production Manager: Amanda Bullock

SPECIAL SALES

This book is available for special discounts for bulk purchases for sales promotions or premiums. Special editions, including personalized covers, excerpts of existing books, and corporate imprints, can be created in large quantities for special needs. For more information, write to Special Markets/Premium Sales, 1745 Broadway, MD 6-2, New York, New York, NY 10019, or e-mail specialmarkets@randomhouse.com.

AN IMPORTANT TIP & AN INVITATION

Although all prices, opening times, and other details in this book are based on information supplied to us at press time, changes occur all the time in the travel world, and Fodor's cannot accept responsibility for facts that become outdated or for inadvertent errors or omissions. **So always confirm information when it matters,** especially if you're making a detour to visit a specific place. Your experiences—positive and negative—matter to us. If we have missed or misstated something, **please write to us.** We follow up on all suggestions. Contact the New York City with Kids editor at editors@fodors.com or c/o Fodor's at 1745 Broadway, New York, NY 10019.

PRINTED IN THE UNITED STATES OF AMERICA

10 9 8 7 6 5 4 3

Be a Fodor's Correspondent

Your opinion matters. It matters to us. It matters to your fellow Fodor's travelers, too. And we'd like to hear it. In fact, we *need* to hear it. When you share your experiences and opinions, you become an active member of the Fodor's community. Here's how you can help improve Fodor's for all of us.

Tell us when we're right. We rely on local writers to give you an insider's perspective. But our writers and staff editors also depend on you. Your positive feedback is a vote to renew our recommendations for the next edition.

Tell us when we're wrong. We update most of our guides every year. But things change. If any of our descriptions are inaccurate or inadequate, we'll incorporate your changes in the next edition and will correct factual errors at fodors.com *immediately*.

Tell us what to include. You probably have had fantastic travel experiences that aren't yet in Fodor's. Why not share them with a community of like-minded travelers? Share your discoveries and experiences with everyone directly at fodors.com. Your input may lead us to add a new listing or a higher recommendation.

Give us your opinion instantly at our feedback center at www.fodors.com/feedback. You may also e-mail editors@fodors.com with the subject line "New York City with Kids Editor." Or send your nominations, comments, and complaints by mail to New York City with Kids Editor, Fodor's, 1745 Broadway, New York, NY 10019.

Happy Traveling!

Tim Jarrell, Publisher

CONTENTS

ABOUT
THIS BOOK

Our Ratings

We wouldn't recommend a place that wasn't worth your time, but sometimes a place is so experiential that superlatives don't do it justice: you just have to be there to know. These sights, properties, and experiences get our highest rating, **Fodor's Choice**, indicated by orange stars throughout this book. Black stars highlight sights and properties we deem **Highly Recommended**, places that our writers, editors, and readers praise again and again for consistency and excellence.

Credit Cards

Want to pay with plastic? **AE, D, DC, MC, V** after restaurant and hotel listings indicate whether American Express, Discover, Diners Club, MasterCard, and Visa are accepted.

Restaurants

Unless we state otherwise, restaurants are open for lunch and dinner daily. We mention dress only when there's a specific requirement and reservations only when they're essential or not accepted—it's always best to book ahead.

Hotels

Unless we tell you otherwise, you can assume that the hotels have private bath, phone, TV, and air-conditioning. We always list facilities but not whether you'll be charged an extra fee to use them, so when pricing accommodations, find out what's included.

Many Listings
★ Fodor's Choice
★ Highly recommended
⊠ Physical address
✛ Directions
⌖ Mailing address
☎ Telephone
🖷 Fax
⊕ On the Web
✉ E-mail
✍ Admission fee
☉ Open/closed times
Ⓜ Metro stations
▭ Credit cards

Hotels & Restaurants
🏨 Hotel
↵ Number of rooms
♨ Facilities
⎢⎢⎢ Meal plans
✕ Restaurant
✍ Reservations
↘ Smoking

Outdoors
⛳ Golf
⛺ Camping

Other
⇨ See also
⊠ Branch address
☞ Take note

WHEN TO GO

New York City weather is a study in extremes. Much of winter brings bone-chilling winds and an occasional snowfall, but you're just as likely to experience mild afternoons sandwiched by cool temperatures. You'll want to venture into Central Park or onto a playground, no matter what the temperature. If you're sitting in a hansom carriage, they'll throw a blanket over you, but if you decide to join the throngs of kids sledding down Cedar Hill, you'll need to dress as if you were on the slopes. In late spring and early summer, streets fill with parades. A light fleece is what you'll need and a packable raincoat. April showers definitely bring May flowers—this is what makes Central Park the true beauty it is when the trees burst into gorgeous color. July–August is another thing. While everyone seems to be outdoors once it gets warmer, sunshine can mean increasing humidity. Bring light clothes for the steamy subway stations but something to cover up when air-conditioners take over. Summertime experiences an exodus of locals that seems to coincide more and more with an influx of international visitors.

September is stunning yellow-and-bronze foliage, the dawn of crisper breezes, and a new cultural season. Kids go back to school, so while early morning can be a wonderfully quiet time to bring your preschool age tots to a museum, they'll be part of the younger scene after 3 PM when playgrounds fill to capacity. Fall temperatures fluctuate from coolish to Indian summer and can soar into the 80s even into October. Schedule around the major holidays, and you'll have more of the city to yourself and at better prices. But if you can't, many parents swear the magic to be had at Christmas and New Year's is worth the expense. Just watch the gleam in your kids' eyes when they see the dancing dolls in the department store windows.

BAD WEATHER PLANS

When dreadful weather strikes, a family visiting NYC needs an accessible destination that can approximate a home base for the entire day. Temperatures in the city can be a study in extremes when it tops 80° or falls below 30°. Wet weather doesn't frighten New Yorkers—but umbrella entanglement and wet feet means you're better off inside. On such days, when it's too hot, too cold, or just too wet, you need an indoor activity everyone can enjoy.

Chelsea Piers. Here's a sports village guaranteed to keep you busy all day with lots of drop-in programs. Little ones can run and jump themselves silly at the Toddler Adventure Center. Older kids and adults can climb a rock wall, improve their batting skills, find a pick-up basketball or soccer game, or play arcade games while they bowl. And, yes, bowling lanes have bumpers so all ages can knock down pins. Not enough? You can roller skate, ice-skate, walk the balance beam, or even grab a mother–daughter manicure at the spa. Manhattan's largest brewery with its river-facing restaurant and kids' corner will keep you energized. A word of caution: in bad weather, you might need to wait for a bus outdoors if there are no taxis.

Times Square. Although spending a day here involves moving from one place to another, you can concentrate on a few activities and stay inside 95% of the time. Some are actually interconnected with kid-friendly restaurants and escalators. Ripley's Believe It or Not sits next to Madame Tussauds. Two mega-movieplexes face each other and there's an arcade to beat all arcades, Dave and Busters, where adults can challenge each other at trivia while kids play all sorts of video and sports games. If culture's more your thing, the New Victory and New Amsterdam theaters are both awesome for families. Keep the boots, raincoats, and umbrellas handy for the two-minute mad dashes this day might require.

American Museum of Natural Science/Rose Center for Earth and Space. Dinosaurs? That's a start. But the classic wildlife dioramas shouldn't be missed. Nor should the Hall of Gems, the rooms of animals, butterflies that land on you, and the terrific food court that really understands kids … and that's before you even venture to the Rose Center. The planetarium show is always enlightening as are the nature movies shown in the IMAX theater. Since you'll have extra time, you can buy tickets for some of the special exhibits: they're usually terrific and most offer timed admissions so you can schedule a movie, lunch, the exhibit and see T. rex, too.

TOP ATTRACTIONS

New York is virtually stuffed with fun activities that can keep you and your kids busy day and night. Here we've tried to cherry-pick ones that make this place a wonderland for the young.

A Day & a Night in the Museum. The hands-down favorite for both visiting and local kids, the American Museum of Natural History could entertain most children for a full week. Trust us, the dinosaurs alone are worth the trip, as is the live seasonal Butterfly Conservatory. There's also an IMAX theater with great nature and science movies, ancient-culture displays, and wildlife dioramas with taxidermied creatures that hit the right mix of fascinating and creepy. And with some planning you can even sleep over under the giant blue whale.

Good Morning Starshine. The appropriately space-age Hayden Planetarium at the Rose Center for Earth and Space is a big bang with kids. It's part of the American Museum of Natural History, but planetarium tickets are sold separately. Kids learning about the solar system will love walking under realistic models of the planets and stars along the Scales of the Universe walkway. Older kids can rock out at the SonicVision light show with music mixed by Moby.

From Lions & Tigers to Cockroaches & Ants. Every borough in New York City has at least one zoo. The country's largest metropolitan wildlife park, the Bronx Zoo, is home to more than 4,000 animals, including endangered and threatened species. Kids will come face-to-face (almost) with gorillas and tigers and adjust to the nocturnal rooms in the World of Darkness. Madagascar's cockroaches add a new dimension as do the ants at the Central Park Zoo. There, you'll also see the playful penguins and polar bears, and watch sea lions slurp their fish before heading over to the Tisch Children's Zoo. Both Central Park zoos are manageable in size for even the youngest of zoo goers.

Seashells, Strikeouts & Sharks by the Seashore. Alongside the creaky amusement park rides and boardwalk beachfront of Coney Island, the New York Aquarium gives another close-up look at the denizens of the deep, more than 10,000 marine species such as sand-tiger sharks and sea otters. From there it's a short trip to Keyspan Park where the Brooklyn Cyclones play in a blissfully intimate setting. Top it off with a yummy Nathan's hot dog with ocean breezes at your back.

Back to the Future. The entry line to get into the futuristic fantasy world at the free Sony Wonder Technology Laboratory is often long. But don't worry—a talking robot will keep your kids entertained while they wait. Inside, there are image-and-sound labs where kids can record their own digital music, make movies, and play games. On every floor, kids swipe their own encoded pass card, which flashes their picture and a voiceprint. It's great high-tech fun.

Water, Water Everywhere. New York has a strong port heritage with lots of boats for the exploring. At the South Street Seaport, kids climb onto the historic lightship, which has an actual lighthouse on top, or set sail on a classic tall ship for a leisurely tour of the harbor. Thrill seekers will want to jump aboard the high-speed Shark or the Beast to zip by the Statue of Liberty and howl into the wind, while others might find the Staten Island Ferry to be more their pace. Although stationary, the *Intrepid* naval carrier and the *Growler* submarine are equally fascinating. A completely different view of the city's attractions comes when on the water. Sail it, ferry it, or (Water) Taxi it—set sail and you'll see.

Get Art Smart. You could visit a museum every day and never run out of options. But with the inexpensive children's admission and—even better—the moments when tickets are free, go ahead and pick a variety of museums for as much or as little time as the kids can han-dle. Workshops tailored for kids at even the most sophisticated of the city's museums are great for instilling a passion about the visual arts. Museums that target kids specifically will let them smudge, wipe, stroke and prepare to be the next Jackson Pollock.

Lights, Camera & the Statue of Liberty. The bright lights of Times Square and the colorful tops of Manhattan's many buildings are probably what elicit the most oohs and aahs from kids of all ages. There are lots of ways to see them, too. A dusk Circle Line cruise around Manhattan skirts by the Statue of Liberty and shows off her lighted-up torch and the illuminated bridges and buildings. From atop the Empire State Building or the Top of the Rock at Rockefeller Center, a magical moment occurs at dusk when the lights blink on throughout the city.

WHAT'S WHERE

1 Lower Manhattan. Serious sightseeing all around: Wall Street and Financial District, historic South Street Seaport, ferries to Ellis Island, Governors Island, and the Statue of Liberty, Ground Zero, the Brooklyn Bridge, Battery Park City esplanade, and Hudson River Park and playgrounds can exhaust you with options.

2 Chinatown & Little Italy. A touristy immersion into Chinese and Italian culture: Chinese herb shops, lots of restaurants, bubble teas and bizarre markets, Italian cafés, gelaterias, and cheap shops keep families happily exploring.

3 SoHo, NoLita & TriBeCa. Fashionistas, foodies, and artists: those in the know come here for trendy shopping and dining. But don't miss SoHo's striking cast-iron buildings, the Children's Museum of the Arts, or the Fire Museum for family fun.

4 The East Village & the Lower East Side. Here's the stomping ground for Punks and Goths. Teens and tweens love St. Marks Place and "Alphabet City" (avenues A, B, C, and D). But kids of all ages dig Tompkins Square Park's dog runs, the illuminating Lower East Side Tenement Museum, and Eldridge Street Synagogue.

5 Greenwich Village. The Village is a mélange of NYU students, young families, and musicians along winding streets. Hit Washington Square Park on a good day to see every resident spill out of their apartment for a day in the sunshine. The scene is B.Y.O.D. (bring your own dog).

6 Chelsea. Center of Manhattan's gay community and art scene, Chelsea also has scores of ethnic restaurants and the wonderful Chelsea Piers sports complex.

7 Union Square, Murray Hill & Gramercy. Catch the superb greenmarket at busy Union Square Park, or hit the urban heights of the Empire State Building. Wonderful big-store and boutique shopping can be had here, or soak up the peaceful, residential Murray Hill and Gramercy Park.

WHAT'S WHERE

8 Times Square & Midtown West. Broadway theaters, neon signs, over-the-top arcades and attractions—this is what people picture when they think of NYC. But break away to 9th Avenue for cheap eats or the Time Warner Center for shopping, great snacks, and a lovely view of the park.

9 Rockefeller Center & Midtown East. Put on some comfortable shoes! The attractions go on for blocks here: Rockefeller Center, swanky 5th Avenue shops, St. Patrick's Cathedral, the New York Public Library, Grand Central Terminal, and the Chrysler Building are just a few.

10 The Upper East Side. Museum Mile brings most visitors this way (the Met and the Guggenheim, among others sit here). You can also find the small Central Park Zoo, Carl Schurz Park, and Madison Avenue shopping.

11 The Upper West Side. It's a different pace here—the neighborhoods are residential with lots of strolling families. Check out the Children's Museum, Central Park and Riverside Park, the American Museum of Natural History, and Lincoln Center on a summer night chockablock with swing dancers.

12 Harlem. This center of African-American and Hispanic-American culture is undergoing a renaissance. You'll find lovely brownstones, gospel brunches, stick-to-your-ribs soul food, and the Museo del Barrio among other highlights.

13 Brooklyn & the Outer Boroughs. Great fun is had outside Manhattan. Brooklyn's got Coney Island, Prospect Park, Brooklyn Botanic Gardens. The Bronx boasts Yankee Stadium, Arthur Avenue (aka the real Little Italy), and the Bronx Zoo. Queens is a great parade of ethnic restaurants: Greek, Indian, Caribbean, Indian. And Staten Island has its magical ferry ride.

W. 120th St.

Marcus Garvey Park

E. 121st St.

HARLEM
12

MORNINGSIDE HEIGHTS

W. 112th St.   Morningside Park   W. 113rd St.
W. 110th St.   W. 111th St.

EAST HARLEM

E. 115th St.

E. 110th St.

E. 109th St.

Harlem Meer

E. 107th St.

W. 108th St.
W. 106th St.
W. 104th St.   **11** UPPER WEST SIDE
W. 102nd St.

E. 106th St.
E. 103rd St.
E. 101st St.
E. 99th St.

W. 100th St.
W. 98th St.

E. 97th St.

W. 96th St.
W. 94th St.
W. 92nd St.
W. 90th St.
W. 88th St.

Jacqueline Kennedy Onassis Reservoir

E. 95th St.
E. 93rd St.
E. 91st St.
E. 89th St.

YORKVILLE

Riverside Park

E. 87th St.
E. 86th St.

W. 86th St.
W. 84th St.
W. 82nd St.
W. 80th St.
W. 78th St.

CENTRAL PARK

E. 85th St.
E. 83rd St.
E. 81st St.
E. 79th St.

American Museum of Natural History

Metropolitan Museum of Art

W. 76th St.
W. 74th St.
W. 72nd St.
W. 70th St.

The Lake

E. 77th St.
E. 75th St.
E. 73rd St.

E. 71st St.
E. 69th St.
E. 67th St.
E. 65th St.
E. 63rd St.
E. 61st St.

10 UPPER EAST SIDE

E. 72nd St.

W. 68th St.
W. 66th St.
W. 64th St.

Lincoln Center

W. 62nd St.
W. 61st St.

E. 64th St.
E. 62nd St.

Queensboro Br.

W. 59th St.
Columbus Circle
W. 57th St.
W. 55th St.

Central Park S.
E. 59th St.

E. 57th St.
E. 55th St.
E. 53rd St.
E. 51st St.
E. 49th St.

MIDTOWN

8
E. 54th St.

W. 52nd St.
W. 50th St.
W. 48th St.
W. 46th St.

Rockefeller Center

9
E. 47th St.

TUDOR CITY

13

W. 44th St.
W. 42nd St.
W. 40th St.

Port Authority Bus Terminal

TIMES SQUARE

E. 45th St.
E. 43rd St.
E. 41st St.

Grand Central Terminal

MURRAY HILL

Javits Convention Center

GARMENT DISTRICT

W. 38th St.
W. 36th St.
W. 34th St.
W. 32nd St.

Public Library

Empire State Building

Madison Square Garden

Penn Station

Herald Square

0   1/4 miles

0   400 meters

Hudson River

Riverside Dr.
West Side Highway
Eleventh Ave.
Tenth Ave.
Ninth Ave.
Eighth Ave.
Seventh Ave.
Broadway
Avenue of the Americas (Sixth Ave.)
Fifth Ave.
Madison Ave.
Park Ave.
Lexington Ave.
Third Ave.
Second Ave.
First Ave.
FDR Dr.

West End Ave.
Amsterdam Ave.
Columbus Ave.
Central Park W.
Manhattan Ave.
Central Park W.
6th Ave.
Broadway

IF YOUR KID LIKES

Dinosaurs

These thunderous prehistoric creatures still roam Manhattan in force, much to the delight of dino fanatics. Check out the dinosaur fossils at the American Museum of Natural History. Unlike other museums that display casts, the fossils here are the real bones put together as real dinosaurs. In the Discovery Room kids can actually touch some of the fossils and artifacts from the museum's vast collection. The gift shop lets you take home your own personal fossil with toys from plush Triceratops to sparks-shooting T-Rex. If that's not enough, the labyrinthine FAO Schwarz stocks various dino-theme playthings and the Times Square Toys "R" Us immediately conjures up *Jurassic Park* with a giant animatronic T. rex. For a more intimate post-prehistoric toy experience head to the toy and clothes boutique Dinosaur Hill, named after these powerful creatures but selling so much more.

Techno Gadgets

Growing up in the age of the Internet means many kids acknowledge the entertainment value of modern technology and are fascinated with the circuitry behind the screen. The Sony Wonder Technology Lab indulges future programmers with their chance to create their own video and musical fun. A special key pass to enter the exhibits projects their picture at every stop along with their own voiceprint. As an encore, the Museum of the Moving Image allows kids to peek into the process of making movies and television shows. Interactive exhibits let kids dub their voices into film clips, tweak sound effects, or dance around in front of a green screen loaded with different moving backgrounds. When they've grown weary of playing director or with the video games in the museum's arcade, they can succumb to a dose of commercial technomania and experiment with gadgets at the city's mega-electronic palaces: Sony Style, the Apple Stores, or Nintendo World.

The Princess Treatment

For many little girls, New York City conjures up images of Eloise, the precocious Plaza-living little lady who received the royal treatment wherever she went. For more of the same, your own princess can do high tea at Alice's Tea Cup surrounded by ephemeral butterflies or have a date with her doll at the American Girl Café where precious and cute are the name of the game. Shopping at tween girl faves like Juicy, Miss Sixty, and Paul Frank add some haute couture and ensure a well-dressed presence at cool-girl evenings watching the Radio City Music Hall Rockettes, *Mamma Mia,* or *The Little Mermaid* musicals, or the dazzling arabesques of the Nutcracker at the New York City Ballet. Older princesses can get a dose of *Gossip Girl* by visiting the Palace Hotel, Serena's ersatz home.

A View from Above

Soaring over Manhattan in a helicopter may be too much for most kids to deal with (and also way too expensive) but there are lots of other bird's-eye views to be had. A free walk over the Brooklyn Bridge puts you smack above the center of the East River with dazzling views of both Manhattan and neighboring Brooklyn at both ends. The highest viewing point in Manhattan, the Empire State Building, gives a thrilling look downward onto the streets and "ants" below. Top of the Rock feeds on this by adding a dramatic view of the Empire State Building itself. A less intense but equally great view can be had from the top floors of the Time Warner Building or from the lobby level of the Mandarin Oriental Hotel in Columbus Circle. Climbing to the top of Belvedere Castle or to the roof of the Metropolitan Museum of Art shows off the enormity of Central Park. For the bravest of all, trying out the trapeze next to the Hudson River may yield the Big Apple's ultimate view as you fly through the air.

The Weird & the Kooky

Manhattan has its share of fun theme-y places for kids. Restaurants of this ilk aren't known for their food but the special effects at Jekyll & Hyde or Mars 2112 will knock their socks off (if they don't terrify them). Odditoriums like Ripley's Believe It or Not or Madame Tussauds will create conversation pieces to last throughout your visit. The Whispering Gallery at Grand Central Terminal, or the crazy assortment of little people sculptures in the 14th Street subway station at 8th Avenue proves that all things weird and wonderful can be spotted all over New York City.

Bright Lights & Action

New York is a force to reckon with when it comes to color and energy. The hub, of course, is Times Square. High-definition electronic billboards hawk everything from Coca-Cola to sexy underwear. Stock market results and news flashes slither around building facades, and much larger-than-life M&Ms and Cup Noodles add blasts of color and movement everywhere. Theater marquees, stores bedecked in lights, and buildings frosted on top with changing colors or inventive light towers seem to never switch off. It's definitely worth keeping the kids up late one night.

FOR FREE

If you think everything in New York costs too much, well, you're right—almost. In fact, the city has tons of free attractions and activities; you just need to know where to look for them. Choose from our list of favorite freebies for families.

Walk across the Brooklyn Bridge (or part of it) for a spectacular view of the Financial District, Brooklyn, the seaport, and Manhattan.

Ride the Staten Island ferry (and back) to see the Statue of Liberty, Ellis Island, and the southern tip of Manhattan from the water.

Catch a free outdoor movie screening in Bryant Park (Manhattan) or at the Socrates Sculpture Garden (Queens) in summertime.

Wander Battery Park City's waterfront promenade; the breeze, fun parks and playgrounds, and passing boats will make you forget you're in the gritty city, though the view of the Statue of Liberty will remind you that you couldn't be anywhere but New York.

Watch wannabe trapeze artists swing and soar at the Trapeze School New York along the Hudson River at Pier 40.

Go catch-and-release fishing at Harlem Meer with free poles and bait to borrow from the Dana Discovery Center.

Taste the treats at the Union Square greenmarket (Monday, Wednesday, Friday, Saturday), where farmers offer samples of organically grown produce, hand-pressed ciders, artisanal cheeses, and fresh bread.

Stroll the Coney Island boardwalk and play on the beach for some old-school kitsch. Annual free events here include the outrageous Mermaid Parade and the July 4 hot-dog-eating contest.

Check out the street performers around New York's parks: breakdancers in Union Square and by Central Park's Bethesda Fountain, nutty unicyclists in Washington Square, and Statue of Liberty clones in Battery Park.

Smell the cherry blossoms in spring at the Central Park Conservatory; or visit any other time for gorgeous, gorgeous flowers, and idyllic gardens.

Attend a storytelling hour at one of the city's kid-friendly bookstores like Barnes & Noble, Borders, or Books of Wonder. FAO Schwarz has them, too.

Exploring
Manhattan

WORD OF MOUTH

"My daughter LOVES going to the top of the Empire State building. We all love a ride on the old fashioned carousel in Central Park or a paddle boat ride on the pond. Check out the schedule for the Park—they do a lot of free summer concerts especially geared towards kids. We also love the dinosaurs and the Planetarium at the Natural History museum."

—Fetch_fenway

SURPRISE: NEW YORK CITY IS one of the most child-friendly cities in the world. For some, that's less believable than a Kung-Fu panda. After all, how could a city like this, a city that never sleeps, be somewhere that kids could fit in and have a blast? But that's the trick. In this city that's a mere 23.7 square mi total, there's something for everyone, at every age. New York City, as we modestly say, is the center of the universe, which means it attracts and caters to all sorts of diverse groups—including families. Kids of all ages fit right in. They live here, they visit here, and they return again and again to the giant toy box of New York City and all its diversions. Home to 8,214,426 residents who represent every nation in the world, NYC is a multicultural capital of style, energy, creativity, independence and warmth (yes, really). People *are* helpful here. It's just that the pace is faster and busier, but proud locals are always happy to share their favorite haunts. And what's not to love? Beautiful parks; 19,000 restaurants and at least twice that many shops; performing arts that range from the traditional to the truly innovative; world-class museums; educational, artistic and sports activities for everyone; and neighborhoods that are a window to the rest of the world. It's a place that's perfect for a family vacation.

For information on museums mentioned in these neighborhoods, consult the Museum chapter (⇨ Ch. 3).

HOW DO I GET AROUND?

BY CAR

Driving Manhattan's crowded streets is about as much fun as chewing on tinfoil. Free parking is often impossible to find, and paid spots are ridiculously expensive. If you arrived in town by car, either stash your car it in your hotel's lot—and look for packages that include free parking (rare), which can save you about $50 per night—or ask your hotel to recommend a good long-term lot. You'll often get a break on the cost of hourly parking if you park the car for a few days, but expect to spend at least $30 a day.

BY SUBWAY & BUS

Close to 5 million people ride New York City's 26 subway routes each day; another 2.4 million clamber onto the city's buses. Significantly less expensive than taxis or car services, the buses and subways are safe, reasonably prompt, and easy to navigate. For a complete rundown on how to use the city's transit services, costs, and route maps, visit www.

mta.info, click on NYC Transit, then select Travel/Tourist Information from the menu. Note that public transit is packed between 8 AM and 9:30 AM and 4 PM and 6 PM, so plan your travels to avoid these times if you can.

Children shorter than 44 inches ride for free on MTA buses and subways. If you're pushing a stroller, don't struggle through a subway turnstile; ask the station agent to buzz you through the gate (the attendant will ask you to swipe your MetroCard through the turnstile nearest the gate). Keep a sharp eye on your young ones while on the subway. At some stations there is a gap between the train doors and the platform. Unfortunately New York riders are not known to give up their seats for children, for someone carrying a child, or for anyone else.

BY TAXI

NYC's licensed street cabs are bright yellow with a prominent NYC Taxi logo on the side and a small plaque—called a medallion—on the hood. These are the only cabs you should accept rides from on the street—nonlicensed "gypsy" cabs can be expensive and are unregulated by the city. If you find yourself in an area where taxis are not frequent, you should call a car service instead.

When the number on the cab's roof sign is lighted, the cab is available. Stand slightly off the curb in the street and stick out your arm to hail the cab. If another person is trying to hail a cab on that corner, it's considered polite to walk a block away or cross the street and try to hail a cab from there, or to wait until the first person gets a ride.

LOWER MANHATTAN

A mix of Wall Street bling, parks, World Trade Center memories, and even ships from the 1800s, Lower Manhattan changes character from day to day and block to block. Crowded with business folks from Monday through Friday, the skyscraper-lined canyons of Wall Street are fairly deserted on the weekend and activity moves to the parks and museums. The remnants of Manhattan's colonial era cluster around the 19th-century brick facades of the South Street Seaport or scatter around the southern tip of the island near Battery Park, an area originally designed to protect the island. On a more somber note, the results of 9/11 (Ground Zero) and several ethnic museums offer up tangible contrasts to the hopes of immigrants and survivors immortalized today by such icons as Ellis Island and the Statue of Liberty.

The city's downtown neighborhoods below Canal Street give you a close-up view of some of the many cultures of Manhattan. There's residential TriBeCa with its urban grittiness and vibrant, bustling Chinatown. Walking from one to another is like entering an entirely different world, each with its own distinct vibe.

THE FINANCIAL DISTRICT, THE SEAPORT & THE WORLD TRADE CENTER AREA

★ Fodor'sChoice **Brooklyn Bridge.** "A drive-through cathedral" is how the critic James Wolcott describes one of New York's noblest and most recognized landmarks, which spans the East River and connects Manhattan to Brooklyn. A walk across the bridge's promenade—a boardwalk elevated above the roadway and shared by pedestrians, in-line skaters, and bicyclists—takes about 40 minutes from the heart of Brooklyn Heights to Manhattan's civic center. It's well worth traversing for the astounding views. The roadway is supported by a web of steel cables, hung from the towers and attached to block-long anchorages on either shore. If the kids are up for it or if you're pushing a stroller, the walk across is a must-do. You can make it less daunting by stopping halfway for a look back at the cinematic skyline of Manhattan. To motivate the kids, promise them sundaes at the Brooklyn Ice Cream Factory on the other side. Ⓜ*4, 5, 6 to Brooklyn Bridge/City Hall; J, M, Z to Chambers St. or A, C to High St.–Brooklyn Bridge.* All ages

★ Fodor'sChoice **Ellis Island.** Between 1892 and 1924, approximately 12 million men, women, and children first set foot on U.S. soil at the Ellis Island federal immigration facility. By the time the facility closed in 1954, it had processed ancestors of more than 40% of Americans living today. The island's main building, now a national monument, reopened in 1990 as the Ellis Island Immigration Museum, and contains more than 30 galleries of artifacts, photographs, and taped oral histories. Check at the visitor desk for free film tickets, ranger tour times, and special programs. The audio tour is worth its $6 price: it takes you through the exhibits, providing thorough, engaging commentary interspersed with recordings of immigrants themselves recalling their experiences. In the American Family Immigration Center, you can search Ellis Island's records for your own ancestors (for a $5 fee); outside is the American Immigrant Wall of Honor where the names of more than 500,000 immigrant Americans are inscribed along a promenade facing the Manhattan skyline. If you have a relative who came through Ellis Island, kids can look up the name on the computer, free, in the main hall to see whether the name is listed on the Wall of Honor. Make a game out of trying to find the name on the wall outside, too, or the names of other famous Americans like Miles Standish or Priscilla Adams. Pick up an "Ellis Island Junior Ranger Program," a free booklet with activities to keep the kids engaged. There's a food court here or you can prearrange a box lunch to pick up if you have a group of 10 or more by calling 221/344–0996. ☎212/363–3200 Ellis Island, 212/561–4500 Wall of Honor information ⊕www.ellisisland.org ⊠Free; ferry $11.50 round-trip, $5 for ages 4–12 ⊙Daily 9–5; extended hrs in summer. 5+up

Federal Hall National Memorial. It's a museum now, but this site has a most notable claim: George Washington was sworn in here as the first president of the United States in 1789, when the building was Federal Hall of the new nation. The museum covers 400 years of New York City's history, with a focus on the life and times of what is now the city's financial district. There's a statue of George Washington planted quite obtrusively on the steps. Kids can be sworn in as a Junior Ranger after picking up a "Federal Hall Junior Ranger" activity book. The building might look familiar to older children—it was modeled after the Parthenon in Greece. ⊠26 Wall St., at Nassau St., Lower Manhattan ☎212/825–6870 ⊠Free ⊙Weekdays 9–5 ⓜ2, 3, 4, 5 to Wall St.; A, C to Broadway/Nassau; J, M, Z to Broad St. 9+up

★ **Ground Zero.** The fenced-in 16-acre work site that emerged from the rubble of September 11th has come to symbolize the personal and historical impact of the attack. A steel "viewing wall" now encircles the site, bound on the north and south by Vesey and Liberty streets, and on the east and west by Church and West streets. Along the east wall are panels that detail the history of lower Manhattan and the WTC site before, during, and after September 11. There are also panels bearing the names of those who perished on 9/11/01 and during the 1993 World Trade Center attack. After years of delays, the process of filling the massive void at Ground Zero with new buildings and a memorial is well under way. The main viewing area is on Liberty Street, but

CHINATOWN

Canal St.

Walker St.

White St.

Asian American
Arts Centre

Columbus
Park

Greenwich St.

Hudson St.

West Broadway

TRIBECA

Franklin St.

Harrison St.

Jay St.
State St.

Leonard St.

Worth St.

Washington
Market Park

Thomas St.   Federal Plaza

Duane St.

Reade St.

Chambers St.   1,2,3   A,C,

Warren St.
Park Pl. W.
Murray St.

Warren St.

Murray St.

Park Pl.

Barclay St.   2,3   N,R,W

Vesey St.

New York
Mercantile
Exchange

World
Financial
Center

North Cove
Yacht
Harbor

BATTERY
PARK
CITY

Esplanade

SouthEnd Ave.

Albany St.

W Thames St.

South
Cove

Third Pl.

Second Pl.

First Pl.

Museum
of Jewish
Heritage

Skyscraper
Museum

Pier A

Hudson River

Ground
Zero

St. Paul's Chapel

Fulton St.

John St.

Cortlandt St.

Liberty St.

Cedar St.

Albany St.

Carlisle

Rector St.

Battery Pl.

Battery Pl.

Battery Pl.

Battery
Park

Church St.

Greenwich St.

West St. (Closed)

West Side Highway

City
Hall

4,5,6

Brooklyn
Bridge
Walkway

Brooklyn
Bridge

Spruce St.

Beekman St.

Ann St.   2,3

South Street Seaport
Historic District

Federal Reserve
Bank of New York

Maiden Lane

Cedar St.

Pine St.

Museum of
American Finance

Wall St.

Hanover Sq.

New York City
Police Museum

Vietnam Veterans
Memorial

Jeanette
Park

Federal Hall
National Memorial

NYSE

Museum of
American Finance

Bowling Green

Beaver St.

Stone St.

Bridge St.

Pearl St.

State St.

Whitehall St.

William St.

Nassau St.

Park Row

Gold St.

Front St.

Water St.

South St.

Water St.

Broad St.

Peck Slip

Beekman St.

FDR Drive

SOUTH STREET
SEAPORT

East River

Staten Island
Ferry

LOWER
MANHATTAN

Brooklyn-
Battery
Tunnel

TO ELLIS ISLAND/
STATUE OF LIBERTY

Lower Manhattan

0   1/8 mi

0   200 meters

TOP LOWER MANHATTAN EXPERIENCES

Honor our history by visiting the World Trade Center site and the Tribute TWC Visitor Center, then take the ferry out to the Statue of Liberty and Ellis Island.

Enjoy the crazy street life, jump on a boat, and catch a glimpse of old New York at the South Street Seaport.

Sample dim sum, soup dumplings, and the tapioca pearls in a bubble tea through a funky straw in Chinatown. (⇨ Ch. 6)

Take a glorious, free ride across New York Harbor on the Staten Island Ferry after spending some time among the street performers and street vendors at Bowling Green.

Look back at one of the greatest views of Manhattan by walking to the center of the Brooklyn Bridge over the East River.

you'll have a better view from the two pedestrian bridges to the World Financial Center itself. You'll need to gently explain to your kids what happened here to put this construction site into context as you walk along its perimeter. An audio tour is available at the Tribute WTC Visitor Center at 120 Liberty Street where there is also a somber thought-provoking exhibit. It may not be appropriate for young children. ⊠*Lower Manhattan* ⊕*www.tributewtc. org or www.nycvp.com for guided tours ($11 to $19 dollars)* ⊡*Free.* 7+up

New York Stock Exchange (NYSE). Unfortunately you can't tour it, but it's certainly worth ogling. At the intersection of Wall and Broad streets, the exchange is hard to miss. The neoclassical building, dating to 1903, has six Corinthian columns supporting a pediment with a sculpture entitled *Integrity Protecting the Words of Man.* If your kids are burgeoning stock brokers or interested in global economics, this might be of interest. ⊠*Lower Manhattan* Ⓜ*2, 3, 4, 5 to Wall St.; J, M, Z to Broad St.* 12+up

SHOP SMART. Ignore the lure of the Seaport mall's chain stores. Focus instead on the Seaport Museum's gift shop, a fun repository of local history and nautical goods.

★ Fodor'sChoice **South Street Seaport Historic District.** This is the city's largest concentration of early-19th-century commercial buildings, wonderfully preserved and set among charming cobblestone streets.

At the intersection of Fulton and Water streets, the gateway to the seaport, is the *Titanic* **Memorial,** a small white lighthouse that commemorates the sinking of the RMS *Titanic* in 1912. Beyond it, Fulton Street turns into a busy pedestrian mall with street performers galore. On the south side of Fulton is the seaport's architectural centerpiece, **Schermerhorn Row,** a redbrick terrace of Georgian- and Federal-style warehouses and counting houses built from 1811 to 1812. Some upper floors house gallery space, and the ground floors are occupied by upscale shops and restaurants.

Also here at 12 Fulton Street is the main lobby of the **South Street Seaport Museum** (☎*212/748–8600* ⊕*www.southst seaport.org* ⊙*Apr.–Oct., Tues.–Sun. 10–6; Nov.–Mar., Fri.–Mon. 10–5*), which hosts walking tours, hands-on exhibits, and fantastic creative programs for children, all with a nautical theme. You can purchase tickets ($10; $5 kids 5–12; free under age 5) at either 12 Fulton Street or Pier 16 Visitors Center.

Cross South Street, once known as the Street of Ships, under an elevated stretch of the FDR Drive to **Pier 16,** where historic ships are docked, including the *Pioneer,* a 102-foot schooner built in 1885; the *Peking,* the second-largest sailing bark in existence; the iron-hulled *Wavertree;* and the lightship *Ambrose.* The Pier 16 ticket booth provides information and sells tickets to the museum, ships, tours, and exhibits. Pier 16 is the departure point for various seasonal cruises.

To the north is **Pier 17,** a multilevel dockside shopping mall with national chain retailers and the jumping off point for the New York Water Taxi and the Shark speedboat ride. The ultra-graphic BODIES . . . The Exhibition has, for now, taken up residence at the Seaport Exhibition Center (11 Fulton Street at Front Street) and is recommended for older kids interested in human anatomy. Parental guidance is definitely advised. ⊠*South Street Seaport, Lower Manhattan* ☎*212/732–7678 events and shopping information* ⊕*www. southstreetseaport.com* ☜*$5 to ships, galleries, walking tours, Maritime Crafts Center, films, and other seaport events BODIES: Adults, $27.50; kids 4–12, $21.50; under 4, free* Ⓜ *A, C, 2, 3, 4, 5, J, M, Z to Fulton St./Broadway Nassau.* All ages (varies by activity)

★ Fodor'sChoice **Staten Island Ferry.** About 70,000 people ride the ferry every day, and you should be one of them. Without having to pay a cent, you get great views of the Statue of Liberty, Ellis Island, and the southern tip of Manhattan. The boat embarks from the Whitehall Terminal at Whitehall and South streets near the east end of Battery Park. The ferry goes to Staten Island, but if you don't want to visit Staten Island you can usually remain onboard for the return trip. Strollers are allowed and there are also snacks for sale onboard. ⛴ *Free* Ⓜ *1 to South Ferry; R, W to Whitehall St.; or 4, 5 to Bowling Green.* All ages

★ Fodor'sChoice **Statue of Liberty.** Liberty Enlightening the World, as the statue is officially named, was presented to the United States in 1886 as a gift from France. The 152-foot-tall figure stands atop an 89-foot pedestal with Emma Lazarus's sonnet "The New Colossus" ("Give me your tired, your poor, your huddled masses . . .") inscribed on a bronze plaque at the base. Over the course of time, the statue has become precisely what its creators dreamed it would be: the single most powerful symbol of American ideals, and, as such, one of the world's great monumental sculptures. Inside the statue's pedestal is a museum. Highlights include the original flame and full-scale replicas of Lady Liberty's face and one of her feet. You're allowed access to the museum only as part of one of the free tours of the promenade (which surrounds the base of the pedestal) or the observatory (at the pedestal's top). The tours are limited so you should order tickets ahead of time—they can be reserved up to 180 days in advance, by phone, or over the Internet. Although the stairs leading to the statue's crown have been closed to visitors since 9/11, you get a good look at the statue's inner structure on the observatory tour. If you're on one of the tours, you'll go through a security check more thorough than any airport screening. Liberty Island has a pleasant outdoor café for refueling. Kids can get a Junior Ranger Booklet, good for a DIY tour of sorts. No large backpacks are allowed on the ferry to the Statue of Liberty. Strollers and backpacks are also not allowed in the monument. Lockers for small items are available on Liberty Island. ☎212/363–3200, 212/269–5755 *ferry information, 866/782–8834 ticket reservations* ⊕*www. statuecruises.com* ⛴*Free; ferry $12 round-trip $5, ages 4–12* ⊙*Daily 9–5; extended hrs in summer.* All ages

City Hall. You just might spot groups of police surrounding news crews on the front steps as they attempt to interview city officials, which is perhaps all you want to know about City Hall. But if the history of local politics is your thing, the hall is open for tours. The pretty park outside is a nice place to sit and catch your breath, especially if you've just walked across the Brooklyn Bridge, but kids won't be able to run around. ⊠*City Hall Park, Lower Manhattan* ☎*212/639–9675* ☎*Free* ⊘*Tours weekdays; reservations required 2 wks in advance* Ⓜ*R, W to City Hall; 4, 5, 6 to Brooklyn Bridge/City Hall; or J, M, Z to Chambers St.* 7+up

St. Paul's Chapel. For more than a year after the World Trade Center attacks, the chapel's fence served as a shrine for visitors seeking solace. People from around the world left tokens of grief and support, or signed one of the large drop cloths that hung from the fence. The ongoing exhibit "Unwavering Spirit: Hope & Healing at Ground Zero" honors the efforts of rescue workers in the months following September 11. Open since 1766, St. Paul's is the oldest public building in continuous use in Manhattan. The chapel, miraculously undamaged on 9/11, is separated from Ground Zero by only a narrow street and its graveyard. The many kids' drawings and messages left here might help explain the horror of the day from a child's perspective. ⊠*209 Broadway, at Fulton St., Lower Manhattan* ☎*212/233–4164* ⊕*www. saintpaulschapel.org* ⊘*Mon.–Sat. 10–5:45, Sun. 8–3:45* Ⓜ*2, 3, 4, 5, A, C, J, M, Z to Fulton St.* 9+up

CHINATOWN & TRIBECA

Chinatown and TriBeCa couldn't be more different. Chinatown is a crowded jumble of people, storefronts, scents and sounds that seems to last all night long. Open-air markets with fresh—or still jumping—seafood or curiously prickly produce tempt with signs written in Chinese. Pagoda shapes frame buildings and even pay phones. In contrast, TriBeCa, while much more urban in architecture and feel, is a serene enclave of shipping docks; 19th-century warehouses turned into shops, galleries, and lofts; and cool restaurants where smaller parks and distinctive architecture make for a city-within-a-city feeling.

★ FodorsChoice **Columbus Park.** People-watching is the thing in this newly restored park. If you swing by in the morning, you'll see men and women practicing tai chi; the afternoons bring intense games of mah-jongg. In the mid-19th century the park was known as Five Points—the point where Mulberry Street, Anthony (now Worth) Street, Cross (now Park) Street, Orange (now Baxter) Street, and Little Water Street

1

(no longer in existence) intersected—and was notoriously ruled by dangerous Irish gangs. The playing fields now have artificial turf and there are restrooms in the reopened historic pavilion along with a Ping-Pong table. If you stick around you may catch the after-school and "Mommy and Me" programs. Ⓜ*N, Q, R, W, 6 to Canal St.* All ages

WHERE CAN I FIND . . . IN LOWER MANHATTAN?

	Location	Description
QUICK MEALS		
Adrienne's Pizzabar	54 Stone St., near Mill La.	Rectangular pizza, salads and baked pastas
GOOD COFFEE		
Picnik	Battery Place in Battery Park	Kiosk by the water with picnic baskets to go
Tea-riffic	55 Mott St., at Bayard St.	Teas of all sorts, hot and cold, including bubble tea
ICE CREAM		
Chinatown Ice Cream Factory	65 Bayard St., near Mott St.	Typical flavors plus lots of Asian specialties
Ice-cream stands and trucks	Bowling Green and South Street Seaport—outdoors	Best bet for kid-pleasing Good Humor–like frozen treats
FUN STORES		
Evelyn's Chocolates	4 John St., near Broadway	Old school confections, hand-dipped chocolates
PLAYGROUNDS		
Teardrop Park	Between Warren and Murray Sts., east of River Terrace	Rocks to climb, sandpits, slide
Nelson A. Rockefeller Park	At north of end of Battery Park City, west of River Terrace	Tiny sculptured creatures everywhere, expansive area. Parkhouse, which loans games and equipment
PUBLIC BATHROOMS		
South Street Seaport Mall	19 Fulton St., Pier 17, 2nd fl.	
World Financial Center, Winter Garden	West St. at Esplanade Plaza, in corner	

★ Fodor'sChoice **Washington Market Park.** This landscaped recreation space with a gazebo and playground—ideal for
permitting the kids to blow off steam—was named after
the great food market that once sprawled over the area.
Across the street at the elementary school are a stout red
tower resembling a lighthouse and a fence with iron ship
figures—reminders of the neighborhood's dockside past.
There's a small greenmarket here on Wednesday and Saturday. ✉*Greenwich St. between Chambers and Duane Sts.,
TriBeCa* Ⓜ*1, 2, 3 to Chambers St.* All ages

SOHO, NOLITA & LITTLE ITALY

SoHo (South of Houston) and NoLita (North of Little Italy)
are shopper's paradises, supertrendy, painfully crowded on
the weekends, and undeniably glamorous. Not too long ago
though, these neighborhoods were quiet warrens of artists'
lofts and galleries, with gorgeous cast-iron buildings thank-
fully saved from the wrecking ball by some urban vision-
aries. (Note: the buildings along Broadway and Greene
Street are prime examples.) Most of the art galleries have
been replaced by cafés and fashion-forward shops but the
neighborhood's Belgian brick cobblestones and turn-of-the-
20th-century lampposts still remain. What's left of Little
Italy is easily walkable: the blocks surrounding the area
near Mulberry Street between NoLita and ultrabusy Canal
Street invite you to pop into bakeries, specialty grocers and
pasta makers that look frozen in time.

SOHO

New York Earth Room. Walter de Maria's 1977 avant-garde
work consists of 140 tons of gently sculpted soil (22 inches
deep) filling 3,600 square feet of space of a second-floor
gallery. It's fun to watch kids puzzle over whether it's art,
and you may find yourself asking the same thing. It's closed
from June to September (perhaps that's when the mush-
rooms and weeds take root?). ✉*141 Wooster St., between
W. Houston and Prince Sts., SoHo* ☎*212/473–072* ⊕*www.
earthroom.org* 🎟*Free* Ⓜ *R, W to Prince St.; B, D, F, V to
Broadway–Lafayette.* 7+up

SoHo, NoLita
& Little Italy

Delancey St.

Eldridge St.

Forsyth St.

Chrystie St.

J,M,Z

S

DiPalo's
Fine Foods

Bowery

NOLITA

Elizabeth St.

LITTLE
ITALY

Grand St.

Broome St.

CHINATOWN

Canal St.

Bayard St.

Pell St.

St. Patrick's
Old Cathedral

Mott St.

Kenmare St.

Hester St.

National Shrine
of San Gennaro

E. Houston St.

Mulberry St.

NYPD
Headquarters

Baxter St.

J,M,Z

Cleveland Pl.

6

Children's
Museum of the Arts

Centre St.

Prince St.

Crosby St.

Howard St.

Lafayette St.

6

B,D,F,V

R,W

SoHo

Broadway

Broome St.

Grand St.

N,R,W,Q

Greene St.

Spring St.

Mercer St.

King of Greene
Street

Wooster St.

Queen of
Greene Street

Canal St.

Lispenard St.

Walker St.

White St.

Franklin St.

Apple Store

West Broadway

West Broadway

Church St.

New York
Earth Room

Thompson St.

W. Houston St.

Sullivan St.

MacDougal St.

C,E

Ave. of the Americas (Sixth Ave.)

Varick St.

A,C,E

King St.

Vandam St.

Dominick St.

Spring St.

Holland Tunnel
Entrance

1

Varick St.

Ericsson Pl.

N. Moore St.

Hubert St.

TRIBECA

J,9

Varick St.

Spring St.

Broome St.

Hudson St.

Greenwich St.

Laight St.

Vestry St.

TO WASHINGTON
MARKET PARK

Greenwich St.

Holland Tunnel

1/8 mi

200 meters

0

0

TOP SOHO/LITTLE ITALY EXPERIENCES

Treat your tots to Italian sweets, from pignoli cookies and creamy cannolis to marzipan-coated cassatas. (⇨ Ch. 6)

Indulge your tween's *Gossip Girl* fantasy and take her around the cool clothing boutiques in SoHo and NoLita. (⇨ Ch. 5)

Shop until your kids drop at the Scholastic Store (on

Broadway between Prince and Spring Sts.), home of all things Clifford (the big red dog), Captain Underpants, and Harry Potter. (⇨ Ch. 5)

Take a whirl around Little Italy during the 11-day Feast of San Gennaro Festival in September, one of the city's liveliest outdoor street fairs.

LITTLE ITALY

National Shrine of San Gennaro. A replica of the grotto at Lourdes is the high point of this church's richly painted interior. Every September the church—officially known as the Most Precious Blood Church (109 Mulberry Street, just off Canal; visit here to enter the shrine on weekdays)—sponsors the Feast of San Gennaro. This makes a good rest stop amid the busy streets of Little Italy and Chinatown. ✉*113 Baxter St., near Canal St., Little Italy* ☎*212/768–9320 festival information, 212/226–6427 church* ⊙*Masses Sat. noon, 5:30; Sun. noon, 2 (Vietnamese)* Ⓜ *N, Q, R, W, 6 to Canal St.; J, M, Z to Canal St.* All ages

EAST VILLAGE & THE LOWER EAST SIDE

Houston Street divides the area south of 14th Street and east of 4th Avenue and the Bowery into the East Village (above) and the Lower East Side (below), two neighborhoods that contain some of the city's funkiest nightlife, restaurants, and shops, all backed up with loads of cultural history. The East Village, best known as the birthplace of American punk and the refuge of artists, activists, and other social dissenters, is also a pastiche of ethnic enclaves, whose imprints are visible in the area's churches, restaurants, shops, and—of course—residents. The Lower East Side has seen waves of immigration of European Jews, Hispanics, and Chinese since the mid-1800s, a legacy excellently captured in the neighborhood's soul, the Lower East Side

Tenement Museum, and the museum at the gorgeously restored Eldridge Synagogue. You can definitely get a sense of the melting pot nature of this neighborhood as you nosh your way through pickles, knishes, bagels, and bialys.

Alphabet City. The north–south avenues east of 1st Avenue, from Houston Street to 14th Street, are labeled with letters, not numbers, which give this area its nickname. The reasonably priced restaurants with their bohemian atmosphere on avenues A, B, and C, and the cross streets in between, attract all kinds. A close-knit Puerto Rican community makes its home along Avenue C with predominantly Latino shops and bodegas, plus a "Nuyorican" café and music venue. Avenue A along the park has a wide variety of ethnic cafés and bars. Avenue B likewise has a growing restaurant scene as does Avenue C, also called Loisaida Avenue (a Spanglish creation meaning Lower East Side. It's pretty edgy here, so for younger kids the only reason to head over is to go Tompkins Square Park. The area might be familiar to older kids who have seen Rent. ⊠ *East Village* Ⓜ*6 to Astor Pl.; L to 1st Ave.; F, V to 2nd Ave.* 12+up

Astor Place Subway Station. At the beginning of the 20th century, almost every Interborough Rapid Transit (IRT) subway entrance resembled the ornate cast-iron replica of a beaux arts kiosk that covers the stairway leading to the uptown 6 train here. Inside, plaques of beaver emblems line the tiled station walls, a reference to the fur trade of the past. Keep your eyes peeled at other stops, too. Kids will appreciate the whimsical art on display in NYC's subway stations, some of it even interactive, although they do little to improve the sometimes-dingy subway surroundings. ⊠*On traffic island at E. 8th St. and 4th Ave., East Village* Ⓜ *6 to Astor Pl.* All ages

St. Marks Place. The longtime hub of the edgy East Village and beatnik, rock and punk music scene, St. Marks Place is the name given to idiosyncratic East 8th Street between 3rd Avenue and Avenue A, filled with loads of people and ethnic cafés. The blocks between 2nd and 3rd avenues have time-tested alternative-clothing punk and Goth boutiques. Younger kids might be frightened by some of the street kids and punk rockers who frequent this block. Ⓜ*6 to Astor Pl.* 12+up

Tompkins Square Park. This leafy spot amid the East Village's crowded tenements is a release valve. The park fills up with locals year-round, partaking in picnics, drum circles, the

0
1/8 mile

0
200 meters

Stuyvesant
Town

Fourth Ave.

E. 15th St.

E. 14th St.
M L

4,5,6,L,
N,Q,R,W

E. 13th St.
The Strand Book Store

E. 12th St.

Third Ave.

Second Ave.

First Ave.

E. 11th St.

Broadway

St. Mark's
Church-in-the-Bowery

E. 10th St.

Stuyvesant St.

Astor Place
Subway Station

E. 9th St.

R, W
M

Sculpture for the Living

St. Marks Pl.

St. Marks Place

Tompkins
Square Park

Astor Pl.
M 6

Fourth Ave.

E. 7th St.

Ave. A

Taras
Shevchenko
Pl.

E. 6th St.

EAST VILLAGE

Merchant's
House Museum

E. 5th St.

Cooper
Square

E. 4th St.

ALPHABET
CITY

Lafayette St.

Gt. Jones St.

E. 3rd St.

Bowery

E. 2nd St.

6
M

Bleecker St.

E. 1st St.

F,V
M

B, D, F, V
M

E. Houston St.

Eldridge St.

Forsyth St.

Allen St.

Orchard St.

Ludlow St.

Essex St.

Norfolk St.

Chrystie St.

Mulberry St.

Mott St.

Elizabeth St.

Stanton St.

LOWER
EAST SIDE

Economy
Candy

Rivington St.

Essex Street
Market

Prince St.

J, M, Z
M

Delancey St.

Lower East Side
Tenement Museum

TO ELDRIDGE ST.
SYNAGOGUE
↓

Broome St.

East Village &
the Lower East Side

TOP EAST VILLAGE & LES EXPERIENCES

Experience New York's Jewish heritage with a visit to the extraordinary Eldridge Synagogue.

Trek among the hipsters, punk rockers, and tattooed and pierced people along St. Mark's Place.

Savor a taste of old NYC with a visit to Bamn! automat at 37 St. Marks Place and 2nd Avenue to select your corn dog or slider from inside a glass window, washed down by an egg cream at Gem Spa across the street.

Watch all dogs go to heaven at the dog runs at Tompkins Square Park. Have you ever seen a park with doggie swimming pools and drinking fountains?

Walk back into NYC's immigrant past at the Lower East Side Tenement Museum. ($\Rightarrow$ Ch. 3)

playground; and two dog runs. The Charlie Parker Jazz Festival, honoring the former park-side resident and noted jazz saxophonist, packs the park in late August. There are three playgrounds here, but be sure to leave before it gets dark. ⊠*Bordered by Aves. A and B and E. 7th and E. 10th Sts., East Village* Ⓜ*6 to Astor Pl.; L to 1st Ave.* All ages

LOWER EAST SIDE

Eldridge Street Synagogue. This was the first Orthodox synagogue erected by the large number of Eastern European Jews who settled on the Lower East Side in the late 19th century. Inside is an exceptional hand-carved ark of mahogany and walnut, a sculptured wooden balcony, jewel-tone stained-glass windows, stenciled walls, and an enormous brass chandelier. A massive renovation of this beloved synagogue was completed in late 2007. The synagogue has a museum, too, with fun hands-on exhibits like "touch tables" that teach about the synagogue and the Lower East Side. Check the Web site for special family-oriented events and tours. ⊠*12 Eldridge St., between Canal and Division Sts., Lower East Side* ☎*212/219–0888* ⊕*www.eldridgestreet.org* ⊡*$10 $6, kids 5–18; under 5, free* ☉*Sun.–Thurs. 10–4; tours on half-hr 10:30 am–3:30 pm* Ⓜ*F to E. Broadway; B, D to Grand St.* 5+up

GREENWICH VILLAGE & CHELSEA

Long the home of writers, artists, bohemians, and *bon vivants*, Greenwich Village (also called the West Village or just the Village) is a singular section of the city. Instead of high-rises and skyscrapers, historic town houses line the small curving streets and peculiar alleys. Streets have names instead of numbers. Primarily residential, the area also has many specialty restaurants, cafés, and boutiques with a warm and charming neighborhood vibe.

NYU students keep the idealistic spirit of the neighborhood alive. The Meatpacking District, in the far northwest part of the Village, has cobblestone streets and an industrial feel. The nabe's original meatpacking tenants are being replaced by a different kind of meat-market life: velvet-rope clubs, trendy restaurants, and trendy-chic shops. To the north, stylish Chelsea has usurped SoHo as the world's contemporary-art-gallery headquarters and has become the center of the city's gay community. It also boasts the city's most comprehensive recreational facility, Chelsea Piers, set along the waterfront, plus a fun food destination, Chelsea Market, with lots of yummy treats in an old brick factory.

GREENWICH VILLAGE

Patchin Place. This little cul-de-sac off West 10th Street between Greenwich and 6th avenues has 10 diminutive 1848 row houses. Around the corner on 6th Avenue is a similar dead-end street, **Milligan Place,** with five small homes completed in 1852. Little kids will feel like giants among these tiny homes. Ⓜ*A, B, C, D, E, F, V to W. 4th St.* All ages

75½ Bedford Street. Rising real-estate rates inspired the construction of New York City's narrowest house—just 9½ feet wide—in 1873. Children may appreciate the dollhouselike dimensions. Most kids won't believe how the furniture fits inside. ✉*75½ Bedford St., between Commerce and Morton Sts., Greenwich Village* Ⓜ *A, B, C, D, E, F, V to W. 4th St.* All ages

★ Fodor'sChoice **Washington Square Park.** NYU students, street musicians, skateboarders, jugglers, chess players, and those just watching the grand opera of it all generate a maelstrom of activity in this physical and spiritual heart of the Village. The 9½-acre park is currently undergoing a major renovation so activities are slightly limited with the

0   1/4 mile

0   400 meters

W. 34th St.   M A,C,E   M 1   M
N,R

Madison Square Garden /Penn Station

W. 31st St.
W. 30th St.
W. 29th St.
W. 28th St.
W. 27th St.

W. 32nd St.

Broadway

Tenth Ave.
Ninth Ave.
Eighth Ave.
Seventh Ave.
Fifth Ave.

Eleventh Ave.

CHELSEA

M   N,R M

W. 26th St.

W. 25th St.
W. 24th St.

W. 24th St.

Madison Square

Avenue of the Americas

1

Chelsea Art Museum

W. 23rd St.   M C,E   M   M F,Q   N,R M

W. 22nd St.

W. 21st St.
W. 20th St.
W. 19th St.

(Sixth Ave.)

Chelsea Piers

M   W. 18th St.

W. 17th St.
W. 16th St.
W. 15th St.

Eleventh Ave.

Chelsea Market

West Side Hwy.

A,C,E,L
M   1,2,3 M W. 14th St.   M F,L

MEATPACKING DISTRICT

W. 13th St.

Forbes Galleries

W. 12th St.   **GREENWICH VILLAGE**
W. 11th St.

Little W. 12th St.
Gansevoort St.
Horatio St.
Jane St.
W. 12th St.
Bethune St.

Greenwich Ave.
Greenwich St.
Eighth Ave.
W. 4th St.
Waverly

Fifth Ave.

Abingdon Square

Patchin Place   **Jefferson Market Library**

Washington Mews

Sheridan Square

W. 8th St.

Bank St.
W. 11th St.
W. 10th St.

Perry St.
Charles St.
Hudson St.
Christopher St.

Washington St.

Washington Arch

Waverly Pl.
Wash. Pl.

Washington Square Park

M
1

A,B,C,D,E,F,V M

Washington Sq. S.

West St.

WEST VILLAGE

Bleecker St.

Father Demo Sq.

New York University

75 1/2 Bedford St.

Seventh Ave. S.
Leroy St.
Carmine St.
Downing St.

Barrow

Morton St.
Leroy St.
Clark St.

Sixth Ave.

MacDougal St.
Sullivan St.
Thompson St.
La Guardia Pl.

W. Houston St.

Promenade

Greenwich Village, the Meatpacking District & Chelsea

TOP VILLAGE/CHELSEA EXPERIENCES

Take in the many street musician performers or grab a game of chess in Washington Square Park.

Watch bread being made at Amy's in Chelsea Market and grab some snacks after meandering through the historic building.

Join the queue at *Sex and the City* fave Magnolia Bakery (at Bleecker St. and 11th) for one of their pastel-frosted cupcakes.

Climb the 30-foot rock wall, skate, bowl, or hit some golf balls at the gigantic Chelsea Piers sports complex.

central fountain area closed off. The playgrounds attract lots of families and pups of all sizes go leash-free inside the dog runs.

The triumphal **Washington Memorial Arch** stands at the square's north end, marking the start of 5th Avenue and commemorating the 100th anniversary of George Washington's presidential inauguration. Washington Square Park offers equal opportunity fun; there are two playgrounds: one for toddlers and one for older kids in addition to game tables, benches, and grassy areas. ⊠*5th Ave. between Waverly Pl. and 4th St., Greenwich Village* Ⓜ*A, B, C, D, E, F, V to W. 4th St.* All ages

CHELSEA

★ Fodor'sChoice **Chelsea Market.** In the former Nabisco plant, where the first Oreos were baked in 1912, nearly two-dozen food wholesalers flank what is possibly the city's longest interior walkway in a single building—from 9th to 10th avenues. The market's funky industrial design—a tangle of glass and metal creates the awning and, inside, a factory pipe has been converted into an indoor waterfall—complements the eclectic—and delicious—assortment of bakers, butchers, florists, and wine merchants inside. Kids will find treats of all types here, from the whimsical cookies at Eleni's to the rich brownies of Fat Witch Bakery to the thick milk shakes at Ronnybrook's Milk Bar. For a peek behind the scenes, look into the gallery window at Amy's Breads. The flipping and kneading of dough is a fascinating sight for children. Music, dance, and game programs happen on weekends. Check the Web site for schedules. ⊠*75 9th Ave., between W. 15th and W. 16th Sts., Chelsea*

CLOSE UP

So Much Fun It's Scary!

1

All things weird and wonderful, all creatures great and squall, all things witty and fantastical, New York City has them all—and on All Hallows' Eve they freak through the streets in New York's Halloween parade. White-sheeted ghouls feel dull compared to fishnets and leathers, sequins and feathers posing and prancing along 6th Avenue in this vibrant display of vanity and insanity.

In 1973 mask maker and puppeteer Ralph Lee paraded his puppets from house to house visiting friends and family along the winding streets of his Greenwich Village neighborhood. His merry march quickly outgrew its original, intimate route and now, decades later, it parades up 6th Avenue, from Spring Street to 21st Street, attracting 50,000 creatively costumed exhibitionists, artists, dancers, musicians, hundreds of enormous puppets, scores of bands, and more than 2 million spectators. Anyone with a costume can join in, no advance registration required, although the enthusiastic interaction between participants and spectators makes it just as much fun to watch. It's a safe "street event" for families and singles alike, and a joyful night unlike any other.

The parade lines up on 6th Avenue between Canal and Spring streets from 6:30 PM to 8 PM. The walk actually starts at 7 PM, but it takes about two hours to leave the staging area. It's best to arrive from the south to avoid the crush of strollers and participants. Get there a few hours early if you can. Costumes are usually handmade, clever, and outrageous, and revelers are happy to strike a pose. The streets are crowded along the route, with the most congestion below 14th Street. Of course the best way to truly experience the parade is to march—if you're not feeling the face paint, you can volunteer to help carry the puppets. For information, contact ⊕ *www.halloween-nyc.com.*

—Jacinta O'Halloran

☏ *212/243–6005* ⊕ *www.chelseamarket.com* ◷ *Daily weekdays 7–9, weekends 7–8* Ⓜ *A, C, E, L to 14th St.* All ages

★ Fodor's Choice **Chelsea Piers.** A phenomenal example of adaptive reuse, this sports-and-entertainment complex along the Hudson River between 17th and 23rd streets (entrance on 23rd) is the size of four 80-story buildings lying flat. There's pretty much every kind of sports activity going on inside and out from golf to ice-skating, roller-skating, rock climbing, swimming, kayaking, bowling, gymnastics, and

basketball (☎*212/336–7873 or 866/211–3805*). . This is
the perfect rainy-day destination: kids of all ages will find
something to do. Pricing varies by activity from the Toddler Adventure Center and up. There are batting cages for
your little Derek Jeters, a diving pit filled with foam for
the toddlers, or balance beams for budding Olympians.
When the weather's nice, aspiring Tony Hawks can try out
the challenging ramps in the Skate Park, just a bit north of
the complex. ✉*Piers 59–62 on Hudson River from 17th to
23rd Sts.; entrance at 23rd St., Chelsea* ☎*212/336–6666*
⊕*www.chelseapiers.com* Ⓜ*C, E to 23rd St.* All ages

WHERE CAN I FIND . . . IN GREENWICH VILLAGE AND CHELSEA?

	Location	Description
FUN STORES		
Alphaville	226 W. Houston, near Varick St.	Classic toys and games
Tah-Poozie	50 Greenwich Ave., between Charles and Henry Sts.	Tchotchkes to the max
Space Kiddets	26 E. 22nd St., between Broadway and Park Ave.	Vintage toys and other gear
PLAYGROUNDS		
Washington Square Park	W. 4th St. near 5th Ave.	2 for different age groups
Hudson River Park	Pier 51 near West. St.	Boat-theme, sprinklers, climbing stuff
PUBLIC BATHROOMS		
Hudson River Park	Pier 51 at Jane St.	Changing tables
Christopher St. Pier	Christopher St. and West Side Hwy.	Changing tables
ICE CREAM		
Pinkberry	170 8th Ave., near 19th St.	Frozen yogurt with candy and fruit toppings
Australian Homemade	22 E. 8th St., at University	Rich ice cream and Belgian chocolates

UNION SQUARE WITH GRAMERCY PARK, MURRAY HILL & THE FLATIRON DISTRICT

Union Square is the beating heart of Manhattan. The square hosts everything from concerts to protest rallies to the farmers' market, and the surrounding neighborhoods each borrow its flavor while maintaining their own vibe and identity. The haste and hullabaloo of the city calm considerably as you stroll through the tree-lined neighborhoods of Murray Hill, the Flatiron District, and Gramercy, east of 5th Avenue between 14th and 40th streets. On Broadway, 5th and 6th avenues have some of the city's best shopping and larger stores. Murray Hill is a charming residential neighborhood—between 34th and 40th streets from 5th Avenue to 3rd Avenue—with some high-profile haunts, including the Morgan Library and King Kong's favorite hangout, the Empire State Building. Worth a look, beautiful Gramercy Park is unfortunately open only by key to residents of the area.

★ Fodor'sChoice **Empire State Building.** This landmark is the city's tallest building. Its pencil-slim silhouette, recognizable virtually worldwide, is an art deco monument to progress, a symbol for New York City, and a star in some great romantic scenes: the building has appeared in more than 200 movies. You might just find yourself at the top of the building with *Sleepless in Seattle* look-alikes or even the building's own King Kong impersonator.

■TIP→**Thanks to advance ticketing on the Internet, you can speed your way to the observatory on the 86th floor and avoid at least one long line.** If this is your first visit, rent a headset with an audio tour from Tony, a fictional but "authentic" native New Yorker, available in eight languages. The 86th-floor observatory (1,050 feet high) is outdoors and spans the building's circumference. This is the deck to go to, to truly see the city. Don't be shy about going outside into the wind (even during the winter) or you'll miss half the experience. Just hang on tightly to your kids (and your hats)! Bring quarters for the high-powered binoculars: on clear days you can see up to 80 mi. If it rains, you can view the city between the clouds and watch the rain travel sideways around the building from the shelter of the enclosed walkway. The advantage of paying the extra $15 to go to the 102nd floor is that this observatory affords a quieter

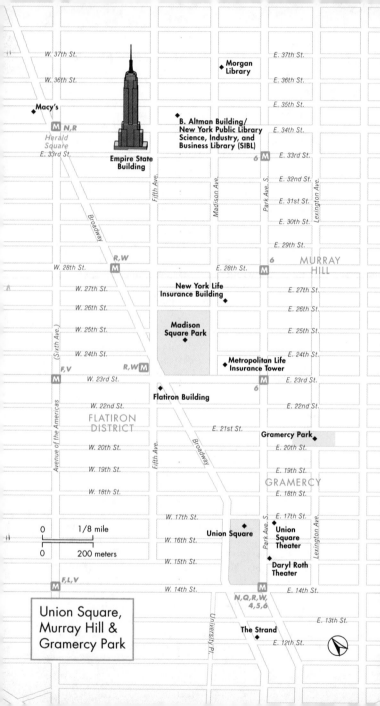

W. 37th St.
W. 36th St.

Macy's

M N,R
Herald
Square
E. 33rd St.

Empire State
Building

Broadway

R,W
M
W. 28th St.

W. 27th St.

W. 26th St.

W. 25th St.

W. 24th St.

(Sixth Ave.)

Avenue of the Americas

R,W M
W. 23rd St.

W. 22nd St.

FLATIRON
DISTRICT

W. 20th St.

W. 19th St.

W. 18th St.

F,V
M

Fifth Ave.

E. 37th St.

Morgan
Library

E. 36th St.

E. 35th St.

B. Altman Building/
New York Public Library
Science, Industry, and
Business Library (SIBL)

E. 34th St.

6 M E. 33rd St.

Madison Ave.

Park Ave. S.

E. 32nd St.

E. 31st St.

Lexington Ave.

E. 30th St.

E. 29th St.

E. 28th St.

6 M

MURRAY
HILL

New York Life
Insurance Building

E. 27th St.

E. 26th St.

Madison
Square Park

E. 25th St.

E. 24th St.

Metropolitan Life
Insurance Tower

E. 23rd St.

6

Flatiron Building

E. 22nd St.

E. 21st St.

Gramercy Park

E. 20th St.

Fifth Ave.

Broadway

E. 19th St.

GRAMERCY

E. 18th St.

0   1/8 mile
0   200 meters

W. 17th St.

W. 16th St.

Union Square

Park Ave. S.

E. 17th St.

Union
Square
Theater

W. 15th St.

Daryl Roth
Theater

F,L,V
M

W. 14th St.

M
N,Q,R,W,
4,5,6

Lexington Ave.

E. 14th St.

Union Square,
Murray Hill &
Gramercy Park

University Pl.

The Strand

E. 13th St.

E. 12th St.

TOP UNION SQUARE AREA EXPERIENCES

Check out the lights atop the Empire State Building and try to guess what's being celebrated that day before riding to the top to see the lights of Manhattan.

Hike through the "18 miles" of books at the Strand looking for some of your old favorites.

Search for seasonal treats and sample the wares at the famous Green Market at Union Square Park on Monday, Wednesday, Friday, and Saturday.

Plant yourself in Madison Square Park at 23rd Street at Madison Avenue for a gorgeous view of the turn-of-the-20th century Manhattan skyline surrounding it.

indoor and less-crowded circular walk-around from which to view the city. Express tickets can be purchased for front-of-the-line admission for an extra $45.

Time your visit for early or late in the day—morning is the least crowded time, and at night the city lights are dazzling. A good strategy is to go up just before dusk and witness nightfall. There's no coat check here, and no large bags or backpacks can be brought inside. A small snack bar on the 86th floor is helpful after waiting in line. You may need to lift up small kids to see over the walls outside, so hold on tightly as it's very windy, or stay in the enclosed, indoor area. The 102nd floor is also a calmer choice for kids who might be scared outside. ✉*350 5th Ave., at E. 34th St., Murray Hill* ☎*212/736–3100 or 877/692–8439* ⊕*www.esbnyc.com* ☎*$19 adults; $17, ages 12–17; $13, ages 6–11* ☼*Daily 8 AM–2 AM; last elevator up leaves at 1:15 AM* Ⓜ*B, D, F, V, N, R, Q, W to 34th St./Herald Sq.; or 6 to 33rd St.* 5+up

Although some parents blanch when they discover both how much it costs and how it lurches, the second-floor **NY SKYRIDE** is a favorite of the seven- and eight-year-old set. The ride yields a movie, motion, and sights, rolled up into New York's only aerial virtual-tour simulator. Make sure your kids understand that they'll be rocking and rolling on this ride or they might get quite nervous. There are definitely more authentic (and less costly) ways to see the city. ☎*212/279–9777 or 888/759–7433* ⊕*www.skyride. com* ☎*$29.50; $22.50, ages 12–17; $16, ages 6–11; $45;*

$37, ages 12–17; $19, ages 6–11, Combo Skyride and observatory ⊙*Daily 10–10.* 5+up

Flatiron Building. Covered with a limestone and white terra-cotta skin in the Italian Renaissance style, the building's odd shape resembled a clothing iron, hence its nickname. This architectural gem and landmark has a cartoon quirki-ness that kids can admire, and it serves as an easy point of orientation. ✉*175 5th Ave., bordered by E. 22nd and E. 23rd Sts., 5th Ave., and Broadway, Flatiron District* Ⓜ*R, W to 23rd St.* 9+up

★ **Macy's.** Yes, this is indeed the world's largest store with 11 floors, 2 million square feet of selling space. Chance a ride on one of the narrow wooden escalators inside; installed in 1902, they were the first escalators ever used in an American store.

   ■TIP➔ **Visit in April during Macy's flower show, when more than 30,000 varieties of flowers and plants blanket the store. The store windows at Christmastime are some of the city's best and fabulous for kids of all ages.** There are lots of restaurants inside and a good children's department to boot. ✉*W. 34th St. between Broadway at 6th and 7th Aves., Murray Hill* ☎*212/695–4400* ⊕*www.macys.com* ⊙*Hrs vary seasonally; Mon.–Sat. 10–9:30, Sun. 11–8* Ⓜ*B, D, F, V, N, R, Q, W to 34th St./Herald Sq.; 1, 2, 3 to 33rd St.* All ages

★ Fodor'sChoice **The Strand.** Serious bibliophiles flock to this mon-strous book emporium with some 2 million volumes (the store's slogan is "18 Miles of Books"). The stock includes both new and secondhand books plus thousands of col-lector's items. You won't find every title you're looking for here, but the discounted prices make for up that. Upstairs on the second floor is a great kids section, very specifically categorized. This is the only section in the store where there are some seats that both parents and kids can use. ✉*828 Broadway, at E. 12th St., Union Square* ☎*212/473–1452* ⊙*Mon.–Sat. 9:30 AM–10:30 PM, Sun. 11–10:30* Ⓜ*N, Q, R, W, 4, 5, 6, L.* All ages

★ **Union Square.** A park, farmers' market, and meeting place, this pocket of green space sits in the center of a bustling residential and commercial neighborhood. Statues in the park include George Washington and Abraham Lincoln.

Union Square is at its best on Monday, Wednesday, Friday, and Saturday (8–6), when the largest of the city's **greenmar-kets** brings farmers and food purveyors from the tristate

1

area. Browse the stands of fruit and vegetables, flowers, plants, fresh-baked pies and breads, and cheeses. Be sure to ask for samples. Between Thanksgiving and Christmas, artisans sell unique gift items including toys and children's clothing in candy-cane striped booths at the square's south-west end. Plenty of kid-friendly stores, including a huge Barnes and Noble, a Babies R Us, and Virgin Megastore ring the park. ✉*E. 14th to E. 17th Sts., between Broadway and Park Ave. S, Flatiron District* Ⓜ*N, Q, R, W, 4, 5, 6, L to Union Sq./14th St.* All ages

WHERE CAN I FIND . . . IN UNION SQUARE?

	Location	Description
FUN STORES		
Abracadabra Superstore	19 W. 21st St., near 5th Ave.	Costumes, gag gifts, and theatrical makeup
Forbidden Planet	840 Broadway, at 13th St.	Science fiction everything, comics books galore
PLAYGROUNDS		
Union Square Park	16th St. and Broadway	2 playgrounds–one for toddlers, one for older kids
Madison Square Park	Near Madison Ave. and 25th St.	Climbing, slides, sprinklers
ICE CREAM		
Pinkberry	7 W. 32nd St., between 5th Ave. and Broadway	Tart frozen yogurt with fun add-ons
Shake Shack	Madison Square Park, at 23rd St. and Madison Ave.	Frozen custard made the old way
PUBLIC BATHROOMS		
Macy's	W. 34th St., 6th and 7th Aves.	
Babies R Us	24–30 Union Sq. E	2nd floor, changing tables

MIDTOWN

Midtown is what most people think of when they think of New York City—a bustling center of skyscrapers, media, shopping, transportation, and tourism. It has more major landmarks that your kids might recognize—Grand Central

Terminal, Rockefeller Center, Times Square, Carnegie Hall, Radio City Music Hall, and the United Nations—than any other part of the city.

Rockefeller Center appears in almost every movie filmed in the city; 5th Avenue is probably the best-known shopping street in the world; Grand Central Terminal is one of the busiest buildings in the city with an incredible Zodiac ceiling and great food; and the renowned Museum of Modern Art, along with several other museums, are all here, too.

Whirling in a chaos of flashing lights, honking horns, and shoulder-to-shoulder crowds, Times Square is the most frenetic and colorful part of New York City. It's a magnet for all ages with its bright neon lights, Broadway theaters, street entertainers, and megastores with names that kids will quickly recognize like Quiksilver, M&Ms, MTV, Hershey, Toys R Us, and Planet Hollywood.

Bryant Park. An oasis amid skyscrapers, this is one of Manhattan's most popular parks. Lining the perimeter of the sunny central lawn, tall London plane trees cast welcome shade over stone terraces, formal flower beds, gravel pathways, and kiosks selling everything from sandwiches to egg creams. In summer you can check out live jazz and comedy concerts. Free outdoor film screenings on Monday at dusk attract a huge crowd of picnickers watching classic films like Romany Holiday alfresco. (Come early to save a spot on the lawn.) On the south side of the park is an old-fashioned **carousel** (☞ 2), where kids can ride fanciful rabbits and frogs instead of horses. Come late October, the park rolls out the artificial frozen **pond** (⊙*Late Oct.– mid-Jan., Sun.–Thurs. 8 am–10 pm, Fri. and Sat. 8 am– midnight*) for ice-skating. Rental for skates and locker will run you $20 ($10 for skates, $10 for a lock to close your "free" locker). Surrounding the ice rink are the Christmas market–like stalls of the **Holiday Shops** (⊙*Late Nov.–Jan. 1*), selling goods from around the world. An extra-special treat: weather permitting, the Outdoor Reading Room is an area behind the café near 42nd Street with books to borrow while you're at the park. Kids get their own small-size chairs to sit back and soak up some literature as well as the fresh air. There's also free Wi-Fi. ✉*6th Ave. between W. 40th and W. 42nd Sts., Midtown West* ☎*212/768–4242* ⊕*www.bryantpark.org* ⊙*Oct.–Apr., daily 7–7; May–Sept., weekdays 7 AM–8 PM, weekends 7 AM–11 PM* Ⓜ*B, D, F, V to 42nd St.; 7 to 5th Ave.* All ages

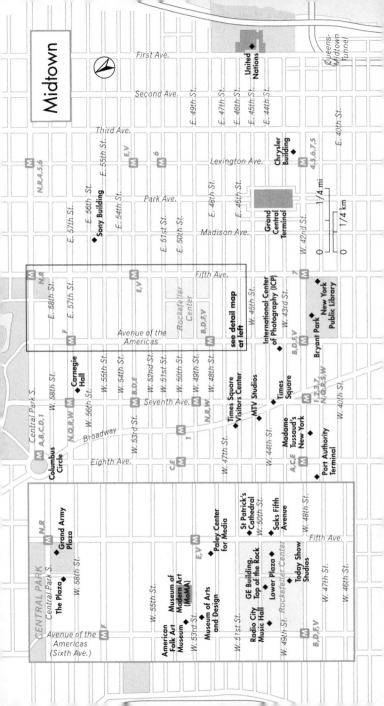

Midtown

First Ave.

Second Ave.

Third Ave.

Lexington Ave.

Park Ave.

Madison Ave.

Fifth Ave.

Avenue of the Americas

Seventh Ave.

Broadway

Eighth Ave.

E. 40th St.
E. 44th St.
E. 45th St.
E. 46th St.
E. 47th St.
E. 49th St.

E. 48th St.
E. 50th St.
E. 51st St.
E. 54th St.
E. 55th St.
E. 56th St.
E. 57th St.
E. 58th St.

W. 40th St.
W. 42nd St.
W. 43rd St.
W. 46th St.
W. 47th St.
W. 48th St.
W. 49th St.
W. 50th St.
W. 51st St.
W. 52nd St.
W. 53rd St.
W. 54th St.
W. 55th St.
W. 56th St.
W. 57th St.
W. 58th St.

United Nations

Queens-Midtown Tunnel

Chrysler Building

4,5,6,7,S

Grand Central Terminal

Sony Building

Rockefeller Center

see detail map at left

International Center of Photography (ICP)

Bryant Park

New York Public Library

E,V

B,D,F,V

7

Carnegie Hall

Times Square Visitors Center

MTV Studios

Times Square

Madame Tussaud's New York

Port Authority Terminal

1,2,3,7 N,Q,R,S,W

A,C,E

N,R,A,5,6

N,R

F

C,E

1

N,R,W

Central Park S.

A,B,C,D,1

Columbus Circle

0   1/4 mi

0   1/4 km

CENTRAL PARK

Central Park S.

Avenue of the Americas (Sixth Ave.)

W. 46th St.
W. 47th St.
W. 48th St.
W. 50th St.
W. 55th St.
W. 58th St.

Grand Army Plaza

The Plaza

N,R

Paley Center for Media

St Patrick's Cathedral

Saks Fifth Avenue

Fifth Ave.

American Folk Art Museum

Museum of Modern Art (MoMA)

Museum of Arts and Design

E,V

GE Building, Top of the Rock

Lower Plaza

Today Show Studios

Radio City Music Hall

W. 49th St.—Rockefeller Center

B,D,F,V

F

TOP MIDTOWN EXPERIENCES

Stand on one of the islands in the center of Times Square and look up while doing a 360.

Whisper to a friend in the mind-boggling Whispering Gallery at Grand Central Terminal near the entrance of the Oyster Bar.

Take a break at Rockefeller Center any time of year—catch an early-morning concert at the Today Show, try ice-skating at the iconic rink under the famous Christmas tree, or ogle the red carpet set-up outside of Radio City Music Hall.

Visit the newly restored Plaza Hotel, the stomping grounds of the legendary Eloise and familiar to viewers of the movie Home Alone 2.

Shop, shop, shop—NBA Store, American Girl Place, H&M, Abercrombie & Fitch—all your tweens' and teens' favorites are here. (⇨ Ch. 5)

★ **Chrysler Building.** The former Chrysler headquarters wins many a New Yorker's vote for the city's most iconic and beloved skyscraper. American eagle gargoyles sprout from the 61st floor and the pinnacle, whose tiered crescents and spiked windows radiate out like a magnificent steel sunburst. This building is absolutely breathtaking especially when illuminated at night. It's an iconic part of Manhattan's skyline and makes for a great photo op with the kids in the foreground. ⊠405 Lexington Ave., at E. 42nd St., Midtown East Ⓜ 4, 5, 6, 7, S to 42nd St./Grand Central. 7+up

★ FodorsChoice **Grand Central Terminal.** Grand Central is not only the world's largest (76 acres) and the nation's busiest (500,000 commuters and subway riders use it daily) railway station, but also one of the world's greatest public spaces. You can best admire Grand Central's exquisite beaux arts architecture from its ornate south face on East 42nd Street, modeled after a Roman triumphal arch. Crowning the facade's Corinthian columns and 75-foot-high arched windows, a graceful clock keeps time for hurried commuters. Inside is the majestic **Main Concourse with its sweeping staircases.** Overhead, a celestial map of the twinkling fiber-optic constellations covers the robin's egg–blue ceiling. During rush hour you'll be swept into the tides and eddies of human traffic, which swirl around the central information kiosk, a popular meeting place. If you visit during Christmas, your family will be treated to an amazing laser show projected among the galaxies on the ceiling. See if your kids will notice that the constellations are painted backward. If you look carefully, you'll see one dirty patch of blue on the ceiling, showing what it looked like before the massive restoration of recent years.

Despite its grandeur, Grand Central still functions primarily as a railroad station. Underground, more than 60 ingeniously integrated railroad tracks lead trains upstate and to Connecticut via Metro-North Commuter Rail. The subway connects here as well. ■TIP→ **Before you head for a snack at the Dining Concourse downstairs, stop by the wonderous Whispering Gallery at the end of the ramp where the Oyster Bar and Restaurant is located. If you whisper into the wall where three tiled, vaulted corridors meet, your kids can hear what you say by pressing their ears to the wall across the way.**

Older kids might enjoy the free tour of the station, which happens every Wednesday at 12:30. They'll get a very special bird's-eye view of the commotion below as they walk across one of the skybridges that run inside the high windows on the side of the building. ⊠*Main entrance: E. 42nd St. at Park Ave., Midtown East* ☎*212/935–3960* ⊕*www.grandcentralterminal.com* Ⓜ*4, 5, 6, 7, S to 42nd St./Grand Central.* All ages; tours 9+up.

The Plaza. With two sides of Central Park *and* 5th Avenue at its doorstep, this world-famous 19-story 1907 building sits proudly on a corner pedestal displaying its birthday-cake exterior of white-glazed brick topped with a French mansard roof. The original hotel was home to Eloise, the fictional star of Kay Thompson's children's books, and has appeared in many movies including *Home Alone 2* and *North by Northwest*. After a $400 million renovation, the Plaza reopened in early 2008 as a part-condo, part-hotel hybrid. Bring your little Eloises to have high tea in the oh-so-refined Palm Court or poke around the gift shop for Plaza tokens including children's books. ⊠*5th Ave. at W. 59th St., Midtown West* ☎*212/759–3000* Ⓜ*N, R, W to 5th Ave./59th St.* 7+up

★ Fodor'sChoice **Rockefeller Center.** If Times Square is New York's crossroads, Rockefeller Center is its communal gathering place, where the entire world converges to snap pictures, skate on the ice rink, peek in on a taping of the *Today show* at NBC Studios, shop, eat, and take in the monumental art deco structures and public sculptures from the past century. Totaling 49 shops, 28 restaurants (1.4 million square feet in all) the complex runs from 47th to 52nd streets between

5th and 7th avenues. Special events and huge pieces of art dominate the central plazas in summer, and in December an enormous twinkling tree towers above (visit ⊕www. rockefellercenter.com for a schedule).

The **Lower Plaza** provides access to the marble-lined corridors underneath Rockefeller Center where you'll also find public restrooms. In inclement weather, you can walk, shop, and dine for blocks underground. ⊠*Between 5th and 6th Aves. and W. 49th and W. 50th Sts., Midtown West* ☎*212/332–7654 for rink* Ⓜ *B, D, F, V to 47th–50th Sts./ Rockefeller Center.* All ages

Rising up on the Lower Plaza's west side is the 70-story (850-foot-tall) art deco **GE Building.** This is where you'll find **NBC Studios** (☎ 212/664–7174), whose news tapings, visible at street level, attract crowds of all ages. For ticket information for NBC shows or the 70-minute studio tour, visit the NBC Experience Store at the building's southeast corner. Kids love the chance to be filmed while being interviewed by Conan O'Brien or to visit the *Saturday Night Live* studio. If you're an early bird, bring your brood to watch the broadcast of the *Today Show,* between 7 and 9 AM. You might just end up on TV or hear an amazing concert. ⊠*30 Rockefeller Plaza, between 5th and 6th Aves. at 49th St., Midtown West* ⊠*NBC Studio Tour $18.50, $15.50, ages 6–12* ☞*Children under 6 not permitted* ⊙*Tours depart every 30 min Mon.–Sat. 8:30–5:30, Sun. 9:30–4:30* Ⓜ*B, D, F, V to 47th–50th Sts./ Rockefeller Center.* 7+up

FRUGAL FUN. The free four-floor **Sony Wonder Technology Lab** in the Sony Building (⊠*550 Madison Ave., between E. 55th and E. 56th Sts., Midtown East* ☎*212/833–8100* ⊕*www.sonywondertechlab. com* ⊙*Tues.–Sat. 10–5, Sun. noon–5; last entrance 30 min before closing*) lets kids program robots, edit music videos, or take a peek inside the human body. There's a High Definition Theater and, of course, Playstation games to try and a movie-making area. Entrance to each floor is with a super-cool personalized swipe card encoded with each visitor's picture and recorded voice. Admission is free but call at least seven days ahead for reservations, as it's very popular.

St. Patrick's Cathedral. The country's largest Catholic cathedral (seating approximately 2,400) this 1859–79 Gothic edifice is among New York's most striking churches (note the 330-foot spires). Take the requisite photo of your kids on the 5th Avenue steps, then quietly enter the cathedral during off-hour times to soak up the magnificence. ⊠*5th Ave. between E. 50th and E. 51st Sts., Midtown East* ☎*212/753–2261 rectory* ⊕*www.ny-archdiocese.org* ☉*Daily 8* AM–*8:45* PM Ⓜ*E, V to 5th Ave./53rd St.* 5+up

★ **Times Square.** Here it is: the square that comes to mind when people use the words "bright lights, big city." Times Square has all the hustle and bustle a big city is known for, topped off with moving billboards, three-story-high TV screens, and piles of neon. Locals avoid it at all costs, but if it's your first time here, there's no doubt you'll want to take a stroll through. Just be ready for crowds, traffic, and lots of street performers and hustlers.

Times Square today is a family-friendly, open-air promenade of familiar brand names in theme park–like settings, from ESPN Zone to one of the world's largest McDonald's. It's all great fun for a while—especially with kids (whose hands you must *never* release because of the wall of people you'll encounter). The Toys "R" Us alone will captivate, with their huge Ferris wheel. Older kids might also get a kick out of the waxwork celebrity figures at Madame Tussauds museum, which is around the corner on West 42nd Street. ⊠*Broadway and Seventh Ave. from 42nd Str. To 47th St.* Ⓜ*N, Q, R, W, S, 1, 2, 3, 7* All ages

Times Square Visitors Center. Times Square has the city's first comprehensive visitor center. Stop by for ATMs, Metro-Cards, free Internet, sightseeing, and theater tickets, a video camera that shoots and e-mails instant photos, and (most important!) free restrooms. Free walking tours of the area start here Friday at noon. ⊠*1560 Broadway, between W. 46th and W. 47th Sts., Midtown West* ☎*212/768–1560* ☉*Daily 8–8* Ⓜ*1, 2, 3, 7, N, Q, R, S, W to 42nd St./Times Sq.* All ages

★ Fodor'sChoice **Top of the Rock.** Rockefeller Center's multifloor observation deck, first opened in 1933, and closed in the early 1980s, reopened in 2005. Arriving just before sunset affords a view of the city that morphs before your eyes into a dazzling wash of colors, with a bird's-eye view of the tops of the Empire State Building, the Citicorp Building, and the Chrysler Building, and sweeping views northward to Central Park and south to the Statue of Liberty. Transparent elevators lift you to the 67th-floor interior viewing area. An escalator leads to the outdoor deck on the 69th floor for sightseeing through nonreflective glass safety panels. Or, take another elevator (or stairs) to the 70th floor for a 360-degree outdoor panorama of New York City on a deck that is only 20 feet wide and nearly 200 feet long. Reserved-time ticketing eliminates long lines. The rooftop is very narrow and very exposed so it may not be suitable for younger kids or those afraid of heights. But you can opt to stay inside instead. The breezeway on the 69th floor is mesmerizing for kids: motion-reacting colored lights switch off and on as you walk around the room. Dance around!—it's a great *Saturday Night Fever* moment to share with your family! ✉*Entrance on 50th St., between 5th and 6th Aves., Midtown West* ☎877/692–7625 *or* 212/698–2000 ⊕*www.topoftherocknyc.com* ✆*Solo visits (one visit in a day)$18,* $13, *ages 6–12; for dawn–dusk visits (twice in one day) $30, children $15* ◷*Daily 8–midnight; last elevator at 11* PM Ⓜ*B, D, F, V to 47th–50th Sts./Rockefeller Center.* 5+up

★ **United Nations Headquarters.** Officially an "international zone" and not part of the United States, the U.N. Head-quarters sit on a lushly landscaped, 18-acre tract on the East River, fronted by flags of member nations.

The main reason to visit is the 45-minute guided tour (given in 20 languages), which includes the **General Assembly** and major council chambers. The tour includes displays on war, nuclear energy, and refugees, and passes corridors overflowing with imaginatively diverse artwork. If you just want to wander around, the grounds include a beautiful riverside promenade, a rose garden with 1,400 specimens, and sculptures donated by member nations. Kids can add to their stamp collection with a wide variety of United Nations stamps sold at the post office and can also mail a post card to their friends from here. If it's a working day, all 191 UN member flags will be flying. Many gifts given to the UN are on display including a model of Sputnik I and a moon rock. ✉*Visitor entrance: 1st Ave. and E. 46th St., Midtown East* ☎212/963–8687 ⊕*www.un.org* ✆*Tour $13.50 adults; $7.50, ages 5–14; $9, students with ID* ☞*Children under 5 not admitted* ◷*Tours weekdays 9:45–4:45, weekends 10–4:30, no weekend tours Jan. and Feb.; tours in English leave General Assembly lobby every 30 min* Ⓜ*4, 5, 6, 7, S to 42nd St./Grand Central.* 5+up

New York Public Library (NYPL) Humanities and Social Sciences Library. This 1911 masterpiece of Beaux Arts design is one of the great research institutions in the world, with 6 million books, 12 million manuscripts, and 2.8 million pictures. It's worth a visit inside for a peaceful (and free!) alternative to Midtown's bustle especially when combined with a stroll through adjacent **Bryant Park.** Or, just chill by the library's grand 5th Avenue entrance to people-watch from the block-long marble staircase.

There are women's rooms on the ground floor and third floor, and a men's room on the third floor. There's a great photo op with your kids in front of the library's two lion mascots, Patience and Fortitude. Also check out the original Winnie-the-Pooh, Eeyore, Tigger, Piglet, and Kanga toys, recently moved to this location. ⊠*5th Ave. between E. 40th and E. 42nd Sts., Midtown West* ☎*212/930–0800, 212/869–8089 for exhibit information* ⊕*www.nypl.org* ⊙*Mon., Thurs.–Sat. 11–6, Sun. 1–5, Tues. and Wed. 11–7:30; exhibitions until 6* Ⓜ*B, D, F, V to 42nd St.; 7 to 5th Ave.* 5+up

WHERE CAN I FIND . . . IN MIDTOWN?

	Location	Description
QUICK MEALS		
Ellen's Stardust Diner	24 W. 45th St., near 5th Ave.	'50s-style diner with trains and singing waitstaff
Daisy May's	623 11th Ave., at 46th St.	Casual BBQ at picnic tables with red velvet cupcakes
PLAYGROUNDS		
Bryant Park	41st St. between 5th and 6th Aves.	Carousel only
ICE CREAM		
'witchcraft	11 W. 40th St., at Bryant Park	Gourmet ice-cream sandwiches by Top Chef Tom Colicchio
Cold Stone Creamery	253 W. 42nd Street	Great creations with mix-ins
PUBLIC BATHROOMS		
World of Disney	511 5th Ave., at 55th St.	Downstairs, changing tables
FAO Schwarz	767 5th Ave., at 58th St.	Nursing area (lower level)
Time Warner Center	Columbus Circle at 59th St.	Upstairs

CENTRAL PARK

The literal and figurative center of Manhattan, Central Park has 843 acres of meandering paths, tranquil lakes, ponds, and open meadows. Twenty-five million people use Central Park each year; on an average spring week-end day, a quarter-million children and adults flood these precincts from all over Manhattan, frolicking in the 21 playgrounds, walking dogs, and watching the world go by from more than 9,000 benches. For softball and soc-cer players, strollers, joggers, ice- and roller skaters, rock climbers, bird-watchers, boaters, picnickers, and outdoor performers, it's an oasis of fresh air and greenery that's the best backyard any kid could ever want. There's also a nice choice of hot dog stands, ice-cream vendors, and cafés to grab a snack plus a small amusement park in the summer months. If there's snow, kids of all ages run out to go sledding or snow tubing on every hill. Restrooms are scattered throughout, many near the playgrounds. Don't be afraid to ask for directions—this is Manhattan's proverbial community center.

Balto. Shiny in places from constant touching, this bronze statue commemorates a real-life sled dog who led a team of huskies that carried medicine for 674 mi across the ice to Nome, Alaska. Have your kids do what thousands of kids before have done: rub the dog's nose and paws. ✉*East of Center Dr. near Literary Walk and E. 67th St., Central Park*. All ages

Belvedere Castle. Standing regally atop Vista Rock, Belve-dere Castle overlooks the Delacorte Theater and picnickers and softball players on the Great Lawn. It's particularly beautiful during the fall foliage months. If you enter the castle from the lower level, you can visit the Henry Luce Nature Observatory, which has nature exhibits, children's workshops, and educational programs. Kids can pretend they're surveying their own kingdom as they climb to the top of this Shrek-like castle. At the base of the castle is Turtle Pond, an island where various kinds of turtles nest. Restrooms are to the West, next to the Delacorte Theatre. ✉*Midpark at 79th St. Transverse, Central Park*. 3+up

Bethesda Fountain. There's a reason this ornate fountain, off the 72nd Street transverse, shows up in so many movies set in New York City: the view from the staircase above is one of the most beautiful in the city. It's a great place to meet, sit, admire the lake beyond with its swans and boaters, or grab a snack. Kids will enjoy running up and down the stairs (under your supervision, of course) or watching the many street entertainers. (Check out the tango dancers on certain summer afternoons!) ⊠*Midpark at 72nd St., Tranverse, Central Park.* All ages

Central Park Wildlife Center. If you saw the film Madagascar, you may recognize the Central Park Zoo, officially known as the Central Park Wildlife Center. Here, the penguins and polar bears play at the Polar Circle, monkeys frolic in the open-air Temperate Territory, and the Rain Forest showcases flora and fauna that you wouldn't expect to see in Manhattan. An unusual exhibit is the ant colony—even New York City's zoo has a sense of humor. Stick around to see the sea lion feedings (call for times) and to watch the animals dance to a variety of nursery rhymes at the Delacorte Musical Clock just outside, on the hour and half-hour from 8 AM to 5 PM. North of the clock is Tisch Children's Zoo, where kids can pet and feed sheep, goats, rabbits, cows, and pigs. Enter through the trunk of a make-believe tree and arrive at rhe Enchanted Forest, filled with huge "acorns," a climbable "spider's web," and hoppable "lily pads." Monkeys play the bells on top of the Delacorte Clock on the hour as well. Both the Children's Zoo and the Central Park Zoo are small enough that kids will enjoy them without the usual "zoo exhaustion." There are various family programs scheduled throughout the year. A wonderful "kid feeding" spot, the Leaping Frog Café packages kid meals in a keepsake bag. ⊠*Entrance at 5th Ave. and E. 64th St., Central Park* ☎*212/439–6500* ⊕*www. centralparkzoo.org* ⊠*$8; $3, ages 3–12.* All ages

Cleopatra's Needle. This weathered hieroglyphic-coveredobelisk began life in Heliopolis, Egypt, around 1500 BC, but has nothing to do with Cleopatra—it's just New York's nickname for the work. It was eventually carted off to Alexandria by the Romans in 12 BC. Ask your kids if they can name another place where there's another one of these (answer: London or Paris) or what country was known for the writing on it. It may also resemble a miniature Washington Monument to them. ⊠*E. Park Dr. north of 79th St. Transverse,Central Park.* 7+up

Conservatory Garden. Walking along 5th Avenue to 105th Street, you'll see a magnificent wrought-iron gate that marks the entrance to this formal garden. As you walk through it, you enter a different world, a quiet place that's

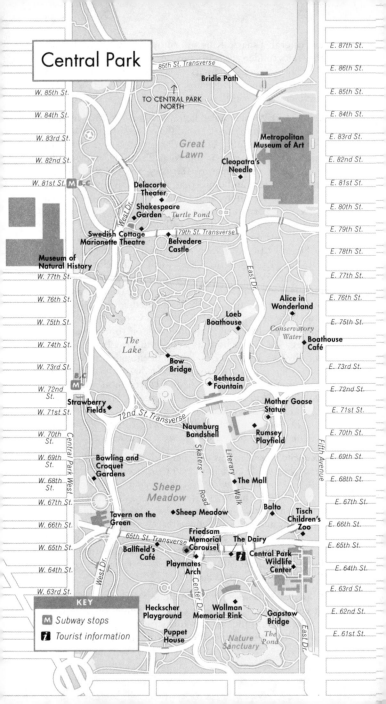

Central Park

E. 87th St.

E. 86th St.

85th St. Transverse

Bridle Path

E. 85th St.

W. 85th St.

↑ TO CENTRAL PARK NORTH

E. 84th St.

W. 84th St.

W. 83rd St.

Great Lawn

Metropolitan Museum of Art

E. 83rd St.

W. 82nd St.

Cleopatra's Needle

E. 82nd St.

W. 81st St. Ⓜ Ⓑ Ⓒ

E. 81st St.

Delacorte Theater

West Dr.

Shakespeare Garden

Turtle Pond

E. 80th St.

Swedish Cottage Marionette Theatre

79th St. Transverse

E. 79th St.

Belvedere Castle

E. 78th St.

Museum of Natural History

East Dr.

W. 77th St.

E. 77th St.

W. 76th St.

Alice in Wonderland

E. 76th St.

Loeb Boathouse

W. 75th St.

Conservatory Water

E. 75th St.

W. 74th St.

The Lake

Boathouse Café

W. 73rd St.

Bow Bridge

E. 73rd St.

Bethesda Fountain

W. 72nd St.

Ⓑ Ⓒ
Ⓜ

E. 72nd St.

Strawberry Fields

72nd St. Transverse

Mother Goose Statue

W. 71st St.

E. 71st St.

Naumburg Bandshell

Rumsey Playfield

W. 70th St.

E. 70th St.

Skaters' Road

Literary Walk

W. 69th St.

Bowling and Croquet Gardens

E. 69th St.

W. 68th St.

The Mall

E. 68th St.

W. 67th St.

Central Park West

Sheep Meadow

Balto

E. 67th St.

Fifth Avenue

Tavern on the Green

Sheep Meadow

Tisch Children's Zoo

W. 66th St.

65th St. Transverse

Friedsam Memorial Carousel

E. 66th St.

W. 65th St.

Ballfield's Café

The Dairy

E. 65th St.

🛈

Central Park Wildlife Center

Playmates Arch

W. 64th St.

E. 64th St.

West Dr.

Center Dr.

W. 63rd St.

E. 63rd St.

KEY

Heckscher Playground

Wollman Memorial Rink

Gapstow Bridge

E. 62nd St.

Ⓜ *Subway stops*

🛈 *Tourist information*

Puppet House

Nature Sanctuary

The Pond

E. 61st St.

East Dr.

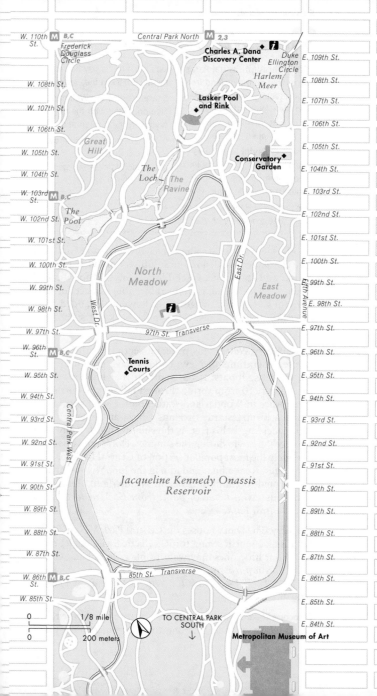

TOP CENTRAL PARK EXPERIENCES

Stroll through Central Park's incredibly gorgeous (and free) Conservatory Garden, savoring the exquisite flowers and glance at the many weddings always happening here.

Visit the playful polar bears Ida and Gus at the Central Park Zoo before you grab a spot to watch the sea lion feeding.

Go fishing at Harlem Meer and then snap a picture with your kid's catch of the day before tossing it back in the water.

Skate around the Wollman Memorial Rink with the city skyline in the background.

Catch the marionette show at the Swedish Cottage for old-fashioned entertainment pre-YouTube style.

positively idyllic for strolling and slowing down. Girls will love the Secret Garden in the south section with its foundation and statue of two children. A second fountain of three women dancing is rimmed by enough space for kids to roam and admire the gorgeous flowers. An added plus: there are large clean restrooms in the back of the gardens. ⊠*Near 5th Ave. and E. 105 St.,Central Park.* 7+up

Conservatory Water. This peaceful section of the park is where generations of New Yorkers have grown up racing model sailboats. It's a tradition that happens every Saturday at 10 from spring through fall. At the north end is the Alice in Wonderland statue; on the west side of the pond, a bronze statue of Hans Christian Andersen, the Ugly Duckling at his feet, is the site of Saturday morning storytelling hours during the summer. Don't miss this—it's definitely the most popular section of Central Park for kids of all ages. Rent a boat and join in the fun. You might also be tempted to climb on Alice in Wonderland along with your kids. ⊠*East side of park, from E. 73rd to E. 75th Sts., Central Park.* All ages

The Dairy. The Dairy houses the Central Park Visitor's Center. It's also worth seeing for its eclectic Swiss-chalet exterior. Your little ones may want to play Hansel and Gretel here. ⊠*Midpark south of 65th St. Transverse, Central Park* ☎*212/794–6564 visitor center* ⊕*www.nycgovparks. org.* All ages

Delacorte Theater. At the southwest corner of the Great Lawn is this fan-shaped theater, home to the summer Shakespeare in the Park festival. Tweens fascinated with *Shakespeare in Love* can find the bard in full force here. ✉*Midpark near W. 81st St.,Central Park* ☎*212/539–8750* ⊕*www. publictheater.org.* 12+up

Friedsam Memorial Carousel. Also known as the Carousel, this ride was built in 1908. It has 58 nearly life-size hand-carved horses and remains a favorite among young and old. Its original Wurlitzer organ plays calliope waltzes, polkas, and standards. There are also two chariots for lit-tler kids not able to sit on the horses. Admission $2 for a 3½-minute ride. ✉*Midpark south of 65th St. Transverse, Central Park.* All ages

Great Lawn. This stretch hums with action on weekends, warm days, and most summer evenings, when its baseball fields and picnic grounds fill with city folks and visitors alike. Its 13 acres have endured millions of footsteps, thousands of baseball games, hundreds of downpours, dozens of concerts, firework displays, and even a papal mass.Kids can run around, play Frisbee, do cartwheels, or just hang out in their strollers. Keep them away from the softball games, though, so the kids won't get hurt. No dogs are allowed on the Great Lawn. ✉*Midpark between 81st and 85th Sts., Central Park.* All ages

Harlem Meer. Yes, there are fish in Central Park. At Harlem Meer, the third-largest body of water in the park, you can borrow fishing poles at the Dana Discovery Center (identification required) from mid-April through October and try your hard at catching the largemouth bass, catfish, golden shiners, and bluegills that are stocked in the water's 11 acres. The fishing is great fun, the poles and bait are free, and it's catch-and-release. The Discovery Center is in a restored boathouse and also hosts environmental, arts-and-crafts and science programs for kids year-round. There's a nearby playground and even a small sandy beach area. ✉*Between 5th and Lenox Aves. at Central Park N, Central Park* ☎*212/860–1370 Charles A. Dana Discovery Center.* 5+up

Jacqueline Kennedy Onassis Reservoir. A popular gathering place for locals and visitors alike; rain or shine, you'll see runners of all ages and paces heading counterclockwise around the 1.58-mi cinder path that encircles the water. The path in turn is surrounded by hundreds of trees that burst into color in the spring and fall. From the top of the stairs at 90th Street just off 5th Avenue you have a

360-degree panorama of the city's exciting skyscrapers and often-brilliant sunsets. On the south side are benches so you can rest and recharge.Tell the kids to watch for celebs like Madonna who have been known to jog here with their trainers. ✉*Midpark from 85th to 96th Sts., Central Park.* All ages

Loeb Boathouse. At the brick neo-Victorian boathouse on the park's 18-acre Lake, you can rent a rowboat or bicycle as well as ride in an authentic Venetian gondola. The attached café is a worthy pit stop. Helmets and tag-alongs can all be rented. ✉*Midpark at E. Park Dr., Central Park* ☎*212/517–2233* ⊕*www.thecentralparkboathouse.com.* All ages

The Mall. This is arguably the most elegant area of Central Park. The mall's southern end, known as Literary Walk, is lined with statues of authors and artists such as Robert Burns and William Shakespeare. Park your baby in the stroller next to you while you sit on the bench and watch the world go by or listen to the nearby drumming circle ✉*Midpark between 66th and 72nd Sts., Central Park.* All ages

The Pond. Swans and ducks cruise on its calm waters, and if you follow the shoreline to Gapstow Bridge and look southward, you'll see much of New York City's skyline. This is a lovely area for a picnic with the kids. Point out the juxtaposition of park and pond with cityscape—it's something that makes New York City really remarkable. ✉*Central Park S and 5th Ave., Central Park.* All ages

Sheep Meadow. The only "beach" that some native New Yorkers have ever known, this area is one of the largest expanses of open space to the west of the Mall. Join in on a Frisbee or football game, or admire the tenacity of kite flyers. There's free Wi-Fi here now, and kids can chill along with the locals after a hard day of sightseeing. No radios are allowed. Sheep Meadow Café, a snack bar by day and more serious restaurant at dinnertime, is popular among both humans and dogs. ✉*East of West Dr. and W. 72nd St., Central Park.* All ages

Strawberry Fields. Across from the Dakota apartment building on Central Park West, this spot is named after the Beatles 1967 classic, "Strawberry Fields Forever." It stands as an informal memorial to John Lennon. Fans make pilgrimages to walk the curving paths, reflect among its shrubs, trees, and flower beds, and lay flowers on the black-and-white

"Imagine" mosaic. On December 8, hundreds of Beatles fans mark the anniversary of Lennon's death by gathering here. Teenagers familiar with the Beatles and John Lennon shouldn't miss this site. ⊠*W. Park Dr. and W. 72nd St., Central Park.* 12+up

Swedish Cottage. Marionette theater is performed in this traditional Swedish schoolhouse every day but Monday to the delight of young park visitors. ⊠*W. Park Dr. north of 79th St. Transverse, Central Park* ☎*212/988–9093* ✉*Marionette theater tickets $8 adults; $5 children.* 3+up

Wollman Memorial Rink. Wollman Memorial Rink sits inside the park against a backdrop of Central Park South skyscrapers. You can rent skates, buy snacks, and have a perfect city-type outing. There's a lively feeling here with lots of great music playing and a terrace so you can watch if you're not skating. It's not as busy as the rink at Rockefeller Center, so it might be better for smaller skaters. In summer, the rink is taken over by the lively Victorian Gardens Amusement Park with rides and games just for kids (free for kids under 3, per-ride charge or one-price for the full day). There's also a grill nearby for burgers and drinks, and the usual array of wandering vendors sell cotton candy and other temptations. ⊠*E. Park Dr. south of 65th St. Transverse, Central Park* ☎*212/439–6900* ⊕*www.wollman skatingrink.com* ✉*$11; $5, children.* 5+up

UPPER EAST SIDE

The Upper East Side is a mix of old money and a lively singles and young family scene. Alongside Central Park, between 5th and Lexington avenues, from the 60s to the 90s are some of the city's ritziest homes and boutiques.

Gorgeous residential Park Avenue may evoke scenes from the elite private schools of *Gossip Girl*. Nearby 5th Avenue is home to "Museum Mile," a stretch of art and treasures that includes the Metropolitan Museum of Art, the Guggenheim, the Jewish Museum, and many others. Superb kids' and adult boutiques line Madison Avenue.

East of Lexington Avenue you can find a younger residential scene, with an incredible range of family-friendly eateries and shops. The remnants of the city's German heritage can be found in Yorkville, with shops and restaurants near 86th street and 2nd Avenue. Along the East River lies one of the city's most beautiful parks and promenades, Carl Schurz

Park, adjacent to the mayor's figurative (and sometimes literal) residence, Gracie Mansion.

★ FodorsChoice **Carl Schurz Park.** Astride the East River, this park is so tranquil you'd never guess you're directly above the FDR Drive. Walk along the promenade, where you can take in views of the river and the Roosevelt Island Lighthouse across the way; to the north are Randall's and Ward's islands and the Triborough Bridge—as well as the more immediate sight of locals pushing strollers, or exercising their dogs. There's a wonderful playground at the 84th Street end with climbing equipment, sprinklers, swings, and other diversions appropriate for toddlers and older children. You'll also find chess tables, a basketball court, and grassy "beach" areas for lounging and suntanning. At the park's 86th Street entrance you'll see the grounds of a Federal-style wood-frame house that belies the grandeur of its name—Gracie Mansion.

The official mayor's residence, **Gracie Mansion** (⊠*Carl Schurz Park, East End Ave. opposite 88th St., Upper East Side* ☎*212/570–4751* ☜*$7; students free* ☉*45-min guided tours by advance reservation only; Wed. 10–2* Ⓜ *4, 5, 6 to 86th St.*) was built in 1799 and is one of New York's oldest wooden structures. Tours of the interior—which you must schedule in advance—take you through its history and colorful rooms furnished over centuries and packed with American objets d'art. Nine mayors have lived here since 1942 but New York City's most recent mayor Michael Bloomberg wasn't one of them; he chose to stay in his own 79th Street town house, though he used this house for meetings and functions. Explain to older kids that this part of the city was once considered "the country," and boats used to pull up to Gracie Mansion. They'll find it hard to believe. ⊠*Carl Schurz Park spans East End Ave. to East River, E. 84th to E. 90th Sts., Upper East Side* Ⓜ*4, 5, 6 to 86th St.* 9+up

Although **Roosevelt Island** (the 2-mi-long East River slice of land that parallels Manhattan from East 48th to East 85th streets) is now a quasi-suburban enclave, it's still a fun offbeat trip. On a small park at the island's north tip is a lighthouse built in 1872. Riverside esplanades provide nice panoramas of Manhattan. You can get here by a fun four-minute ride on the **Roosevelt Island Tramway,** the only commuter cable car in North America, which lifts you 3,000 feet in the air with views of midtown Manhat-

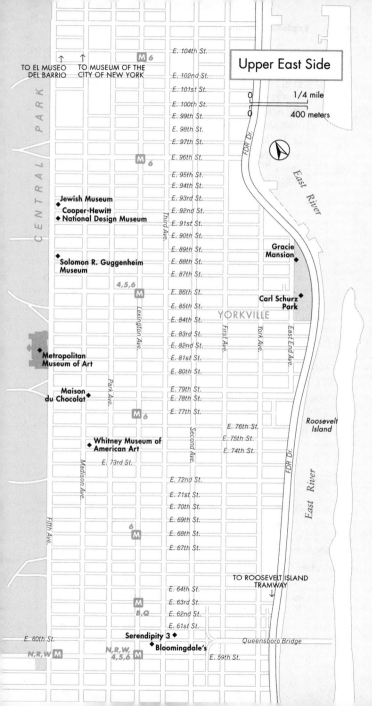

Upper East Side

0   1/4 mile
0   400 meters

E. 104th St.
E. 102nd St.
E. 101st St.
E. 100th St.
E. 99th St.
E. 98th St.
E. 97th St.
E. 96th St.
E. 95th St.
E. 94th St.
E. 93rd St.
E. 92nd St.
E. 91st St.
E. 90th St.
E. 89th St.
E. 88th St.
E. 87th St.
E. 86th St.
E. 85th St.
E. 84th St.
E. 83rd St.
E. 82nd St.
E. 81st St.
E. 80th St.
E. 79th St.
E. 78th St.
E. 77th St.
E. 76th St.
E. 75th St.
E. 74th St.
E. 73rd St.
E. 72nd St.
E. 71st St.
E. 70th St.
E. 69th St.
E. 68th St.
E. 67th St.
E. 64th St.
E. 63rd St.
E. 62nd St.
E. 61st St.
E. 60th St.
E. 59th St.

TO EL MUSEO DEL BARRIO
TO MUSEUM OF THE CITY OF NEW YORK

CENTRAL PARK

FDR Dr.

East River

M 6
M 6

Jewish Museum
Cooper-Hewitt
National Design Museum

Solomon R. Guggenheim Museum

Gracie Mansion

4,5,6
M

Carl Schurz Park

YORKVILLE

Metropolitan Museum of Art

Maison du Chocolat

M 6

Whitney Museum of American Art

Third Ave.
Lexington Ave.
Park Ave.
Madison Ave.
Fifth Ave.
Second Ave.
First Ave.
York Ave.
East End Ave.

Roosevelt Island

6
M

Roosevelt Island

East River

TO ROOSEVELT ISLAND TRAMWAY

M
B,Q

Serendipity 3
Bloomingdale's

Queensboro Bridge

N,R,W M
N,R,W
4,5,6 M

TOP UPPER EAST SIDE EXPERIENCES

Stop to watch canines of all sizes at the Carl Schurz Park dog runs as your family strolls along the beautiful riverside.

Let the kids swirl down the spiral ramp at the Guggenheim (5th Avenue and 88th Street). (⇨ Ch. 3)

Indulge your sweet tooth with a frozen hot chocolate at Serendipity or bags of goodies from Dylan's Candy Bar.

Find the precious kids' clothes you won't find elsewhere along Madison Avenue from the 80s to the 90s. (⇨ Ch. 5)

tan and Queens. Red buses service the island, 25¢ a ride. Kids go gaga over this Disney-like tramway ride, which gives you the feeling of a helicopter ride without the scariness. ⊠*Tramway entrance at 2nd Ave. and either 59th St. or 60th St., Upper East Side* ☎*212/832–4543* ☎*$2 each way*; students with permits ride for $2 round-trip ⊙*Sun.– Thurs. 6 AM–2 AM, Fri. and Sat. 6 AM–3:30 AM; leaves every 15 min* Ⓜ*F to Roosevelt Island.* All ages

WHERE CAN I FIND . . . ON THE UPPER EAST SIDE?

	Location	Description
ICE CREAM		
Ciao Bella	27 E. 92nd St., near Madison Ave.	Rich unusual ice cream and sorbet flavors
Dylan's Candy Bar	1011 3rd Ave., near 61st St.	An ice-cream bar with floors and floors of candy, too
FUN STORES		
Homboms	1500 1st Ave., near 78th St.	Toys, games, crafts at many different prices
Mary Arnold Toys	1010 Lexington Ave., between 72nd and 73rd Sts.	Madame Alexander dolls, Steiff bears and unusual toys
PLAYGROUNDS		
Carl Schurz Park	East End Ave. and 84th St.	Toddler-friendly playground, climbing equipment
John Jay Park	E. 76–78th Sts. and East River	Toddler and preschool play areas, swimming pool
E. 96th Playground	Central Park off 5th Ave.	Tire swings, treehouse, toddler area, climbing structures, sprinklers

UPPER WEST SIDE

1

Stretching from West 59th Street to roughly West 100th Street, the Upper West Side still is a primarily residential neighborhood and family-oriented. On weekends, stroller-pushing parents cram the sidewalks and shoppers jam the gigantic food emporiums like Zabar's and Fairway and an eclectic mix of stores that line Broadway and Columbus Avenue. The varied outdoor cafés on Amsterdam Avenue have lots of strollers and bikes parked outside. Families, nannies with their charges, singles, and just about every-body else head to Riverside Park the neighborhood's com-munal backyard or to the Western fringes of Central Park, both with lots of creatively themed playgrounds. Lively avenues, quiet tree-lined side streets with beautiful brown-stone town houses, and terrific restaurants and museums, all in a relatively compact area, make this the perfect neigh-borhood to experience life the way the locals do.

Columbus Circle. This busy traffic circle at Central Park's southwest corner anchors the Upper West Side and makes a good starting place for exploring the neighborhood if you're coming from south of 59th Street. The central 700-ton granite monument (capped by a marble statue of Chris-topher Columbus) serves as a popular meeting place. The benches and beautiful fountain make it a lovely place for tired kids and adults alike to relax for a bit. You'll almost forget that you're sitting in the middle of one of the city's busiest intersections.

To the west looms the **Time Warner Center,** its 80-story twin glass towers holding an array of shops on the first three floors, restaurants on the third and fourth floors, a huge Whole Foods grocery store, and clean restrooms. The complex also includes the Mandarin Oriental Hotel and the performing arts center **Jazz at Lincoln Center** (☎*212/258–9800* ⊕*www.jalc.org*), **which offers the pop-ular Jazz for Young People concert series for ages 6 and up on Saturday. Call for schedules.** Ⓜ*A, B, C, D, 1 to 59 St./Columbus Circle.* All ages

Riverside Park. Walking around concrete and skyscrapers all day, you can easily miss this expansive waterfront park just blocks away. Riverside Park borders the Hudson from 72nd to 159th streets. Designed by Olmsted and Vaux of Central Park fame, it is often outshone by Olmsted's "other" park. But with its waterfront bike and walking paths and lighter crowds, Riverside Park holds its own.

One of the park's loveliest attributes is a half-mile water-front promenade, a rare spot in Manhattan where you can walk right along the river's edge. Reach it by heading through an underpass beneath the West Side Highway at the park's entrance at West 72nd Street and Riverside Drive (look for the **statue of Eleanor Roosevelt**). The promenade takes you past the **79th Street Boat Basin,** where you can watch a flotilla of houseboats bobbing in the water. Above it, a ramp leads to the **Rotunda,** home in summer to the Boat Basin Cafe, an open-air spot for a burger and river views. At the end of the **promenade and up** a staircase, a community garden explodes with flowers. Strollers fit comfortably at the Boat Basin Café and chaperoned kids can walk around the rotunda while you wait for your meal. A nice variety of playgrounds, complete with restrooms, are usually filled with nannies, babies, and school-age kids throughout the day. ⊠ *W. 72nd to W. 159th Sts. between Riverside Dr. and Hudson River, Upper West Side* Ⓜ*1, 2, 3 to 72nd St.* All ages

Cathedral Church of St. John the Divine. Despite the fact that it is only two-thirds complete, this is still the largest Gothic-style cathedral in the world. The 162-foot-tall dome crossing could comfortably contain the Statue of Liberty (minus its pedestal). The cathedral's **Great Rose Window,** made from more than 10,000 pieces of colored glass, is the largest stained-glass window in the United States. Encircling the Peace Fountain on the grounds outside are whimsical animals cast in bronze from pieces sculpted by children. Kids 12 and up can do the Vertical Tour, 124 feet up a spiral staircase to the top. Reserve in advance as space is limited. On some Saturdays, there are medieval arts workshops for families. ⊠ *1047 Amsterdam Ave., at W. 112th St., Morningside Heights* ☎ *212/316–7540, 212/662–2133 box office, 212/932–7347 tours* ⊕ *www.stjohndivine.org* ☞ *Tours $5* ☉ *Daily 9–6; tours Tues.–Sat. at 11, Sat. at 12:45, Sun at 2. A vertical tour with a climb of 124 feet to top is given on Sat. at noon and 2; reservations required. $15; $10 for students. Sun. services at 9, 11, and 6* Ⓜ*1 to 110th St./Cathedral Pkwy.* 5+up

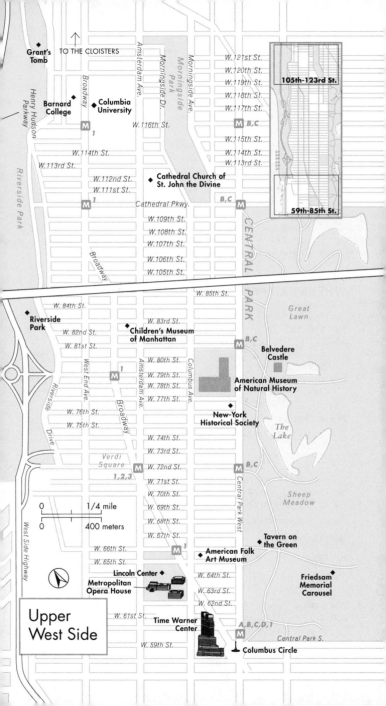

TOP UPPER WEST SIDE EXPERIENCES

Play in one of the animal-theme playgrounds of Riverside Park, a park that seems to stretch for miles and miles and miles, or climb in the Safari Playground or Wild West Playground near Central Park West.

Treat the young ladies in your family to a special afternoon tea at Alice's Tea Cup (102 W. 73rd St.) and buy them a pair of butterfly wings for dress-up when they get home. (⇨ Ch. 6)

Let your kids join you on a treasure hunt at the Sunday flea market on Columbus Avenue between 76th and 77th streets where they can find cool jewelry, posters, and other goodies.

Stare down Tyrannosaurus rex and the rest of the dinosaurs in the amazing Fossil Hall at the American Museum of Natural History. Can you find the mummified dinosaur eggs? (⇨ Ch. 3)

WHERE CAN I FIND . . . IN THE UPPER WEST SIDE?

	Location	Description
FUN STORES		
West Side Kids	498 Amsterdam Ave., near 84th St.	Creative toys for all ages
Robot Village	252 W. 81st St., between Broadway and West End	If you've ever thought of having your kids build a robot
PLAYGROUNDS		
Riverside Park	Elephant Playground: 76th St. and Riverside Dr.	Shade, sandbox, elephant sprinklers, basketball courts nearby
	Dinosaur Playground: 97th St. and Riverside Dr.	Dinosaur climbing structures, rings
PUBLIC BATHROOMS		
Riverside Park	Near all playgrounds	See list above
ICE CREAM		
Grom	2165 Broadway, near 76th St.	Italian gelati and fruit sorbets
Emack and Bolio's	389 Amsterdam Ave., between 78th and 79th Sts.	Fabulous ice cream with great toppings

HARLEM

Harlem is known throughout the world as a center of culture, jazz, and African-American life. Today's Harlem is considerably safer than it was 10 years ago with more and more renovated and new buildings joining historic jewels such as the Apollo Theatre, architecturally splendid churches, and cultural magnets like the Studio Museum in Harlem, El Museo del Barrio, and the Schomburg Center for Research in Black Culture. Sunday is a popular day to visit Harlem as wonderful soul food restaurants often feature gospel brunches.

Former president Bill Clinton's New York office is at 55 West 125th Street close to outposts of Starbucks, Old Navy, the Body Shop, MAC Cosmetics, and H&M. Outside the shops, the sidewalk is a continuous traffic jam of pedestrians and street vendors. The colorful grates in front of the many shops show off amazing street art creations.

The city's north–south avenues take on different names in Harlem: 6th Avenue is Malcolm X Boulevard (or Lenox Avenue), 7th Avenue is Adam Clayton Powell Jr. Boulevard, and 8th Avenue is Frederick Douglass Boulevard; West 125th Street, the major east–west street, is called Dr. Martin Luther King Jr. Boulevard.

Abyssinian Baptist Church. This 1923 Gothic-style church holds one of Harlem's richest legacies as the first African-American Baptist church in New York State. Among its legendary pastors was Adam Clayton Powell Jr., a powerful orator and Civil Rights leader and the first black U.S. congressman. Today, sermons by pastor Calvin Butts are fiery and the seven choirs are excellent. Dress your best and expect to line up early on Sunday. Well-behaved kids are welcome. ✉*132 Odell Clark Pl., W. 138th St., between Adam Clayton Powell Jr. Blvd., 7th Ave., and Malcolm X Blvd., Lenox Ave./6th Ave., Harlem* ☎*212/862–7474* ⊕*www.abyssinian.org* ⊙*Sun. services at 9 and 11* Ⓜ*2, 3 to 135 St.* 7+up

Hamilton Heights. In this area of elegant stone row houses in mint condition, stop by Hamilton Grange, the recently relocated and restored Federal-style mansion of former president Alexander Hamilton, now facing out on Saint Nicholas Park. The simple elegance of the house should impress older kids studying American history. ✉*St. Nicho-*

las Park between 128th and 141st Sts., Harlem Ⓜ*1, B, C to 145th St.* 12+up

Marcus Garvey Park. At the center of this historic, tree-filled public square, atop a 70-foot-high outcrop of Manhattan schist (the same bedrock that anchors our skyscrapers) stands a 47-foot cast-iron **watchtower**, the last remnant of a citywide network used to spot and report fires in pre-telephone days. Around it, an **Acropolis** provides great views of Manhattan Do not let kids roam the Acropolis alone, as there can sometimes be homeless people. The park has both toddler and older-kid playgrounds. ✉*Interrupts 5th Ave. between W. 120th and W. 124th Sts., Madison Ave. to Mt. Morris Park W, Harlem* ⊕*www.east-harlem.com/parks_mg.htm* Ⓜ*2, 3 to 125th St.* 7+up

Strivers' Row. Some of the few remaining private service alleys that once ran behind the city's town houses (where deliveries would arrive via horse and cart) lie behind these elegant 1890s Georgian and neo-Italian homes, visible through iron gates. Note the gatepost between No. 251 and 253 on West 138th Street that says, "Private Road. Walk Your Horses." Although younger kids will be bored, older kids might appreciate this snapshot of Harlem's best architecture. ✉*W. 138th and W. 139th Sts. between Adam Clayton Powell Jr. and Frederick Douglass Blvds., Harlem* Ⓜ*B, C to 135th St.* 12+up

TOP HARLEM EXPERIENCES

Enjoy real soul food at one of the many restaurants here, some with gospel music or jazz as well. (⇨Ch. 6)

Visit the Sugar Hill/Hamilton Heights historic district and survey Manhattan from above. You'll see Manhattan's oldest house, the Morris-Jumel Mansion, where George Washington slept and a Disney-like row of homes around the corner.

Walk along 125th Street and absorb the energy of Harlem while also scouting out the colorful painted grates in front of the stores.

Dress in your Sunday best to get a taste of a gospel service at one of the many churches.

Side Trips

2

WORD OF MOUTH

"We then walked across the Brooklyn Bridge. The weather was perfect, not a cloud in the sky, until we reached the end of the bridge. It started getting dark, and by the time we reached Grimaldi's, it was pouring. There was a small line to get in, but . . . we only had to wait about 5 minutes for their fabulous pizza. NOTE: Our daughter had eaten a hot dog at the beginning of the Brooklyn Bridge. She then proceeded to eat 3 pieces of a large pizza, followed by a cannoli!"

—april04

MANY TOURISTS MISS OUT ON seeing the outer boroughs of New York City, and that's a shame. They're easily reached by subway and they have some of the city's best restaurants, museums, and attractions. Brooklyn is the largest and most populous of all the boroughs, with 2.5 million residents. If it were independent of New York, it would be the fourth-largest city in the country. Diverse neighborhoods share a down-to-earth character: they are the province of families, singles, and upwardly mobile couples looking for a less-expensive and often more interesting alternative to Manhattan. Restaurants are incredibly varied with lots of Italian, Russian, and seafood choices; and there are picturesque brownstone buildings and beachfront communities, too. Brooklyn's museums, parks, and aquarium are fantastic spots for kids.

Queens is a pastiche of neighborhoods, each with a distinct culture. Thanks especially to the borough's strong immigrant population (almost 50%), you can also find some of New York City's most interesting cuisine from Italian and Asian to Greek and Indian. The former World's Fair Grounds is the place to come for a park, museums, gardens, sports, and a zoo—all in one place.

As for the Bronx, in addition to being the home of Yankee Stadium, it has one of the world's finest botanical collections and the largest metropolitan zoo in the country. The borough is pretty spread out, though, so take advantage of the free Bronx Trolley, which departs from Manhattan on weekends from April through October and offers hop on–hop off service to all major attractions.

Staten Island is legally a part of New York City, but, in many ways, it's a world apart. Reached by a drive over the Verrazano-Narrows Bridge or by a scenic 24-minute ferry trip from Lower Manhattan, the borough has a small children's museum, a zoo, and a historic village replicating New York's rural past. It's worth a trip just for the view of the Manhattan skyline and the Statue of Liberty.

TOP BROOKLYN EXPERIENCES

Take the subway all the way to Coney Island where you can catch some minor league baseball, build sandcastles on the beach, test your fearlessness on the famous Cyclone roller coaster, and eat the hot dogs that made Nathan's a New York legend.

Enjoy a lazy day in Prospect Park, pedal boating or birdwatching, or simply kicking back and playing catch on the gorgeous grounds.

Board the New York Water Taxi from Manhattan to DUMBO's Fulton Ferry Landing for a taste of everything Brooklyn: ice cream at the

Brooklyn Ice Cream Factory, fabulous pizza at Grimaldi's, and chocolate from Jacques Torres. Work off those calories by playing in the wonderful new waterfront parks.

Walk across the Brooklyn Bridge from Brooklyn this time to get an entirely different perspective of the experience of the NYC skyline rising up to greet you (see Lower Manhattan).

Crawl around in the Discovery Garden at the Brooklyn Botanic Garden and cool off by the "dancing" fountain at the nearby Brooklyn Museum.

BROOKLYN

BROOKLYN HEIGHTS

Brooklyn's toniest neighborhood, and a designated historic district, offers residents a stunning view of the Manhattan skyline from the **Brooklyn Heights Promenade.** First developed in the mid-1800s as the business center of the then-independent city of Brooklyn, it boasts historic cobblestone streets of gorgeous brownstones. Neighborhood pride is strong here and record high real estate prices akin to those of Manhattan have kept the neighborhood truly beautiful. It's a great neighborhood to wander around in with cute shops and restaurants. It's also adjacent to the New York Transit Museum where kids can happily climb in and out of old subway cars and buses, set in a former subway station.

Brooklyn Borough Hall. Built in 1848, this Greek Revival landmark is one of Brooklyn's handsomest buildings and Brooklyn's original City Hall. It is also the site of the **Brooklyn Tourism & Visitors Center** (☎718/802–3846), which has historical exhibits, a gift shop, and helpful information. It's open weekdays 10–6 and summer Saturdays 10–4. On

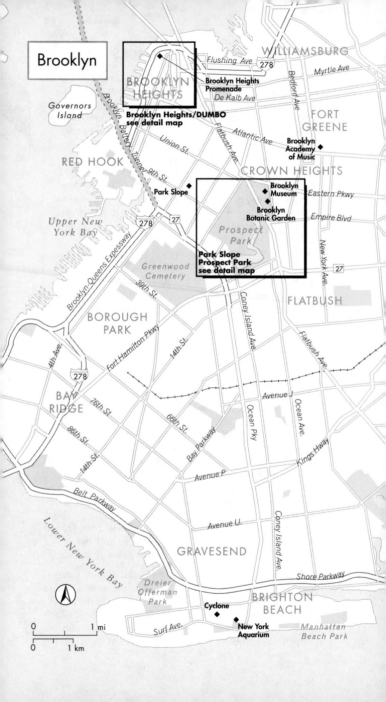

Brooklyn

WILLIAMSBURG

Flushing Ave. 278

Myrtle Ave.

BROOKLYN HEIGHTS

Brooklyn Heights Promenade

De Kalb Ave.

Brooklyn Heights/DUMBO see detail map

Governors Island

Bedford Ave.

FORT GREENE

Brooklyn Academy of Music

RED HOOK

Union St.

Atlantic Ave.

CROWN HEIGHTS

Flatbush Ave.

Brooklyn Battery Tunnel

9th St.

Park Slope

278

27

Brooklyn Museum

Eastern Pkwy

Brooklyn Botanic Garden

Empire Blvd.

Upper New York Bay

Prospect Park

Park Slope Prospect Park see detail map

New York Ave.

27

FLATBUSH

Greenwood Cemetery

39th St.

BOROUGH PARK

Brooklyn-Queens Expressway

Fort Hamilton Pkwy.

14th St.

Coney Island Ave.

Flatbush Ave.

4th Ave.

278

BAY RIDGE

76th St.

86th St.

66th St.

Bay Parkway

Ocean Pky

Avenue J.

Ocean Ave.

14th St.

Avenue P.

Kings Hwy.

Belt Parkway

Avenue U.

Coney Island Ave.

Lower New York Bay

GRAVESEND

Dreier Offerman Park

Shore Parkway

Cyclone

BRIGHTON BEACH

0   1 mi

0   1 km

Surf Ave.

New York Aquarium

Manhattan Beach Park

Tuesday and Saturday a greenmarket sets up on the flag-stone plaza in front. Free tours offered on Tuesday at 1 PM might be interesting to middle-schoolers studying American history. ⊠*209 Joralemon St., between Court and Adams Sts.* ☎*718/802–3700* ⊕*www.visitbrooklyn.org* ⊠*Free* Ⓜ*2, 3, 4, 5 to Borough Hall; R, M to Court St.* 9+up

WHAT IT COSTS				
¢	$	$$	$$$	$$$$
RESTAURANTS				
under $10	$10–$17	$18–$24	$25–$35	over $35

Price per person for a median main course or equivalent combination of smaller dishes. Note: if a restaurant offers only prix-fixe (set-price) meals, it has been given the price category that reflects the full prix-fixe price.

★ Fodor'sChoice **Brooklyn Heights Promenade.** Stretching from Orange Street in the north to Remsen Street in the south, this esplanade provides enthralling views of Manhattan. Find a bench and take in the skyline, the Statue of Liberty, and the Brooklyn Bridge. To your left is Governors Island, a former Coast Guard and Army base now partially a national park. At the south end of the promenade, near Montague Street, is a small playground. Although closer to Brooklyn, Governors Island is reachable on weekends by free ferry from Lower Manhattan, seasonally. Ⓜ*2, 3 to Clark St.; A, C to High St.* All ages

Brooklyn Historical Society. The Brooklyn Historical Society displays memorabilia, artifacts, art, and interactive exhibitions. Upstairs is an impressive library with an original copy of the Emancipation Proclamation. Recent exhibits have included old illustrated children's books printed in Brooklyn such as Alice in Wonderland and Mother Goose. ⊠*128 Pierrepont St., at Clinton St., Brooklyn Heights* ☎*718/222–4111* ⊕*www.brooklynhistory.org* ⊠*$6; $4 for students* ⊙*Wed.–Sun. noon–5* Ⓜ*2, 3, 4, 5 to Borough Hall; A, C, F to Jay St.; M, R to Court St.* 7+up

Plymouth Church of the Pilgrims. Built in 1849, this Protestant Congregational church was a center of abolitionist sentiment, thanks to the stirring oratory of the church's first minister, Henry Ward Beecher (brother of Harriet Beecher Stowe, who wrote *Uncle Tom's Cabin*). Because it provided refuge to slaves, the church was known to some as the Grand Central Depot of the Underground Railroad. A fragment of Plymouth Rock is in an adjoining arcade. The church provides an interesting glimpse into Civil War life for students of American history. ⊠*Orange St., between Henry and Hicks Sts., Brooklyn Heights* ☎*718/624–4743* ⊕*www.plymouthchurch.org* ☉*Service Sun. at 11; tours by appointment* Ⓜ *2, 3 to Clark St.; A, C to High St.* **9+up**

Transit Museum. Step down into a 1930's subway station where you'll find more than 60,000 square feet devoted to the history of public transportation. Kids can interact with the collection of vintage trains and turnstiles, sit behind the wheel of city buses, and laugh over old advertisements and signs. The gift store is a treasure trove of NYC-themed souvenirs to bring home. ⊠*Boerum Pl. at Schermerhorn St., Brooklyn Heights 11201* ☎*718/694–1600* ⊕*www.mta. info/mta/museum/web* ☎*$5, kids and seniors $3* ☉*Tues.– Fri. 10–4, Sat. and Sun. noon–5.* **All ages**

WHERE TO EAT

$$ ✕**Henry's End.** *American.* At this neighborhood favorite, the casual decor belies the quality of the food and the extensive wine list you'll find here. Wild game such as elk, kangaroo, and ostrich take center stage during the winter months; seasonal seafood and foraged vegetables star in spring. Your kids might be a bit freaked out by the menu, and the space is not suitable for larger families. The restaurant will, however, make appetizer portions of entrées and usual kid-pleasers like chicken fingers and pasta. ⊠*44 Henry St., near Cranberry St., Brooklyn Heights* ☎*718/834–1776* ▤*AE, DC, D, MC, V* ☉*No lunch* Ⓜ*2, 3 at Clark St.; A, C at High St.*

$ ✕**Noodle Pudding.** *Italian.* Ignore the unappetizing name; the food is great at this cozy restaurant serving some of the best authentic regional Italian food in the city. Locals especially rave about the osso bucco served with goat cheese polenta. It does get crowded, but that means it's noisy enough you can bring the kids. ⊠ *38 Henry St. , nr. Middagh St. Brooklyn Heights* ☎*718/625–3737* ☜*No reservations accepted* ▤ *No credit cards* ☉*Dinner only.*

$ ✕**Teresa's.** *Polish.* This busy mom-and-pop coffee shop serves well-prepared Polish and American food. Fill up on spinach blintzes, delicate orange ricotta pancakes, pierogi, or kielbasa. Smaller yummy dishes like potato pancakes and apple fritters are great for kids who can talk to their hearts

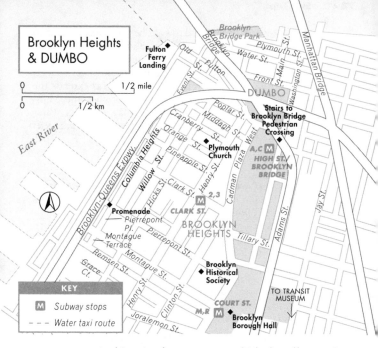

Brooklyn Heights
& DUMBO

0   1/2 mile
0   1/2 km

KEY

Ⓜ Subway stops

- - - Water taxi route

content in this noisy, fun restaurant, which also offers sandwiches, burgers, and chicken dishes. ✉80 Montague St., near Hicks St., Brooklyn Heights ☎718/797–3996 ═AE, D, MC, V Ⓜ2, 3 to Clark St.; M, R at Court St.

DUMBO

Downhill from Brooklyn Heights is the neighborhood called DUMBO (Down Under the Manhattan Bridge Overpass), an area with striking views of both Manhattan and the Brooklyn Bridge. The area's historic warehouses have been turned into spacious loft apartments and art studios, and families have now taken up residence in luxury condos. The area has a funky under-the-bridge feel to it, cobblestones streets, a developing waterfront park area with a beach, and some beloved food destinations: the fancy River Café, Grimaldi's Pizzeria, and Brooklyn Ice Cream Factory, conveniently located by the New York Water Taxi stop.

Empire-Fulton Ferry State Park. This 9-acre park has picnic tables and benches to accompany great views of the nearby bridges and the Manhattan skyline. The large playground includes a replica of a boat for make-believe voyages across the East River. From April to October, the park is home to a wide range of arts performances, and on Thursday nights in July and August, Movies with a View projects New York classic films on an outdoor screen with no cover charge. The Brooklyn Bridge Park work-in-progress extends the waterfront park area between the Brooklyn and Manhattan bridges and adds additional play areas. ✉ *Water St., at Dock St.* ☎*718/858–4708* ⊕*nysparks.state.ny.us* ✆*Free* ⊙*Daily dawn–dusk* Ⓜ*A, C to High St.; F to York St.* **All ages**

WHERE TO EAT

$ ✕**Grimaldi's Pizzeria.** *Pizza.* This classic New York–style parlor serves excellent pizza pies from its coal ovens. Grimaldi's popularity allows them to be picky: no slices, no reservations, no credit cards, and no empty tables (expect a wait). Impatient foodies have been known to phone in a to-go order, swoop past the lines, and then enjoy their pizza in the nearby Brooklyn Bridge Park. Go as early as possible if you have your heart set on eating indoors. ✉*19 Old Fulton St., between Front and Water Sts., DUMBO* ☎*718/858–4300* ⌂*Reservations not accepted* ⊟*No credit cards* Ⓜ*A, C at High St.; 2, 3 at Clark St.; F at York St.*

$$ ✕**Superfine.** *Mediterranean.* This spacious neighborhood hangout serves Mediterranean-American cuisine alongside a giant orange-felt pool table. Locals especially love Sunday Bluegrass brunches, when they can enjoy breakfast burritos spiked with real New Mexican chilies while listening to live bands. The menu changes daily, so call ahead if you're concerned about picky eaters. ✉*126 Front St., at Pearl St., DUMBO* ☎*718/243–9005 AE, D, MC, V* ⊙*Closed Mon.* Ⓜ*F to York St.*

SHOPPING

At **Jacques Torres Chocolate** (✉*66 Water St.* ☎*718/875–9772* ⊕*www.mrchocolate.com*), feel like Charlie getting a peek at the Oompa Loompas as you peer into the small factory while munching on a few unusual-flavored chocolate bonbons and sipping a thick, rich cup of hot chocolate. The staff will happily warm up some cookies for your kids.

Forget the touristy "I Heart NY" shirts. Pick up souvenirs they'll actually wear at **Neighborhoodies** (✉*26 Jay St.* ☎*718/722–7277 Ext. 201* ⊕*www.neighborhoodies.com*), where locals swear allegiance by emblazoning sweatshirts and other clothing with their favorite nabe. Kids can get custom-printed T-shirts, hoodies, and bibs.

CARROLL GARDENS/COBBLE HILL/BOERUM HILL

The three adjacent neighborhoods of Carroll Gardens, Cobble Hill, and Boerum Hill—on Atlantic Avenue's south side—form a quiet residential area of leafy streets lined with 19th-century town houses. The action swirls around Court Street's restaurants, bookstores, and old-fashioned bakeries, as well as on Smith Street, a famed restaurant row augmented by fresh, fashionable boutiques.

Atlantic Avenue between Court and Clinton streets is a rapidly gentrifying Middle Eastern enclave, which includes the emporium Sahadi's. After you purchase some baklava or olives, go to the corner of Atlantic and Court to stand where George Washington watched the disastrous Battle of Brooklyn unfold or descend through a manhole cover to tour Brooklyn's underground railroad tunnel, currently being excavated. (Advance reservations requested, *718/941–3160).*

WHERE TO EAT

$ ✕ **Lucali.** *Café.* Considered by many to be the best pizza in Brooklyn, Lucali is a humble pizza salon with a very brief menu: just pizzas and calzones. But it's simplicity will knock your socks off: thin crispy crust support a soft bubble of cheese and faint basil. Get ready for a wait, the cult following here doesn't match the small supply of tables. If your kids are too hungry, take them for a stroll back around Court Street for more Italian options. ✉*575 Henry St., at Carroll St., Carroll Gardens* ☎718/858–4068 ▭*Cash only* Ⓜ *F, G to Carroll St.*

$$$ ✕ **Saul.** *American.* Owner Saul Bolton's experience as a cook at famed Le Bernardin shows; the dynamic menu of seasonal specials features first-rate ingredients from the city's best purveyors. The food is so good that patrons only wish the portions were larger. Weekdays, opt for the bargain $30 prix-fixe menu. The restaurant is willing to make basic dishes for kids like pasta, steak, chicken, and veggies. ✉*140 Smith St., Carroll Gardens* ☎718/935–9844 ▭*AE, D, DC, MC, V* ☺ *No lunch* Ⓜ *F, G to Bergen St.*

$ ✕ **Sweet Melissa Patisseire.** *Café.* If your family wakes up with a raging sweet tooth, take them here for a decadent brunch of sweet muffins, croissants, and scones. Later in the day a kids menu of smaller sandwiches provides a solid lunch. If you're just strolling by it's worth stopping into the "Crémerie" next door for a scoop of raspberry truffle ice cream. ⊠*276 Court St., between Butler and Douglass Sts., Cobble Hill* ☎*718/855–3410* ⊟*AE, DC, MC, V* Ⓜ *F, G to Bergen St.*

FORT GREENE

One of Brooklyn's most racially diverse neighborhoods, Fort Greene has long been a home to artists and musicians. The area is in the midst of a cultural renaissance, anchored by the venerable Brooklyn Academy of Music (BAM), with new performance centers like the Mark Morris Dance Center or places to learn arts close up like the glassblowing classes at UrbanGlass.

The **Brooklyn Academy of Music** (BAM) is a comprehensive arts center with diverse and cutting-edge offerings in opera, theater, dance, music, film, and more. The movie theater shows both art-house and mainstream films.

BAM also holds performances at the nearby **Harvey Theater** (⊠*651 Fulton St.*), a 1904 vaudeville house whose renovation purposefully retained some of its crumbling beauty. The BAMkids Film Festival in spring includes film and other performing arts offerings just for kids. Check the Web site for musical shows (hip-hop, alternative rock) and films appropriate for different age groups. But leave your littlest ones at home; children under 5 are not permitted. ⊠*Peter Jay Sharp Bldg., 30 Lafayette Ave., between Ashland Pl. and St. Felix St., Fort Greene* ☎*718/636–4100* ⊕*www.bam. org* Ⓜ*C to Lafayette Ave.; 2, 3, 4, 5, B, Q to Atlantic Ave.; D, M, N, R to Atlantic Ave.–Pacific St.* 9+up

WHERE TO EAT

$$ ✕**BAMcafé.** *American.* Starting two hours before BAM performances, enjoy casual fare on the mezzanine level, often with live music on the weekend. On Friday and Saturday when there is no performance, BAMcafé opens at 8 PM with a limited menu. Older well-behaved kids may enjoy the live performances. It's not suitable for young children. ⊠*30 Lafayette Ave., at Ashland Pl., Fort Greene* ☎*718/623–7811* ⊟*AE, DC, D, MC, V* Ⓜ*D, M, N, R to Pacific St.; 2, 3, 4, 5, B, Q to Atlantic Ave.; C to Lafayette Ave.; G to Fulton St.*

$ ✕**Smoke Joint.** *Southern.*Up the hill from BAM, this relative newcomer serves "real New York Barbecue," which translates to a mix of regional specialties like incredibly moist smoked chicken, spicy dry-rubbed beef short ribs, collard greens, and meaty barbecued beans, along with local beers and sodas. Several kinds of sauces are served on the side, and the counter service couldn't be friendlier. Non-BBQ lovers can munch on hot dogs and burgers instead. ⊠*87 S. Elliot Pl., Fort Greene* ☎*718/797–1011* ⌂*Reservations not accepted* ▤*AE, D, MC, V* ⊘*Closed Mon.* Ⓜ *D, M, N, R to Pacific St.; 2, 3, 4, 5, B, Q to Atlantic Ave.; C to Lafayette Ave.; G to Fulton St.*

PARK SLOPE/PROSPECT HEIGHTS/PROSPECT PARK

This family-friendly neighborhood with row upon row of beautiful brownstones is full of academics, writers, and couples pushing designer strollers. Follow dog walkers and bicyclists to 526-acre **Prospect Park,** designed by the same landscapers as Central Park and from which the neighborhood streets "slope" down. Cafés and local designer boutiques are plentiful along 7th and 5th avenues. Adjacent to the park are two of Brooklyn's main attractions: the **Brooklyn Botanic Garden,** a must-see during its springtime Cherry Blossom Festival, and the **Brooklyn Museum,** known for its Egyptian art collections.

★ **Brooklyn Botanic Garden.** A major attraction at this 52-acre botanic garden is the Japanese Hill-and-Pond Garden—complete with a 1-acre pond and blazing red *torii* gate. The Japanese cherry arbor nearby turns into a breathtaking cloud of pink every spring, and the Cherry Blossom Festival is among the park's most popular events. Also be sure to wander through the Cranford Rose Garden and the Fragrance Garden, designed especially for the blind.

The Steinhardt Conservatory holds desert, tropical, temperate, and aquatic vegetation, as well as a display charting the evolution of plants over the past 140 million years. Near the conservatory are a café and a gift shop. Free garden tours are given every weekend at 1 PM. Entrances to the garden are on Eastern Parkway, next to the subway station; on Washington Avenue, behind the Brooklyn Museum; and on Flatbush Avenue at Empire Boulevard. Free drop-in family programs include Discovery Tuesdays, Thirsty Garden Thursdays, Storytelling Saturdays and Tremendous Trees. The highlight for any kid, the Discovery Garden, has trails, plants and garden creatures to explore plus enclosed spaces for toddlers to play in. There are lots of turtles, ducks, and giant koi in the Japanese Garden. Martial arts demonstrations are part of the Cherry Blossom

Festival. The Children's Garden has been welcoming families since 1913. ⊠*900 Washington Ave., between Crown and Carroll Sts., Prospect Heights* ☎*718/623–7200* ⊕*www. bbg.org* ☜*$5; $4 for students; free under 12; free all day Tues. and Sat. before noon. Weekend combo ticket with Brooklyn Museum $14* ⊙*Apr.–late Oct., grounds Tues.– Fri. 8–6, weekends 10–6, conservatory daily 10–5:30; late Oct.–Mar., grounds Tues.–Fri. 8–4:30, weekends 10–4:30; conservatory daily 10–4* Ⓜ *2, 3 to Eastern Pkwy.; B, Q to Prospect Park.* All ages

Across Grand Army Plaza from the park entrance is the **Brooklyn Public Library** (☎*718/230–2100* ⊕*www.brooklyn publiclibrary.org* ⊙*Tues.–Thurs. 10–9, Fri. and Sat. 10–6, Sun. 1–6*), a sleek, modern temple of learning with gold-leaf figures on the facade celebrating art and science. The building is meant to resemble an open book, with the entrance at the book's spine. Check the Web site for kids events like Tween Time, which offer a program of games, crafts, and music.

★ **Brooklyn Museum.** Next to the Brooklyn Botanic Garden, the Brooklyn Museum has more than 1 million pieces in its permanent collection and is the second-largest art museum in the United States after the Met. Notable for its extensive Egyptian art collections (including mummies kids love), it holds one of the best assortments in the world. On the first Saturday of each month, starting at 5 PM, the museum resembles a giant block party when it throws its doors to offer free art, music, dancing, film screenings, and readings. The 30-foot-tall replica of the Statue of Liberty in the Sculpture Garden and the dancing fountain in front of the museum are kid faves. Try to visit on warmer days so you can really appreciate both and sit on the strips of grass with other families. On weekends, four- to seven-year-olds and their parents can participate in Arty Facts, a drop-in art program at various times. The First Saturdays evening is appropriate for all ages and takes place every month except September. The museum café has a good selection of family fare. ⊠*200 Eastern Pkwy., at Washington Ave., Prospect Heights* ☎*718/638–5000* ⊕*www.brooklynmuseum.org* ⌨*$8 suggested donation. $4 for students; free under 12. Weekend combo ticket with Brooklyn Botanic Garden $14* ⊙*Wed.–Fri. 10–5, weekends 11–6; 1st Sat. every month 11–11; call for program schedule* Ⓜ *2, 3 to Eastern Pkwy./ Brooklyn Museum.* All ages

Prospect Park. Brooklyn residents are passionate about Prospect Park in the same way that Manhattanites cherish Central Park. Designed by Frederick Law Olmsted and Calvert Vaux, the park was completed in the late 1880s. It's popular with families and hosts events on major holidays including a Halloween Haunted Walk and festival, New Year's Fireworks, and Earth Day Weekend with lots of children's activities. The 60-acre Prospect Lake has graceful swans and ducks. A carousel, open from April to October, features 51 carved wooden horses, along with a lion-, giraffe-, deer-, and dragon-drawn chariots. (It's at the entrance at the intersection of Empire Boulevard and Flatbush Avenue.)

The 3⅓-mi circular drive is closed to cars at all times except during weekday rush hours. Families with children should head straight for the eastern side where most kids' attractions are clustered. (☎*718/965–8999 events hotline* ⊕*www. prospectpark.org*)

The park's north entrance is at **Grand Army Plaza,** where the Soldiers' and Sailors' Memorial Arch honors Civil War veterans. (Look familiar? It's patterned after the Arc

dren's Museum (✉*145 Brooklyn Ave. , Crown Heights* ☎*718/ 735-4400* ⊕ *www.brooklynkids.org* ☜ *$7.50* ☉ *Weekends 10–6, Wed.–Fri. 1–6 pm, closed Mon. and Tues.*) now housed in a sparkling new Viñoly-designed "green" building. Here kids can become astronauts, run a bakery, create African-patterned fabric, and even become DJs, mixing the rhythms of the outdoors to make music.

WHERE TO EAT

$ ✕**al di là.** *Italian.* This northern Italian hot spot is consistently packed, and it's easy to understand why: affordable prices, a relaxed and charming environment, and simple yet soulfully comforting cuisine. The no-reservations policy ensures that the place always has a buzz around it from waiting patrons. Even if you arrive when the restaurant opens, your table may not be available for ages. This is not the best place to take fidgety, hungry kids. ✉*248 5th Ave., at Carroll St., Park Slope* ☎*718/783–4565* ⌔*No reservations accepted* ▭*MC, V* ☉ *Closed Tues. No lunch* F at 15th St.–Prospect Park; M, R at Union St.

$$ ✕**applewood.** *New American.* Lavish devotion to seasonal
★ ingredients plus supporting local farmers plus relaxed service in a pretty pale-yellow dining room plus simple flavors layered in interesting ways all adds up to one thing—an amazing restaurant. The menu changes constantly; recent highlights have included a melt-in-your-mouth crispy braised pork belly served with creamy apples. The country-style feel is comfortable for kids. Brunch is an especially good time to visit for the restaurant's kids' menu with surprisingly low prices. ✉*501 11th St., at 7th Ave., Park Slope* ☎*718/768–2044* ▭*D, MC, V* ☉*Closed Mon. No lunch Tues.–Sat.* Ⓜ *F at 7th Ave.*

¢ ✕**Tom's Restaurant.** *American.* For friendly service and great luncheonette fare like fluffy banana-walnut pancakes served with homemade flavored butters and egg creams, head three blocks north of the Brooklyn Museum to this family-owned, 70-year-old restaurant. On weekends, lines are long, but your wait is eased by free coffee and orange slices. The restaurant keeps the little ones happy as well with free cookies while they wait. ✉*782 Washington Ave., at Sterling Pl., Prospect Heights* ☎*718/636–9738* ⌔*Reservations not accepted* ▭*No credit cards* ☉ *Mon.–Sat. 6 AM–4 PM; closed Sun.* Ⓜ *2, 3 to Grand Army Plaza.*

SHOPPING

Seventh Avenue is Park Slope's main shopping street, with long-established restaurants, bookstores, shops, cafés, and bakeries. More fun, however, are the restaurants and shops along 5th Avenue.

Bierkraft (⊠*191 5th Ave., near Union St.* ☎*718/230–7600*) sells cheeses, olives, and some impressively pricey chocolate. The ice-cream sandwiches using two brownies as "bread," are a hit with sweet lovers of any age. At **Brooklyn Superhero Supply Co.** (⊠*372 5th Ave. at 7th St.* ☎*718/499–9884* ⊕*www.superherosupplies.com*) young superheroes can purchase capes, grappling hooks, secret identity kits, and more from staff who never drop the game of pretend. Proceeds benefit the nonprofit organization 826NYC and free drop-in tutoring center in a "secret lair" behind a swinging bookcase. As a bonus, kids can try on capes and be blasted by fans while having their pictures taken. And you can feel good about buying that jar of "anti-gravity"; 862NYC helps kids 6–13 with creative and writing skills.

CONEY ISLAND

★ **Fodor's**Choice A picture of crowds, carnival rides, and summer fever, Coney Island has a boardwalk, a 2½-mi-long beach, amusement parks, and the **New York Aquarium.** Eating a Nathan's Famous hot dog (1310 Surf Avenue) and strolling seaside has been a classic New York experience since 1916. And then there are the freakish attractions at **Sideshows by the Seashore** and the **Coney Island Museum,** the heart-stopping plunge of the granddaddy of all roller coasters—the **Cyclone**—and the thwack of bats swung by the minor-league team, the Cyclones, at **Keyspan Park.** A fireworks display lights up the sky Friday night from late June through Labor Day.

Cyclone. One of the oldest roller coasters still operating, this world-famous wood-and-steel colossus was inaugurated in 1927. Although the neighborhood is changing, this is the real original Coney Island deal and shouldn't be missed (even if only to watch . . .), Thrill-seeking kids can get pretty banged up on this ride, so seat them next to a larger adult who can provide both a safety net and a cushion. ⊠*1000 Surf Ave., at W. 10th St., Coney Island* ☎*718/372–0275* ☎*$6 per ride* ☉*Memorial Day–Labor Day, open daily, call for seasonal hrs* Ⓜ*D, F, N, Q to Coney Island Stillwell Ave.* 12+up

Deno's Wonder Wheel Amusement Park. You get a new perspective atop the 150-foot-tall Wonder Wheel, built in 1920. Though it appears tame, its swinging cars will quicken your heart rate. (You can also opt to ride a "stable" car.) Other rides include the Spook-a-rama, the Thunderbolt, and bumper cars. At this writing, there were 17 kiddie rides to amuse the under 10 set. ✉ *3059 Denos Vourderis Pl., at W. 12th St., Coney Island* ☎718/372–2592 ⊕*www. wonderwheel.com* ✑*$5 per ride, 5 rides for $20* ⊙*Memorial Day–Labor Day, daily 11–midnight; Apr., May, Sept., and Oct., weekends noon–9* Ⓜ*D, F, N, Q to Coney Island Stillwell Ave.* 5+up

Keyspan Park. Indulge your kids' love of baseball at a Brooklyn Cyclones game. The team is a minor league Class A affiliate of the Mets. This is a wonderful place to catch a baseball game. The 6,500-seat stadium is intimate, there are great views of the amusement park and the beach, and the giveaways are always fun souvenirs for kids. The trick is getting the affordable tickets. ✉*1904 Surf Ave., between 17th and 19th Sts., Coney Island* ☎718/449–8497 ⊕*www. brooklyncyclones.com* ✑ *$5–$12* ⊙*Games June–Sept.; call for schedule* Ⓜ*D, F, N, Q to Coney Island Stillwell Ave.* All ages

New York Aquarium. Home to more than 8,000 creatures of the ocean, New York City's only aquarium is also the nation's oldest. Tropical fish, sea horses, and jellyfish luxuriate in large tanks; otters, walruses, penguins, and seals lounge on a replicated rocky Pacific coast; and a 90,000-gallon tank is home to several different types of sharks. Kids can take a simulated submarine ride on the Deep Sea 3-D ride, open April through October. Special programs geared to families happen throughout the year such as early-morning animal feedings. The Touch Tank lets kids under 10 explore a variety of creatures, from May through October. Everyone gets a thrill from the sea lions at the Aquatheater shows. Note that some of the exhibits are outdoors so you many want to save a visit for a warmer or sunny day. Call ahead to confirm hours. ✉*W. 8th St. and Surf Ave., Coney Island* ☎718/265–3474 ⊕*www. nyaquarium.com* ✑*$13; ages 2–12 and seniors $9; under 3 free* ⊙*Early Apr.–Memorial Day and Labor Day–early Nov., weekdays 10–5, weekends 10–5:30; Memorial Day–Labor Day, weekdays 10–6, weekends 10–7; Nov.–early Apr., daily 10–4:30; last ticket sold 45 min before close* Ⓜ*F, Q to West 8th St.* All ages

Sideshows by the Seashore and the Coney Island Museum. Step right up for a lively circus sideshow, complete with a fire-eater, sword swallower, snake charmer, and contortionist. Upstairs, the small museum has Coney Island memorabilia and a great deal of tourist information. Both of these may be too intense and frightening for younger kids, although it's certainly a one-of-a-kind experience for the curious. ⊠*1208 Surf Ave., at W. 12th St., Coney Island* ☎*718/372–5159* ⊕*www.coneyisland.com* ⊠*Sideshow $5; museum 99¢* ☉*Sideshows: Memorial Day–Labor Day, Wed.–Fri. 2–8, weekends 1–11; Apr., May, and Sept., weekends 1–8. Museum: weekends noon–5. Hrs vary, so call ahead* Ⓜ*D, F, N, Q to Coney Island Stillwell Ave.* 9+up

WHERE TO EAT

The fried clams, hot dogs with spicy mustard, and ice-cold lemonade from **Nathan's Famous** (*American* ⊠*1310 Surf Ave., at Stillwell Ave.* ☎*718/946–2202*) have been nearly inseparable from the Coney Island experience since it opened in 1916. Another branch on the boardwalk is open from May through September. If you need a spot to sit, head to this second branch. If not, just do as the locals do and chow down on your hot dog while standing and indulging in great people-watching—a sideshow unto itself.

QUEENS

L.I.C. & ASTORIA

Just for the museums and restaurants alone, a short trip to **Long Island City** and **Astoria** makes for a good kids' excursion. Long Island City (L.I.C. for short) has three cool art centers, each different from the next: the MoMA-affiliated **P.S. 1 Contemporary Art Center** in a former school building, which has both interesting exhibits and interesting spaces; the **Noguchi Museum,** a more serene garden and gallery setting better suited for older kids; and **Socrates Sculpture Park,** where children of all ages are encouraged to climb on the art (what a novelty!).

Astoria is the center of New York's Greek community and offers up terrific dining and food shopping, mostly notably on Broadway between 31st and Steinway streets. It is also home to a mix of other ethnic communities, from Eastern European and Irish to Asian and Latino, creating an interesting array of small-restaurant choices that take you on a culinary tour around the world. Astoria also has some-

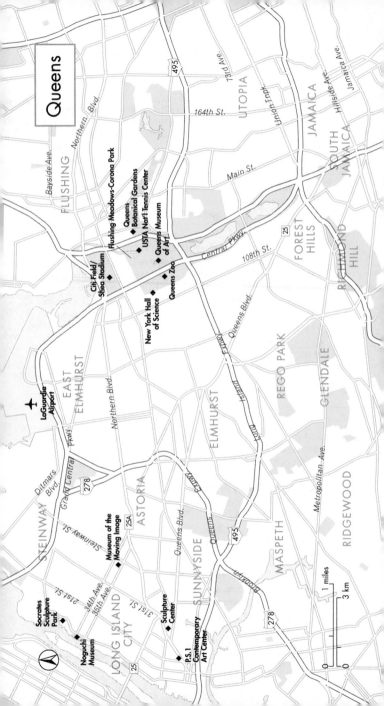

Queens

Bayside Ave.

Northern Blvd.

FLUSHING

164th St.

495

UTOPIA

73rd Ave.

Jamaica Ave.

Hillside Ave.

Jamaica Ave.

JAMAICA

Union Tpk.

SOUTH JAMAICA

Main St.

Flushing Meadows-Corona Park

Queens Botanical Gardens

USTA Nat'l Tennis Center

Queens Museum of Art

Central Pkwy.

108th St.

FOREST HILLS

RICHMOND HILL

25

Citi Field/ Shea Stadium

Queens Zoo

New York Hall of Science

Queens Blvd.

Long Island Expwy.

REGO PARK

GLENDALE

LaGuardia Airport

EAST ELMHURST

Northern Blvd.

ELMHURST

Metropolitan Ave.

RIDGEWOOD

Ditmars Blvd.

Grand Central Pkwy.

278

STEINWAY

Steinway St.

Museum of the Moving Image

25A

ASTORIA

34th Ave.

85th Ave.

31st St.

21st St.

Queens Blvd.

SUNNYSIDE

495

Long Island Expwy.

MASPETH

278

1 miles

3 km

Socrates Sculpture Park

Noguchi Museum

LONG ISLAND CITY

25

Sculpture Center

P.S. 1 Contemporary Art Center

TOP QUEENS EXPERIENCES

Share in New York City's major-league baseball fever with the Mets at the brand-new Citi Field.

Climb up and down the stairs from room to room at the P.S. 1 Contemporary Art Center where changing outdoor exhibits can be as interesting as the indoor ones.

Do what you've never been allowed to do: climb all over and sit on the crazy art cre-

ations at the outdoor Socrates Sculpture Park.

Learn by having fun at the wonderful New York Hall of Science where science reigns on the playground and both teaches and entertains indoors.

Play video games, make your own flipbooks, and learn about film and TV at the Museum of the Moving Image.

thing that no kid should miss when visiting New York: the **American Museum of the Moving Image** with hands-on exhibits about film, TV and digital media that can entertain all ages on both sunny and rainy days.

TOP ATTRACTIONS

Noguchi Museum. In 1985, the Japanese-American sculptor Isamu Noguchi transformed this former photo-engraving plant into a place to display his modernist and earlier works. A peaceful central garden with a water and stone sculpture called "The Wall" is surrounded by gallery buildings, providing room to show more than 250 pieces done in stone, metal, clay and other materials. The museum is about a mile from subway stops; check the Web site for directions. On Sunday, a shuttle bus leaves from the northwest corner of Park Avenue and 70th Street in Manhattan, hourly, beginning at 12:30; the round-trip costs $10. It can be a leisurely walk here, but it's not particularly scenic. Best to find a taxi if you can. The museum sometimes offers Art for Tots and Art for Families programs with hands-on activities. ⊠*9–01 33rd Rd., at Vernon Blvd., Long Island City* ☎*718/204–7088* ⊕*www.noguchi.org* ☜*$10; students, $5; under 12, free* ☉*Wed.–Fri. 10–5, weekends 11–6* Ⓜ*N, W to Broadway.* 7+up

★ **Fodor's**Choice **P.S. 1 Contemporary Art Center.** A pioneer in the "alternative-space" movement, P.S.1 rose from the ruins of an abandoned school in 1976 as a sort of community arts center for the future. Now a partner of MoMA, P.S.1

presents experimental and formally innovative contemporary art. The building is enormous, and every available corner is used; discover art not only in galleries but also on the rooftop spaces, in the boiler room, and even in the bathrooms. Fun exhibits that kids would enjoy have included an outdoor slide and outdoor water sculptures. (Be sure to check the age appropriateness of certain shows as some contain controversial subjects and adult content). There is a spacious café with brownies and other treats. ⊠*22–25 Jackson Ave., at 46th Ave., Long Island City* ☎*718/784-2084* ⊕*www.ps1.org* ⊠*$5 suggested donation* ⊙*Thurs.–Mon. noon–6* Ⓜ*7 to 45th Rd.–Courthouse Sq.; E, V to 23rd St.–Ely Ave.; G to Court St.* 3+up

Museum of the Moving Image. Step inside the world of movie- and television-making at this museum full of Hollywood memorabilia. Exhibitions range from the history of the film camera to the (literally) head-spinning special effects of *The Exorcist.* Try your hand at interactive stations that allow you to dub your voice into *Titanic,* create stop-action sequences, and more. Those wishing to improve their Space Invaders or Pac-Man score should head to the darkened video arcade on the ground floor (games are moving images, too). Next door at the Kaufman-Astoria Studios is where Sesame Street is filmed. Kids can create flipbook of themselves using a video camera that captures staccato images. A major renovation will add some new attractions—be sure to call for details and check the schedule for the Family Motion workshops held on weekends. ⊠*35th Ave. at 36th St., Astoria* ☎*718/784-0077* ⊕*www.movingimage. us* ⊠*$10; free after 4 on Fri.* ⊙*Wed. and Thurs. 11–5, Fri. 11–8, weekends 11–6:30; screenings weekends and Fri. 7:30* Ⓜ*R, V, to Steinway St.; N, W to 36th Ave.* 5+up

Socrates Sculpture Park. In 1985, local artist Mark di Suvero and other residents rallied to transform what had been an abandoned landfill and illegal dump site into this 4½-acre waterfront park devoted to public art. Today a superb view of the river and Manhattan frames changing exhibitions of contemporary sculptures and multimedia installations. One big difference from the usual museum rules: children are actually encouraged to touch the art and climb on it! Kids can watch artists work their craft in this outdoor studio and museum and then climb onto (or in) an old station wagon that is actually a work of art. Exhibits change frequently and kids' workshops led by artists-in-residence are held on some Saturdays. Come on a Wednesday in July or August, bring a picnic, and stay for an evening movie screening. ✉ *3205 Vernon Blvd., at Broadway, Long Island City* ☎ *718/956–1819* ⊕ *www.socratessculpturepark.org* ✈ *Free* ☉ *Daily 10–dusk* Ⓜ *N, W to Broadway, then walk west or take Q104 bus along Broadway to Vernon Blvd.* **7+up**

WHERE TO EAT

End your day with dinner at one of Astoria's legendary Greek restaurants (on or near Broadway) or venture to the Middle Eastern restaurants farther out on Steinway Street. Some are more kid-friendly than others, so judge by how many families you see inside.

$ ✕**Kabab Café**. *Middle Eastern*. This charming and eccentric 16-seat Egyptian-Mediterranean café excels at satisfyingly interesting home-style dishes. The meze plate is good for kids to share with hummus, falafel, and bread. ✉ *25–12 Steinway St., Astoria* ☎ *718/728–9858* ⚂ *Reservations not accepted* ⊟ *No credit cards* ☉ *Closed Mon.* Ⓜ *N, W to Astoria–Ditmars Blvd.*

$$ ✕**S'Agapo**. *Greek*. This well-regarded Greek taverna is two blocks away from the Museum of the Moving Image, making it convenient for a combo-trip. Kid-favorites include the pita bread and possibly the best hummus in the city. The restaurant is off the main street and a bit quieter for kids who might be tired after visiting the museum and playing so many video games. ✉ *34–21 34th Ave., Astoria* ☎ *718/626–0303* ⚂ *Reservations essential* ⊟ *AE, MC, V* Ⓜ *36th Ave. to Broadway, Steinway St. to Crescent St.*

JACKSON HEIGHTS

Even in the diverse borough of Queens, Jackson Heights stands out for being a true multicultural neighborhood. In just a few blocks surrounding the three-way intersection of Roosevelt Avenue, 74th Street, and Broadway, you can find shops and restaurants catering to the area's strong Indian, Bangladeshi, Colombian, Mexican, and Ecuadorian communities. Point out the gorgeous saris in the window, introduce your kids to some wonderful Indian breads, and simply absorb the blend of cultures that makes up this distinctive neighborhood.

WHERE TO EAT

$ ✕ **Delhi Palace.** *Indian.* There are dozens of daily Indian buffets offered in the neighborhood, but Delhi Palace's $8 spread, served daily from 11:30 to 4 and until 5 on weekends, stands out from the competition. This is a great option for letting kids sample lots of different dishes. Tuck into the vegetarian dishes like the raita dip and the chickpeas. ✉ *37–33 74th St., between Roosevelt and 37th Aves.* ☎ *718/507–0666* ▭ *AE, DC, MC, V* Ⓜ *E, F, 7 to 74th St.– Broadway; G, R, V to Jackson Heights–Roosevelt Ave.*

$$ ✕ **Jackson Diner.** *Indian.* A perfect unfancy introduction to Indian cuisine can be had here. Popular choices for kids include chicken tandoori, papadum crackers, and fluffy Nan bread. There are lots of curry dishes, some extremely hot and others mild enough for the little ones, as well as vegetarian specialties. ✉ *37–47 74th St., between Roosevelt and 37th Aves.* ☎ *718/672–1232* ▭ *No credit cards* Ⓜ *E, F, 7 to 74th St.-Broadway; G, R, V to Jackson Heights-Roosevelt Ave.*

SHOPPING

Patel Brothers (✉ *37–27 74th St., near 37th Ave.* ☎ *718/898–3445*). It's easy to lose hours browsing the gleaming aisles of Indian groceries, including dozens of varieties of lentils, spices in bulk, and an entire aisle devoted to rice. Ask for assistance in picking out some exotic sweets or snacks that your kids might like.

Sahil Sari Palace (✉ *37–39 74th St., between Roosevelt and 37th Aves.* ☎ *718/426–9526*) is filled with endless bolts of colorful silks and ready-to-wear sequined saris and tunics. Buy enough fabric for your own little princess and have a sari made to take home.

FLUSHING & CORONA

Bustling Flushing is the center of Asian life outside of Manhattan. Just take the 7 train and get off on Main Street where you can find fascinating grocery stores and enjoy some of the best and least expensive Chinese and Korean cuisine in the city.

Next door, quiet Corona has great neighborhood Italian and Latino restaurants, and one of Queens' real contributions to children, some of the best Italian ices anywhere.

Citi Field. The brand-new home of the New York Mets, Citi Field sits next door to its predecessor, Shea Stadium. Catch the "Amazin' Mets" here from April through September. Watch for special cap nights and other promotions, when goodies and memorabilia are given out. ⊠*Roosevelt Ave., off Grand Central Pkwy.* ☎*718/507–8499* ⊕*www.mets. com* Ⓜ *7 to Willets Pt./Shea Stadium.* 5+up

Flushing Meadows–Corona Park. The gleaming Unisphere (an enormous 140-foot-high steel globe) standing regally over this 1,255-acre park is one of the remnants of the World's Fair held here in 1964, a symbol of global independence. Weighing 700,000 pounds, it's surrounded by fountains in the summer and lots of rollerbladers and skateboarders.

Many New Yorkers head to a specific attraction, such as a Mets game at Citi Field or the NY Hall of Science and its outdoor playground, but this is a park that offers much more, especially for families. Here are not only typical grassy knolls, barbecue pits, and sports fields, but also an art museum, a petting zoo, golf and minigolf, and even a model plane field. The flat grounds are ideal for family biking; rent bikes near the park entrance or Meadow Lake from March to October. There's enough to do here for more than one day, so you'll need to pick and choose your family's favorite activities. ∎TIP→ **Although the park is great in daytime, avoid visiting once it gets dark; there has been some crime in this area.** All ages

New York Hall of Science. In nearby Corona Park, the New York Hall of Science has more than 400 hands-on exhibitions and 60,000 feet of outdoor space that make science a playground for inquisitive minds of all ages. Climb aboard a replica of John Glenn's space capsule, throw a fastball and investigate its speed, make monstrous bubbles, and learn about the effects of light. Open from April through New Year's Eve, the outdoor Science Playground teaches the principles of motion, balance, sounds, and sight with fun interactive exhibits that include a giant seesaw, speaking tubes, and a climbing space net. The Sports Challenge puts science in motion as you test your adeptness at balance, reaction time, climbing, racing, pitching, leaping, and bouncing through familiar sports activities. Adults will also want to get in on the fun. ⊠*111th St. at 46th Ave., Flushing* ☎*718/699–0005* ⊕*www.nyscience.org* ⊠*$11; $8, children 2–17; free Fri. 2–5 and Sun. 10–11 Sept.–June* ⊙*Sept.–June, Mon.–Thurs. 9:30–2, Fri. 9:30–5, weekends 10–6; July and Aug., weekdays 9:30–5, weekends 10–6;*

Science Playground, $4. ⓜ*7 to 111th St.; walk 3 blocks south.* 3+up; Science Playground, 5+up

The Queens Zoo. The intimate scale of this zoo makes it especially well suited to young visitors who tire easily. Eleven acres re-create natural habitats of more than 400 North and South American animals, including bears, mountain lions, bison, elk, bald eagles, and pudu—the world's smallest deer. Buckminster Fuller's geodesic dome from the 1964 World's Fair is now the aviary. Across the street is a petting zoo. The daily sea lion feedings are especially fun for kids. The wildlife theater offers shows with audience participation. ✉*53–51 111th St., at 53rd Ave.* ☎*718/271–1500* ⊕*www.wcs.org* ☞*$6; $2, ages 3–12* ☽*Early Apr.–late Oct., weekdays 10–5, weekends 10–5:30; late Oct.–early Apr., daily 10–4:30; last ticket sold 30 min before closing* ⓜ*7 to 111th St.* All ages

Queens Botanical Garden. Built for the 1939 World's Fair, these 39 acres include rose and herb gardens, an arboretum, and plantings especially designed to attract bees and birds. A new environmentally friendly visitor center uses solar energy and recycles rainwater. Special holiday programs are fun especially in the fall with Halloween happenings, bobbing for apples, and a pumpkin patch. Other favorites are the Olfactory Walk with its collection of fragrant shrubs and flowers and the Bee Garden where plants attract colonies of busy bees. ✉*43–50 Main St., Flushing* ☎*718/886–3800* ⊕*www.queensbotanical.org* ☞*Free* ☽*Apr.–Oct., Tues.–Fri. 8–6, weekends 8–7; Nov.–Mar., Tues.–Sun. 8–4:30* ⓜ*7 to Main St.–Flushing.* All ages

USTA Billie Jean King National Tennis Center. Each August and September, this center hosts the U.S. Open, which claims the title of highest-attended annual sporting event in the world. The rest of the year the 45 courts (33 outdoor and 12 indoor, all Deco Turf II) are open to the public for $20–$60 hourly. Make reservations up to two days in advance. Kids as young as 4 years old can take lessons here. Young fans will especially enjoy the earlier qualifying rounds of the Open, some scheduled in the late morning, when some of the younger players compete; if you're in town in August, check the date for the Arthur Ashe Kids' Day, a family-oriented event with tennis clinics, interactive games, musical performances, and chances to meet tennis stars. ✉*Meadows–Corona Park* ☎*718/760–6200* ⊕*www. usta.com* ⓜ*7 to Willets Pt./Shea Stadium.* 5+up

NEED A BREAK? If you're looking for authentic kid-pleasing Queens experiences, you have to check out the **Lemon Ice King of Corona** (✉ 52–02 108th St., at 52nd St., Corona ☎ 718/699–5133). Though there aren't seats or friendly service, none of that will matter as soon as you taste one of the more than 30 flavors of Italian ice, homemade and fresh, from this 65-year-old institution. Try the chocolate, cotton candy, or peanut butter, sure to please the kids.

THE BRONX

Three of the Bronx's most well-known attractions are a healthy walk away from each other: the Bronx Zoo, the New York Botanical Garden, and the Italian section known as Arthur Avenue. Both the Zoo and the Botanical Garden each warrant a full day's visit. A trip to Arthur Avenue will restore your energy after each.

★ Fodor'sChoice **The Bronx Zoo.** When it opened its gates in 1899, the Bronx Zoo only had 843 animals. But today, with 265 acres and more than 4,500 animals (of more than 600 species), it's the largest metropolitan zoo in the United States. Get up close and personal with exotic creatures in outdoor settings that re-create natural habitats; you're often separated from them by no more than a moat or wall of glass. The **Congo Gorilla Forest** (✉$3), a 6½-acre re-creation of a lush, wooded African rain forest with two troops of lowland gorillas, as well as white-bearded DeBrazza's monkeys, okapis, and red river hogs, puts you face-to-face with your distant relatives, protected by a glass wall. At **Tiger Mountain,** an open viewing shelter lets you get incredibly close to Siberian tigers that frolic in a pool, lounge outside (even in cold weather) and enjoy daily "enrichment sessions" with zookeepers. As the big cats are often napping at midday, aim to visit in the morning or evening.

Go on a minisafari via the **Wild Asia Monorail,** open May–October, weather permitting. As you wind your way through lush forest, see Asian elephants, Indo-Chinese tigers, Indian rhinoceroses, gaur (the world's largest cattle), Mongolian wild horses, and several deer and antelope species. ■TIP→ Try to visit the most popular exhibits, such as Congo Gorilla Forest and World of Darkness, early to avoid lines later in the day. In winter the outdoor exhibitions have fewer animals on view, but there are also fewer crowds, and plenty

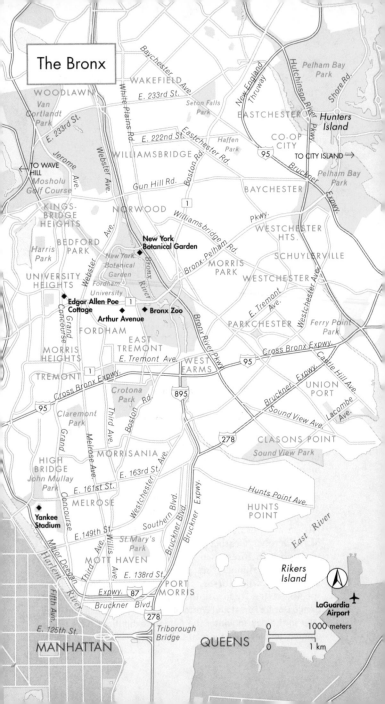

TOP BRONX EXPERIENCES

Spend a day at the Bronx Zoo with the lions, tigers and bears . . . or in Congo Gorilla Forest with your nose pressed up against the glass as the gorillas check you out as well.

Lose yourself at New York Botanical Garden where you can disappear in the giant mazes or behind animal topiaries, or dance among the gorgeous daffodils, roses, and tulips after planting your own plant in the Family Garden.

Munch your way along the Bronx's own Little Italy, Arthur Avenue. Bring your brood to the Arthur Avenue market for stand after stand of fresh sandwiches, pizza, cookies, and yummy gelati.

Point out to your kids the plaques commemorating the stars of Yankees past at Monument Park before you settle in for a game at the brand-new Yankee Stadium.

Take your kids to watch a Tai Chi class, or get your culture on in an art workshop at Wave Hill.

of indoor exhibits to savor. From mid-November to January 1, the zoo is decorated with holiday lights and open until 9 PM. The Skyfari cable car ride is a wonderful way for tired kids to get a bird's-eye view of the park and the animals. The Zoo Shuttle also zips you throughout the park so you don't have to walk. Littler guests will enjoy the funky Bug Carousel with friendly dung beetles and other crawly things to sit on, while all ages will have fun climbing atop a real camel. In the Children's Zoo area, kids can climb a giant spider web, try on a turtle shell, or crawl through a hollow tree. If it rains, there's plenty to do: besides the World of Darkness's nocturnal creatures, you can visit the Reptile House, the Mouse House, and the Monkey House. The zoo's newest permanent exhibit, Madagascar, shows off African animals like crocodiles, tortoises, lemurs, and even cockroaches. It's in the zoo's beaux arts Lion House. There are picnic tables, snack stands, and four cafés. With advance reservations (and a pile of money), your kids can have a sleepover in the Congo Gorilla Forest and drift off next to dozing primates. ⊠*Bronx River Pkwy. and Fordham Rd., Fordham* ☎*718/367–1010* ⊕*www.bronxzoo. com* ⊠*Adults $14; $10, ages 3–12; free Wed., donation suggested; extra charge for some exhibits; parking $8 for cars* ⊘ *Apr.–Oct., weekdays 10–5, weekends 10–5:30; Nov.–Mar., daily 10–4:30; last ticket sold 30 min before closing* Ⓜ*2, 5 to E. Tremont/West Farms, then walk 2*

*blocks to zoo's Wild Asia entrance; 2 to Pelham Pkwy.,
then walk 3 blocks west to Bronx Pkwy. entrance; Bx11
express bus to Bronx Pkwy. entrance.* All ages

★ **Fodor's Choice New York Botanical Garden.** Considered one of
the leading botany centers of the world, this 250-acre garden is one of the best reasons to make a trip to the Bronx.
Built around the dramatic gorge of the Bronx River, the
Garden offers lush indoor and outdoor gardens, acres
of natural forest, as well as classes, concerts, and special
exhibits. The color and perfume of the Rose Garden's
2,700 plants, especially beautiful in June and September,
leave kids giddy; marvel at orchids that look like they
came from *Little Shop of Horrors*; and have a blast in the
Everett Children's Adventure Garden, a 12-acre, indoor-
outdoor museum with mazes, giant animal topiaries with
a splashing fountain, and oversize flowers. In the Wonder
Gallery, children can invent a plant or wander through
vine-covered tunnels, tiny bridges, and a minipond. In the
wondrously named What Stinks exhibit, youngsters learn
how wetlands recycle plants. The Family Garden invites
kids to try their hand at planting and nurturing. Families
can board a tram that scoots around this giant park, letting
you jump off at various points.

The Victorian-style **Enid A. Haupt Conservatory** (⌂$5) houses
re-creations of misty tropical rain forests and arid African
and North American deserts as well as exhibitions, such as
the beloved Holiday Train Show and the Orchid Show. The
Combination Ticket ($13, off-peak days) gives you access
to the Conservatory, Rock Garden, Native Plant Garden,
Tram Tour (perfect for tired little feet), Everett Children's
Adventure Garden, and exhibits in the library.

The most direct and comfortable way for families to reach
the Garden is via **Metro-North Railroad** (⊕*www.mta.info/mnr*)
from Grand Central Terminal (Harlem Local Line, Botanical Garden stop). Round-trip tickets are $5 to $12.50,
depending on time of day. The D or 4 train also goes to
Bedford Park Boulevard, but then you have to walk a ways.
Seasonal programs and workshops for kids of all ages are
offered throughout the year. In the Ruth Rea Howell Family
Garden children play in the dirt, plant seeds, and dig for
worms—bring an extra change of clothes! ⌂*200th St. and
Kazimiroff Blvd., Bedford Park* ☎*718/817–8700* ⊕*www.
nybg.org* ⌂*All-Garden Pass, $20 adults; students, $18 ages
2–12; free under age 2; grounds only, $6; $1, ages 2–12;*

free Sat. 10–noon and Wed.; parking $10 ⊙*Apr.–Oct. and mid-Nov.–1st wk of Jan., Tues.–Sun. 10–6; 2nd wk of Jan.– Mar., Tues.–Sun. 10–5* Ⓜ*B, D, 4 to Bedford Park Blvd.; Metro-North to Botanical Garden.* All ages

Yankee Stadium. Be among the first to visit the new home of the Bronx Bombers, at the classic-looking Yankee Stadium, just next to the old one. Tours of the park are offered— check the Web site for schedules and age requirements. Baseball fans will love walking through Monument Park— it's like a quick museum of the best and greatest of baseball heroes. Try to bring your kids about two hours before a game to watch batting practice and score autographs from the players. The subway will be a lot less crowded that way, too. Buy clear bags if you plan to bring your own snack. Security is very strict here. ⊠*River Ave. at 161st St., South Bronx* ☎*718/293–4300* ⊕*www.yankees.com* Ⓜ *B, D, or 4 to 161st St.–Yankee Stadium.* 5+up

OFF THE BEATEN PATH. A former summer home set on a glorious cliff in the Riverdale section of the Bronx, **Wave Hill** (⊠*Independence Ave. at W. 249th St., Riverdale* ☎*718/549–3200* ⊕*www. wavehill.org*) is now a 28-acre public garden and cultural center that offers year-round programs for adults and families. The center teaches little ones about plants and gardening and has workshops as well. The Saturday morning tai chi classes are legendary and families can participate (or just watch). Seasonal festivals offer arts programs synched with nature themes. It's a beautiful place to add a calming moment to your trip (and maybe run down the hills a little bit). Tickets are $6, but if you come on Saturday before noon or on Tuesday, admission is free. There is no direct subway route here; see the Web site for directions using Metro-North or the Bronx bus lines.

ARTHUR AVENUE (BELMONT)

Belmont, the Little Italy of the Bronx, is a thriving Italian-American community with a lot of family-friendly appeal. Go for the wonderful food—you can create your own picnic, eat in an enclosed European-style market area, or pick from a host of family-style restaurants. The area teems with meat markets, bakeries, and cheesemakers. Thanks to generations of Italian grandmothers who carefully supervise and comment, vendors here wouldn't dare offer anything less than superfresh, handmade foods.

Join the locals who shop for groceries and authentic Italian snacks on Saturday afternoons; most stores are closed on Sunday. There's plenty here that will appeal to young palates: any restaurant can make a kid's favorite pasta dish and the gelato here is among the best in the city. Take more adventurous tots into the small Italian food shops to admire the goods and experiment with new tastes. ⊠*Arthur Avenue between Crescent Ave./E. 184th St. and E. 188th Sts., and 187th St. from Lorillard Pl. to Hughes Ave.* ⊕*www.arthuravenue.com* Ⓜ*B, D, 4 to Fordham Rd., then Bx12 east; 2, 5 to Pelham Pkwy., then Bx12 west. On weekends and holidays Apr.–Oct., free Bronx Tour Trolley leaves from Fordham Plaza Metro-North and West Farms 2/5 stations.* All ages

WHERE TO EAT

$ ✕ **Mario's.** *Italian.* Eat like Don Corleone at this 90-year-old restaurant that was memorialized by Mario Puzo in *The Godfather.* Tuxedoed waiters bring you typical red-sauce fare that regulars rave about, including giant antipasto platters and tangy eggplant Siciliana. Kids can order the usual basics: pasta and chicken as they like. ⊠*2342 Arthur Ave., Belmont* ☎*718/584–1188* ▤*AE, MC, V* Ⓜ*B, D, 4 to Fordham Rd.*

$$ ✕ **Roberto Restaurant.** *Italian.* Go early and brave long lines for huge portions of handmade pastas and risottos at this stylishly casual space with long farmhouse tables. The family-style servings are perfect for lots of kids to share. ⊠*603 Crescent Ave., at Arthur Ave., Belmont* ☎*718/733–9503* ⚲*Reservations not accepted* ▤*MC, V* ☉*Closed Sun.* Ⓜ*2, 5 to Pelham Pkwy.*

NEED A BREAK? At Mike's Deli (⊠*2344 Arthur Ave., inside Arthur Avenue Retail Market, Belmont* ☎*718/295–5033)* prime cuts of meat and charcuterie, friendly service, a convenient location, and Italian sandwiches as big as your head keep customers satisfied. Pull up a seat near the deli counter and try the King David: sopressata, aged parmigiana, roasted peppers, and basil. If you're nice, you might get some samples of salami or cheese to give to your kids. It's also the perfect place to stock up on treats for a wonderful picnic in the park (or at the zoo).

SHOPPING

The covered **Arthur Avenue Retail Market** (✉ *2344 Arthur Ave., at E. 187th St.* ☎ *718/367–5686* ⊕ *www.arthuravenue.com*) houses more than a dozen vendors selling great sandwiches and pizza that kids will adore and other Italian staples for you. Open Monday through Saturday 7–6. There's plenty of space to bring your stroller in here.

STATEN ISLAND

Staten Island is full of surprises, from a premier collection of Tibetan art to a multifaceted historic village with a beautiful botanic garden. There's also a charming zoo, lots of parks, and a very non-Manhattan residential feel. To explore the borough, take the **Staten Island Ferry** from the southern tip of Manhattan. After you disembark, grab an S40 bus to the **Snug Harbor Cultural Center (about 10 minutes)** or take the S74 and combine visits to the **Tibetan Art Museum** and **Historic Richmond Town.**

TOP ATTRACTIONS

★ Fodor'sChoice **Historic Richmond Town.** Explore 27 vibrant historical buildings (19 of which are open to the public) in this 100-acre village, constructed from 1695 to the 19th century. Highlights of most interest to children include the one-room **General Store and the Voorlezer's House,** one of the oldest buildings on the site that was both a residence and the country's oldest elementary school. As you wander around, staff in period dress demonstrate Early American crafts and trades such as printing, tinsmithing, basket making, and fireplace cooking. December brings a monthlong Christmas celebration. Take the S74–Richmond Road bus (30 minutes) or a car service (about $14) from the ferry terminal. The Historical Museum has a terrific exhibit Toys!, an interactive experience for kids, with more than 200 toys from the present to the 1840s. ✉ *441 Clarke Ave., Richmondtown* ☎ *718/351–1611* ⊕ *www.historic richmondtown.org* 🖃 *$5; $3.50, ages 5–17* ⊘ *July and Aug., Wed.–Sat. 10–5, Sun. 1–5; Sept.–June, Wed.–Sun. 1–5* Ⓜ *S74 bus to St. Patrick's Pl.* 5+up

Staten Island Ferry. One of Staten Island's biggest attractions is free—the phenomenal view of Manhattan and the Statue of Liberty afforded by the 25-minute ferry ride across New York Harbor. From Whitehall Terminal at the southern tip of Manhattan, catch the ferry every half hour on weekdays and weekend afternoons. On weekend

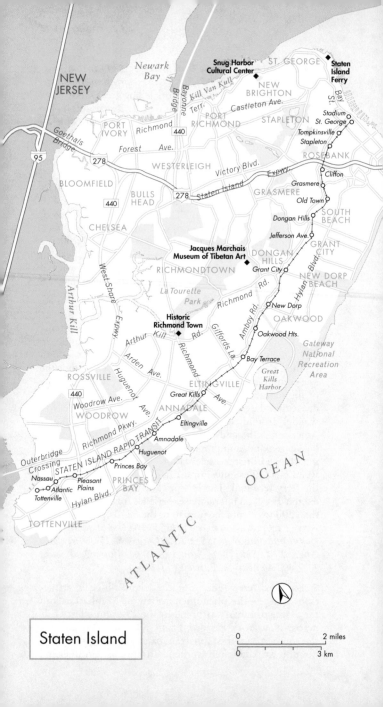

NEW JERSEY

Newark Bay

Bayonne Bridge

Kill Van Kull

Snug Harbor Cultural Center ◆

ST. GEORGE

Staten Island Ferry ◆

NEW BRIGHTON

Castleton Ave.

STAPLETON

Stadium

St. George ○

Bay St.

Tompkinsville ○

Stapleton ○

ROSEBANK

Cliffton ○

Grasmere ○

Old Town ○

SOUTH BEACH

Dongan Hills ○

Jefferson Ave. ○

GRANT CITY

NEW DORP BEACH

Grant City ○

New Dorp ○

OAKWOOD

Oakwood Hts. ○

Bay Terrace ○

Great Kills Harbor

Gateway National Recreation Area

PORT IVORY

Richmond

PORT RICHMOND

440

Goethals Bridge

I-95

278

Forest Ave.

WESTERLEIGH

Victory Blvd.

Staten Island Expwy.

278

GRASMERE

BLOOMFIELD

BULLS HEAD

440

CHELSEA

DONGAN HILLS

Jacques Marchais Museum of Tibetan Art ◆

RICHMONDTOWN

La Tourette Park

Richmond Rd.

Amboy Rd.

Giffords La.

Historic Richmond Town ◆

West Shore Expwy.

Arthur Kill

Arden Ave.

Huguenot Ave.

Richmond Rd.

Hylan Blvd.

ROSSVILLE

440

Woodrow Ave.

WOODROW

Richmond Pkwy.

STATEN ISLAND RAPID TRANSIT

ELTINGVILLE

Amboy Ave.

Great Kills ○

Eltingville ○

ANNADALE

Annadale ○

Huguenot ○

Princes Bay ○

PRINCES BAY

Pleasant Plains ○

Nassau ○

Atlantic ○

Tottenville ○

Hylan Blvd.

TOTTENVILLE

Outerbridge Crossing

Arthur Kill

OCEAN

ATLANTIC

0   2 miles

0   3 km

Staten Island

TOP STATEN ISLAND EXPERIENCES

Board the Staten Island ferry for some of the most memorable views you'll ever have of the Manhattan skyline, the Statue of Liberty, and New York harbor . . . free of charge.

Tour Snug Harbor by boat or by foot to see the maritime artifacts.

Find your colonial alter ego at Historic Richmond Town where buildings, activities, and

characters bring American history to life.

Dress up like a fire fighter or as an actor in a play at the Staten Island Children's Museum.

Find your way out of the Secret Garden maze at the Staten Island Botanical Garden and get lost all over again in the beauty of the outdoor waterfalls, ponds and rose garden.

mornings until 11:30 AM, ferries run every hour on the half hour. From 11:30 AM until 7:30 PM, they run every half hour. Snacks are sold on-board. Ⓜ*Runs between Manhattan's Whitehall Terminal, Whitehall and South Sts., and Staten Island's St. George Terminal ⊕www.siferry.com Ⓜ4 or 5 train to Bowling Green, or R or W train to Whitehall St., 1 to South Ferry.* All ages

ALSO WORTH SEEING

★ **Snug Harbor Cultural Center.** Once part of a sprawling farm, this 83-acre community is Staten Island's most popular attraction. Here you can see maritime art, play and learn in the children's museum, and stroll through lush gardens. After all that, you'll definitely be ready for lunch among the flowers at the charming on-site café.

Made up of 26 mostly restored historic buildings, Snug Harbor's center is a row of striking mid-19th-century Greek Revival colonnaded structures. Main Hall—the oldest building on the property—is home to the **Eleanor Proske Visitors Center** (⊠*$3, including Newhouse Center*). The adjacent **Noble Maritime Collection** (☎*718/447–6490* ⊕*www.noblemaritime.org* ⊠*$5*), an old seaman's dormitory, is now a museum of ocean-inspired artwork with exhibits of model ships as well. A tour boat leaves from the launch here, taking you around the sites of Snug Harbor. The **Staten Island Children's Museum** (☎*718/273–2060* ⊕*www.statenislandkids.org* ⊠*$5* ⊙*School year, Tues.–Fri. noon–5, weekends 10–5; in summer until 8 on Thurs.*) has five galleries with hands-on exhibitions introducing such topics as bugs, great explorations, and storytelling. Portia's Playhouse, an interactive children's theater, brings youngsters on-stage in costume and stage make-up with real stage props and lighting. Ladder 11, a thrill for firefighter fans, invites you to jump on their fire truck, ring the fire bell, and slide down the ladder. And there's much more: Block Harbor is an imaginative play space with blocks and a menagerie of animal toys. In *It's a Dog's Life,* kids learn about the amazing abilities of animals through interactive experiences. Sea of Boats is an outdoor play space with a tugboat, lighthouse, and dinghy. Family workshops are offered as well.

Spread over the cultural center grounds is the **Staten Island Botanical Garden** (☎*718/273–8200* ⊕*www.sibg.org* ☞*Free; $5 for Chinese Garden and Secret Garden* ☉*Daily dawn–dusk; Chinese Garden and Secret Garden Apr.–Sept., Tues.–Sun. 10–5; Oct.–Mar., Tues.–Sun. 10–4*), which includes a perennial garden, orchid collection, 9/11 memorial, 20-acre wetland, rose garden, and sensory garden with fragrant, touchable flowers and a tinkling waterfall. The Chinese Scholar's Garden has reflecting ponds, waterfalls, and a teahouse. Children love the Connie Gretz Secret Garden, especially designed for them, with its castle and maze among the flowers.

From the Staten Island Ferry terminal, take the S40 bus 2 mi (about 7 minutes) to the Snug Harbor Road stop. Or, grab a car service at the ferry terminal. (The ride should cost you about $5.) ✉*1000 Richmond Terr., between Snug Harbor Rd. and Tyson Ave., Livingston* ☎*718/448–2500* ⊕*www.snug-harbor.org* ☞*$3; gardens and galleries combined admission $6; Cultural Center grounds free; Secret Garden: children, $1; adults free, if accompanied by a child Chinese garden: $5, adults; $5, ages 12 and under* ☉*Tues.–Sun. 10–5. Grounds dawn–dusk every day except major holidays.* All ages

WHERE TO EAT

$ ✕**Adobe Blues.** *American.* In this warm terra-cotta restaurant/bar, the Southwestern food mixes with live music on Wednesday nights. Kids can have a basic menu of tacos and enchiladas. ✉*63 Lafayette Ave., off Fillmore St., 25 min from Richmondtown* ☎*718/720–2583* ☜*Reservations not accepted* ▭ *AE, D, MC, V.*

Museums

3

WORD OF MOUTH

"One thing you might try is to integrate [your kids] most recent school curriculum into what you see—if the oldest has studied Medieval Europe, seeing the tapestries and arms and armor at the Met will bring those subjects alive for him/her. If American history was covered this year, Ellis Island and the Tenement Museum will be especially rewarding."

—mp

www.fodors.com/forums

MOST KIDS' IDEA OF THE "worst vacation ever" includes spending hours visiting boring museums. But New York City is far from boring, and the museums are a part of that urban adventure. First of all, you have to have a game plan so kids end up with great memories and not just aching feet and glazed over expressions.

Tap into their favorite subjects. There's a museum for almost every interest you can imagine from fire trucks to outer space. And who can forget the legions of art museums, fascinating to everyone from finger painters to septuagenarian sculptures.

Just visit museums on your kid's terms—keep things bite-size. You could decide to view just one theme part of a museum, like the Egyptian wing, for instance, at the Met. Or look at some of the smaller nonartsy museums, too, like the Intrepid Sea-Air-Space Museum. Sell the concept that museums = fun.

This chapter covers museums that should have something for everyone. There are the heavy-hitters on everyone's must-see list and some of the less-familiar gems. Whichever one or ones you choose to visit, get a sense of what's inside online before you go. Pick exhibits will give you some quality time visiting before your kids get antsy. A number of museums offer scavenger hunts and other interactive activities to keep the entire family engaged. Older kids should bring along their student ID for reduced prices at some venues. And do avail yourselves of the free nights or hours that some museums offer—great for quick, guilt-free 15–30 minutes museum runs.

See the Exploring Manhattan chapter (⇨Ch. 1) for map locations of major museums.

WHAT TO SEE

American Folk Art Museum. Weather vanes, quilts, pottery, scrimshaw, sculpture, and paintings give an excellent overview of the freewheeling folk-art genre, but the exterior is a work of art as well: the eight-story building consisting of 63 hand-cast panels of alloyed bronze, reveals individual textures, sizes, and plays of light. The museum's award-winning gift shop has an outstanding collection of handcrafted items. Exhibits of dolls, carousel horses, weather vanes, and whirligigs are fascinating as well. A family guide, "Hello Folks," available at the front desk, will point out specific points of interest. The museum's

TOP MUSEUM EXPERIENCES

See two titans clash with the opening display of dinosaurs locked in combat at the American Museum of Natural History.

Let kids envision the Metropolitan Museum of Art as a giant dress-up box with the gleaming knights and armor section and the Costume Institute's glorious dresses.

Dive into a movie on the giant IMAX screen following an exploration of the planets at the amazing Hayden Planetarium.

Ask kids to imagine their own make-believe battle while viewing the monumental toy soldier collection at the Forbes Galleries.

Put on your most colorful T-shirt and let the hundreds of gorgeous butterflies at the seasonal American Museum of Natural History butterfly vivarium land on your head, your hands, and your shirt.

award-winning gift shop has an outstanding collection of handcrafted items and unusual toys for sale. Folk Art for Families art workshops follow guided family tours of the museum. Call for schedules. ⊠*45 W. 53rd St., between 5th and 6th Aves., Midtown West* ☎*212/265–1040* ⊕*www.folk artmuseum.org* ⊠*$9 adults; free Fri. 5:30–7:30; students $7; children under 12, free* ☉*Tues.–Thurs. and weekends 10:30–5:30, Fri. 10:30–7:30* Ⓜ*E, V to 5th Ave./53rd St.; B, D, E to 7th Ave.; B, D, F, V to 47th–50th Sts./Rockefeller Center.* All ages

★ **Fodor's Choice American Museum of Natural History.** The towering, spectacularly reassembled dinosaur skeletons that greet you when you enter this museum are practically worth the (suggested) price of admission. But there's tons more, including exhibits of ancient civilizations, animals both stuffed and living (don't miss the live Butterfly Conservatory October– May), a hall of oceanic creatures overlooked by a 94-foot model of a blue whale, and space shows at the adjoining Rose Center for Earth and Space. Families can easily spend an entire day here, so you'll need a game plan to navigate the 46 exhibits scattered through 25 interconnected buildings. Most kids race to the popular Fossil Halls to see the 39-foot-long Tyrannosaurus Rex skeleton and 600 other prehistoric creatures on display. Live animals illustrate the ecology of New York City in the Natural Science Center. Little eyes begin to sparkle when they visit the Hall of Gems, home to the Star of India—it's the world's largest blue star sapphire. The Ross Hall of Meteorites is another great stop with the largest meteorite ever displayed; it can be viewed as well as touched. The Origins of Man exhibit is perfect for grade schoolers studying evolution and natural science. The Rose Center for Earth and Space is home to the Hayden Planetarium holding the incredible Hayden Sphere, some 87 feet in diameter. Educational and entertaining, movies projected on the giant IMAX screen offer a perfect way to rest tired feet. This museum is one of the most popular in the city, and it is recommended that you go early. There may be extra fees for special exhibits and for IMAX Theater showings. For something truly different, prebook a sleepover for your family at the museum. Kids 8–12 and their chaperones sleep on cots under the blue whale in the Hall of Ocean Life. Your kids might feel a little like Ben Stiller in *Night at the Museum*, which is apt as it was filmed here. ⊠*Central Park West at W. 79th St., Upper West Side* ☏ *212/769–5200* ⊕ *amnh.org* ⊜*$20 suggested donation, includes admission to Rose Center for Earth and Space; students $11; children 2–12, $8.50* ⊙⊙*Daily 10–5:45; Rose Center until 8:45 on Fri.* Ⓜ*B, C to 81st St.* All ages

Children's Museum of the Arts. In this bi-level space, children ages 1 to 10 can amuse and educate themselves with various arts-related activities, including diving into a colorful "Ball Pond" (for kids 2–8 only); playacting in costume; music making with real instruments; and art making, from computer art to old-fashioned painting, sculpting, and collage. Kids can learn claymation and animation on select days. The innovative drop-in Wee-Arts Early Childhood program offering experimentation and exploration for ages 1–3. On rainy days or cold weekends, this museum is crowded. ⊠*182 Lafayette St., between Grand and Broome Sts., SoHo* ☏*212/941–9198* ⊕*www.cmany.org* ⊜*$9* ⊙*Wed. and Fri.–Sun. noon–5, Thurs. noon–6* Ⓜ*6 to Spring St.* All ages

Children's Museum of Manhattan. In this five-story exploratorium, children ages 1 to 10 are invited to paint their own masterpieces, float boats down a "stream," and put on shows at a puppet theater. Art workshops, science programs, sing-alongs, and storytelling sessions are held daily. Play Works, an educational play area for children infant–4 is designed in the form of a mini city, "Little West Side." In warmer months, City Splash is an outdoor water play area that teaches kids about water as they splash, pour, float, and play. (Bring a change of clothes and a towel!) On rainy days or cold weekends, this museum is crowded. There is limited stroller storage, and lines for the coatroom are long. ⊠*212 W. 83rd St., between Broadway and Amsterdam Ave., Upper West Side* ☎*212/721–1234* ⊕*www.cmom. org* 🎫*$10; free under age 1* ⊙*Tues.–Sun. 10–5* Ⓜ*1 to 86th St.* All ages

The Cloisters. Perched on a wooded hill in Fort Tryon Park, near Manhattan's northern tip, the Cloisters holds the medieval collection of the Metropolitan Museum of Art. Colonnaded walks connect authentic medieval French cloisters, a French Romanesque chapel, a 12th-century chapter house, and a Romanesque apse. One room is devoted to the 15th- and 16th-century Unicorn Tapestries—a must-see masterpiece of medieval mythology. Three gardens shelter plants similar to those grown during the Middle Ages. Concerts of medieval music are held regularly. No kid can resist playing "castle" here; the setting is definitely more for them than the actual exhibits. Older kids may appreciate the program guides just for them. Check the calendar for the Gallery Workshops for Families program events, held on weekends. ⊠*Fort Tryon Park, Inwood* ☎*212/923–3700* ⊕*www.metmuseum.org* 🎫*$20 suggested donation; free if combined with a same-day visit to the Met (already paid). Students $10; free under age 12* ⊙*Mar.–Oct., Tues.–Sun. 9:30–5:15; Nov.–Feb., Tues.–Sun. 9:30–4:45* Ⓜ*A to 190th St.* All ages

Cooper-Hewitt National Design Museum. More than 2,000 years of international design is on display inside the 64-room mansion, formerly home to industrialist Andrew Carnegie. The 250,000-plus objects here include drawings, textiles, furniture, metalwork, ceramics, glass, and woodwork. Changing exhibitions are drawn from the permanent collection, highlighting everything from antique cutlery and Japanese sword fittings to robotics and animation. In summer some exhibits are displayed in the museum's lush garden. The mansion, built to Carnegie's scale with short doorways, may be more interesting to kids than the exhibits. Tweens will recognize the building and the garden as the site of the Lily van der Woodsen–Bart Bass wedding in *Gossip Girl.* ⊠*2 E. 91st St., at 5th Ave., Upper East Side* ☎*212/849–8400* ⊕*www.cooperhewitt.org* 🎫*$15; students, $10; under 12, free* ⊙*Tues.–Fri. 10–5, Sat. 10–6, Sun. noon–6* Ⓜ*4, 5, 6 to 86th St.* 5+up

El Museo del Barrio. *El barrio* is Spanish for "the neighborhood" and the nickname for East Harlem, a largely Spanish-speaking Puerto Rican and Dominican community. The museum, on the edge of this neighborhood, focuses on Latin American and Caribbean art. The 8,000-object permanent collection includes numerous pre-Columbian artifacts, sculpture, photography, film, and video, and traditional art from all over Latin America. During Museum Mile night in June, a block-party atmosphere burst open with live music and sidewalk chalk for kids. Signs throughout the museum are in English and Spanish. ✉*1230 5th Ave., between E. 104th and E. 105th Sts., Upper East Side* ☎*212/831–7272* ⊕*www.elmuseo.org* 🎟*$6; students $4; under 12, free* ☉*Wed.–Sun. 11–5* Ⓜ*6 to 103rd St.* 12+up

Forbes Galleries. Marvel at the idiosyncratic personal collection of the late publisher Malcolm Forbes, on view in the Forbes Magazine Building. Military music is piped into the displays of warships and ocean liners. A tiny, dramatic diorama captures the adrenaline of the men on the gun deck of the HMS *Victory* during the Battle of Trafalgar. Of the 10,000 toy soldiers depicted in action, you'll see Aztecs resisting Cortez in 1521, Mussolini marching into Ethiopia in 1935, and a skirmish between "cowboys and Indians." There are more than 500 tin, cast iron, and paper lithograph toy boats in the Toy Galleries. Kids might also like the display of original handcrafted versions of the board game Monopoly. There are stools set by some of the higher display windows so little ones can look as well. No strollers are allowed in the galleries; all must be left at the security desk. ✉*62 5th Ave., at E. 12th St., Greenwich Village* ☎*212/206–5548* ⊕*www.forbesgalleries.com* 🎟*Free* ☉*Tues.–Sat. 10–4* Ⓜ*L, N, Q, R, W, 4, 5, 6 to 14th St./Union Sq.* All ages

Intrepid Sea, Air & Space Museum. Formerly the USS *Intrepid,* this 900-foot aircraft carrier is serving out its retirement as the centerpiece of Manhattan's only floating museum. The carrier's most trying moment of service, the day it was attacked in World War II by kamikaze pilots, is recounted in a multimedia presentation. Aircraft on deck include an A-12 Blackbird spy plane, a Concorde, helicopters, and two-dozen other aircraft. Docked alongside, and also part of the museum, is the *Growler,* a strategic-missile submarine. Children can explore the ships' skinny hallways and winding staircases, as well as manipulate countless knobs, buttons, and wheels. For an extra thrill (and an extra $8), kids can try the Navy flight simulator and "land" an aircraft on board. The museum is great on rainy days, too, as there are many interactive exhibits inside. A complete overhaul in 2008 means new exhibits such as the renovated radar room, which was previously "top secret." ✉*Hudson River, Pier 86, 12th Ave. and W. 46th St., Midtown West* ☎*212/245–0072 or 877/957–7447* ⊕*www.intrepidmuseum. org* ⊒*$19.50; free to active and retired U.S. military personnel; children 6–17, $14.50; children 2–5, $7.50; under 2, free* ⊗*Apr.–Sept., weekdays 10–5, weekends 10–6; Oct.– Mar., Tues.–Sun. 10–5; last admission 1 hr before closing* Ⓜ*A, C, E to 42nd St.; M42 bus to pier.* All ages

The Jewish Museum. Within a Gothic-style 1908 mansion, the museum draws on a large collection of art and ceremonial objects to explore 4,000 years of Jewish culture through art. The two-floor permanent exhibition, "Culture and Continuity: The Jewish Journey" displays nearly 800 objects. Most interesting for kids is the re-creation of an ancient synagogue, and the changing exhibits on the fourth floor. Every Sunday the museum hosts drop-in crafts programs at the Family Activity Center from 1 to 4. Family tours are offered on the second Sunday of the month along with kids' concerts and musical theater. Interactive computers play TV programs, including children's programs. Look for "Ari the Lion" signs throughout the museum— he points out fun stuff for young museum-goers. A family audio guide is free for ages 5 and up. ✉*1109 5th Ave., at E. 92nd St., Upper East Side* ☎*212/423–3200* ⊕*www. jewishmuseum.org* ⊒*$12; Sat. free all day; students $7.50; under 12, free* ⊗*Sat.–Wed. 11–5:45, Thurs. 11–8* Ⓜ*6 to 96th St.* All ages

★ Fodor'sChoice **Lower East Side Tenement Museum.** Step back in time and into the partially restored 1863 tenement building at 97 Orchard Street, where you can squeeze through the preserved apartments of immigrants on one of four one-hour tours. This is America's first urban living-history museum dedicated to the life of immigrants. "Getting By" visits the homes of Natalie Gumpertz, a German-Jewish dressmaker (dating from 1878) and Adolph and Rosaria Baldizzi, Catholic immigrants from Sicily (1935). "Piecing it Together" visits the Levines' garment shop/apartment and the Rogarshevsky family from Eastern Europe (1918). The tour through the Confino family apartment is perfect for children, who are greeted by a costumed interpreter playing teenaged daughter. Building tours are limited to 15 people so reserve your tickets in advance. Walking tours of the neighborhood are also held on weekends. The visitor information center and excellent gift shop displays a video with interviews of Lower East Side residents past and present. The Museum's newest tour introduces you to Irish-Catholic immigrant life in New York with the Moore family. No strollers are allowed but you can leave yours at the visitor center. There are no elevators or lockers. ⊠*108 Orchard St., between Delancey and Broome Sts., Lower East Side* ☎*212/431–0233* ⊕*www.tenement.org* ⊠*Tenement and walking tours $17; students $13* ⊙*Tenement tours leave in 40-min intervals, Tues.–Fri, 1–4:45, weekends 11–5, check Web site for full details; Confino apartment tour weekends, hourly 1–3; walking tours Apr.–Dec., weekends 1 and 3. Visitor center and gift shop Mon. 11–5:30, Tues.–Fri. 11–6, weekends 10:45–6* Ⓜ*B, D to Grand St.; F to Delancey St.; J, M, Z to Essex St.* 5+up

Madame Tussauds New York. Join Captain Jack Sparrow's pirate crew, sing along with an American Idol, mix your own R&B hit alongside Usher, or forecast tomorrow's weather with Al Roker. Much of the fun here comes from the photo opportunities—you're encouraged to pose with nearly 200 realistic replicas of the famous and infamous (disposable cameras are on sale). But there's more to do here than just pal around with the waxworks. Interactive options include a karaoke café, a celebrity walk down the red carpet, and a haunted town, the latter populated with both wax figures and real people. Miley Cyrus (Hannah Montana)'s likeness is a magnet for girls. Little Leaguers will love the Ultimate Subway Series where you can throw a pitch as David Wright, Derek Jeter, and fans lead the cheers. The new 4-D Theater will thrill kids with special effects including seat vibration, leg ticklers, water mist, bubbles, air currents, and other surprises. Only the oldest kids should venture into Chamber Live!, which displays scenes from three horror films. ⊠*234 W. 42nd St., between 7th and 8th Aves., Midtown West* ☎*212/512–9600* ⊕*www. madame-tussauds.com* ⊠*$35; ages 4–12, $28; free under age 3* ⊙*Weekdays 10–9, weekends 10–10* Ⓜ*1, 2, 3, 7, N, Q, R, W, S, A, C, E to 42nd St.* 7+up

★ Fodor'sChoice **The Metropolitan Museum of Art.** The largest art museum in the Western Hemisphere, the Met is—naturally—a mecca for art lovers of all stripes. Treasures from all over the world and every era of human creativity comprise its expansive collection. Kids will want to speed past the grand staircase to visit the extensive Egyptian area with its many mummies; or head to the popular Arms and Armor exhibit with its medieval swords and armor (even a suit of children's armor). Follow the museum's unofficial mascot, William the blue hippo (often tricky to find), to the amazingly popular Temple of Dendur, reassembled after being shipped over from its original Egyptian home. Ask at the helpful information desk for guidance about anything interesting for kids, like the colorful impressionist and expressionist paintings by Monet, Seurat, Pissarro, and Van Gogh. The 20th-Century Wing also has lots of bold art that kids might enjoy. Recent exhibits have included pop art and superhero costumes. Strollers are allowed, and free back carriers to use are distributed at the 81st Street entrance. Part of the many family-friendly entice-ments include a Family Audio Guide for kids age 6–12; weekend programs such as "Hello, Met!", "Look Again," or "How Did They Do That," especially designed to pique the curiosity of kids ages 5–12 with hands-on activities. ✉ *5th Ave. at 82nd St., Upper East Side* ☎*212/535–7710* ⊕ *www.metmuseum.org* ✍*$20 suggested donation; students, $10; under 12, free; if you combine this with same-day visit to Cloisters (already paid), admission is free* ⊗ ⊗*Tues.– Thurs. and Sun. 9:30–5:30, Fri. and Sat. 9:30–9* Ⓜ*4, 5, 6 to 86th St.* All ages

Museum of the City of New York. Within a colonial revival building designed for the museum in the 1930s, the city's history and many quirks are revealed through engaging exhibits. Permanent collections detail firefighting, theater, and New York's role as a port. Period rooms include several that John D. Rockefeller Sr. acquired when he bought a fully furnished New York mansion in the 1880s. The historic toys on view include the beloved Stettheimer Dollhouse, a miniature mansion outfitted down to postage-stamp-size artworks imitating 20th-century masters. Don't miss *Timescapes,* a 25-minute media projection, narrated by Stanley Tucci, which innovatively illustrates New York's physical expansion and population changes. The museum hosts New York–centric lectures, films, and walking tours. ▇TIP→When you're finished touring the museum cross the street and stroll through the Vanderbilt Gates to enter the Conservatory Garden, one of Central Park's hidden gems. Long-term exhibitions of greatest appeal are: Perform! showing costumes and props from popular Broadway productions and Trade!, a collection of ship models and other items pertaining to

NYC's history as a port. Past exhibits have included such marvels as seats from the original Yankee Stadium or an original Checker cab. Strollers are OK here. ⊠*1220 5th Ave., at E. 103rd St., Upper East Side* ☎*212/534–1672* ⊕*www.mcny.org* ⚏*$9 suggested donation; $20 families (max 2 adults); $5 students; under 12, free* ☉*Tues.–Sun. 10–5* Ⓜ*6 to 103rd St.* **3+up**

Museum of Jewish Heritage—A Living Memorial to the Holocaust. In a granite 85-foot hexagon at the southern end of Battery Park City, this museum pays tribute to the 6 million Jews who perished in the Holocaust. The museum is built in the shape of a Star of David, with three floors of exhibits demonstrating the dynamism of 20th-century Jewish culture. Visitors enter through a gallery that provides a context for the early-20th-century artifacts on the first floor: an elaborate screen hand-painted for the fall harvest festival of Sukkoth, wedding invitations, and tools used by Jewish tradesmen. Original documentary films play throughout the museum. The second floor details the rise of Nazism and anti-Semitism, and the ravages of the Holocaust. The third floor covers postwar Jewish life. A kids' guide helps explain the seriousness and importance of this museum through role play as detectives. The second floor may be too graphic for younger kids. ⊠*36 Battery Pl., Battery Park City, Lower Manhattan* ☎*646/437–4200* ⊕*www.mjhnyc. org* ⚏*$10; students $5; under 12, free* ☉*Thurs. and Sun.– Tues. 10–5:45, Wed. 10–8, Fri. and eve of Jewish holidays 10–3* Ⓜ*4, 5 to Bowling Green.* **5+up**

★ Fodor'sChoice **Museum of Modern Art.** Described as a "modernist dream world" after its $425 million face-lift in 2004, MoMA, as it is known by most locals, has since become as famous for its architecture as for its collections. Yoshio Taniguchi, the Japanese architect responsible for the redesign, created newly spacious, soaring-ceiling galleries suffused with natural light, where masterpieces like Monet's *Water Lilies,* Picasso's *Les Demoiselles d'Avignon,* and Van Gogh's *Starry Night* can get the oohs and aahs they deserve. The museum offers a variety of guided programs suitable for children of all ages, such as gallery talks, film screenings, and interactive workshops. Call Ford Family Programs (☎ *212/708–2005*) for a schedule. MoMA also offers audio tours where children explain key art pieces in their own words at a kid's level. The colorful Chagalls, Warhols, and Pollocks are great vibrant pieces for kids, the Dalis and Magrittes less so. You'll have to keep them from touching the "melted" Oldenburg Giant Soft Fan, but that's part of the fun. The airy sculpture garden provides a breath of air for little ones tired of being cooped up indoors. Café 2 has a children's menu and high chairs. ✉ *11 W. 53rd St., between 5th and 6th Aves., Midtown East* ☎212/708–9400 ⊕ *www.moma.org* ✎ *$20; students, $12; children under 16, free* ⊗ ⊗*Sat.–Mon., Wed., and Thurs. 10:30–5:30, Fri. 10:30–8. Closed Tues.* Ⓜ *E, V to 5th Ave./53rd St.; B, D, F, V to 47th–50th Sts./Rockefeller Center.* All ages

National Museum of the American Indian. Changing presentations drawn from the National Museum of the American Indian, a branch of the Smithsonian, are exhibited in the beaux arts Alexander Hamilton U.S. Custom House (1907), one of Lower Manhattan's finest buildings. You can see everything without being overwhelmed. The Diker Pavilion for Native Arts and Cultures provides a venue for dance, music, and storytelling programs. The museum gives out a fun family guide with games and a scavenger hunt. Kids will love the entrance where the Welcome Wall let you hear greetings in hundreds of Native American languages. Touch-screen computers, some interactive, help explain the items in each gallery. The "Especially for Kids" film series focuses on the lives of Native American children. ✉*1 Bowling Green, between State and Whitehall Sts., Lower Manhattan* ☎212/514–3700 ⊕*www.americanindian.si.edu* ✎*Free* ⊗*Mon.–Wed. and Fri.–Sun. 10–5, Thurs. 10–8* Ⓜ*4, 5 to Bowling Green.* 7+up

The New Museum. Focused on new art and new ideas, the New Museum reopened here in late 2007. The seven-story, 60,000-square-foot structure here is a glimmering metal mesh-clad assemblage of off-centered boxes. Exhibits change constantly and have included such off-center showcase as the annual "Altoids Curiously Strong Collection," a yearly survey of emerging artists. Start at the Sky Room on the top floor (open on weekends) where kids can run around a bit and survey the skyline, then follow the stairs to each of the floors with their varying, somewhat-quirky exhibits. Be aware that some of the exhibits may not be suitable for younger viewers. ✉*235 Bowery, at Prince St., Lower Manhattan* ☎212/219–1222 ⊕*www.newmuseum. org* ✎*$12, children under 18 free* ⊗*Wed., Sat., and Sun. noon–6, Thurs. and Fri. noon–10* Ⓜ *6 to Spring St. or F, V to 2nd Ave.* 12+up

New York City Fire Museum. In the former headquarters of Engine 30, dating from 1904, retired firefighters volunteer their time to answer visitors' questions about firefighting, from early bucket brigades to current techniques. The collection of firefighting tools from the 18th century to the present includes hand-pulled and horse-drawn engines, pumps, and uniforms. There's also a memorial exhibit with photos, paintings, children's artwork, and found objects relating to the September 11 attacks. Kids will get a charge out of ringing the fire bell and can have their picture taken wearing a real firefighter's helmet and coat. The FDNY Store sells lots of cool memorabilia. For a fire safety learning experience, consider a visit to the FDNY Fire Zone at 34 W. 51st St., too. ✉ *278 Spring St., near Varick St., SoHo* ☎ *212/691–1303* ⊕ *www.nycfiremuseum.org* 🖃 *$5 suggested donation; 12 and under, $1; 6 and under, free* ☉ *Tues.–Sat. 10–5, Sun. 10–4* Ⓜ *C, E to Spring St.* 3+up

New York City Police Museum. Why are police called cops? When was fingerprinting first used to solve a crime? Find the answers at this museum dedicated to New York's finest, set in the first police precinct station in downtown Manhattan (1911). The force's history from colonial times through the present is covered through permanent and rotating exhibits, as well as interactive and sometimes chilling displays, including fingerprinting and forensic art stations. The permanent exhibit "9/11 Remembered" includes a video with interviews with those who were first responders to the attack. Special events include a vintage police car show the first weekend in June, and the first Saturday in October, when kids get to meet police officers and demonstrations take place. Children will marvel at the collection of confiscated items, which include weapons and piles of money. The transportation room displays old patrol cars and motorcycles used by police forces of yore. No kid will want to miss the mock jail cells on the second floor. In the Real Time Crime Center, you can see how lab statistics identify possible suspects. Snap a souvenir picture of your kid wearing a police uniform or let kids take part in a make-believe line-up. (The 9/11-related exhibits may be too disturbing for some.) ✉ *100 Old Slip, near South St., Lower Manhattan* ☎ *212/480–3100* ⊕ *www.nyc policemuseum.org* 🖃 *$7 suggested donation; $5, students and ages 6–18; under 6, free* ☉ *Mon.–Sat. 10–5* Ⓜ *2, 3 to Wall St.* 5+up

New-York Historical Society. Manhattan's oldest museum, founded in 1804, has a collection of 6 million pieces of art, literature, and memorabilia. Special exhibitions shed light on New York's—and America's—history, everyday life, art, and architecture. It's a bit of a jumble but you're bound to stumble across many wonderful things. The permanent collection features a large variety of antique toys. Scavenger hunts and activity packs are available for each exhibition. ⊠2 W. 77th St., at Central Park W, Upper West Side ☎212/873–3400 ⊕www.nyhistory.org ☜ $10; students, $6; under 12, free ⊙Tues.–Thurs. and weekends 10–6, Fri. 10–8 Ⓜ B, C to 81st St. **5+up**

★ Fodor's Choice **The Paley Center for Media.** Formerly the Museum of Television & Radio, the Center documents the history of broadcasting. The main draw here is the computerized catalog of more than 100,000 television and radio programs. You type the name of the song, show, or performer into a computer terminal and then proceed to a semiprivate screening area to watch your selection. Adding to the delight of screening TV shows from yesteryear is the original commercials still embedded in many of the programs; if ads are your thing you can skip the programming altogether and watch different compilations of classic commercials. Tune into some of your favorite cartoons or children's program like the *Wonderful World of Disney* (1954) and let the little ones have a blast from the past. Other favorites include *Saturday Night Live* episodes and commercials from the Superbowl. Reservations are required to watch programs, so make this an early stop in the day. Strollers are welcome here. ⊠25 W. 52nd St., between 5th and 6th Aves., Midtown West ☎212/621–6800 ⊕www. paleymediacouncil.org ☜$10; students, $8; under 14, $5 ⊙Tues., Wed., and Fri.–Sun. noon–6, Thurs. noon–8 Ⓜ E, V to 5th Ave./53rd St.; B, D, F, V to 47th–50th Sts./Rockefeller Center. **5+up**

Solomon R. Guggenheim Museum. Frank Lloyd Wright's landmark museum building is visited as much for its famous architecture as it is for its superlative art. Opened in 1959, shortly after Wright's death, the Guggenheim is acclaimed as one of the greatest buildings of the 20th century. Inside, under a 92-foot-high glass dome, a seemingly endless ramp spirals down past changing exhibitions. The museum has strong holdings of Wassily Kandinsky, Paul Klee, Marc Chagall, Pablo Picasso, and Joan Miro. The ramp is a kid's dream, although the adults may not think so. You'll want to start at the top and try to keep the kids from barreling down the slope as you pass the special exhibits along the walls. Outside is equally fun with its own ramp that would be perfect for kicking a soccer ball around (not that we encourage that!). ✉*1071 5th Ave., between E. 88th and E. 89th Sts., Upper East Side* ☎*212/423–3500* ⊕*www.guggenheim.org* 🎟*$18; students, $15; children under 12 free* ☼*Sun.–Wed. 9–5:45, Fri. and Sat. 9–8. Closed Thurs.* Ⓜ*4, 5, 6 to 86th St.* 5+up

Studio Museum in Harlem. Contemporary art by African-American, Caribbean, and African artists is the focus of this small museum with a light-filled sculpture garden. Its changing exhibits have included "Black Artists and Abstraction" and "Africa Comics." The museum also includes art by children. The relatively brief exhibits may appeal to kids with short attention spans. ✉*144 W. 125th St., between Lenox Ave. and Adam Clayton Powell Jr. Blvd., Harlem* ☎*212/864–4500* ⊕*www.studiomuseuminharlem.org* 🎟*$7 suggested donation; students, $3; under 12, free* ☼*Wed.–Fri. and Sun. noon–6, Sat. 10–6* Ⓜ*2, 3 to 125th St.* 7+up

Whitney Museum of American Art. With its bold collection of American and contemporary art, this museum presents an eclectic mix of more than 16,000 works in its permanent collection. Notable pieces include Hopper's *Early Sunday Morning* (1930), Bellows' *Dempsey and Firpo* (1924), Alexander Calder's beloved Circus mobile, and several of Georgia O'Keeffe's dazzling flower paintings. Note that some of the art may be unsuitable for younger children due to its subject matter, especially some of the movies shown daily. A variety of WhitneyKids family programs are age-appropriate for kids infant–12 with hands-on art workshops and activities for the whole family. ✉*945 Madison Ave., at E. 75th St., Upper East Side* ☎*800/WHITNEY* ⊕ *www.whitney.org* 🎟*$15; students, $10; under 12, free* ☼*Wed., Thurs., and weekends 11–6, Fri. 1–9* Ⓜ*6 to 77th St.* All ages

The Performing Arts

4

WORD OF MOUTH

"We headed to Times Square because we had tickets to Mary Poppins. We had purchased the tickets off of www.broadwaybox.com for $25.00. We were in the top balcony, but still had a great view, especially for the price. The show was fantastic . . . We waited outside of the Stage Door after the show and our daughter was able to get several autographs . . . She was elated. She is 14 and involved in a local theater group at home."

—april04

THEATER IS WHAT COMES TO mind when most families think of New York City and the arts. The Great White Way, Broadway, the glitz of Times Square—most families can't get enough of it. You could see a different play every night, both on Broadway or off-Broadway in a smaller, less well-known theater, or involve your kids in a performance of their own. What kid wouldn't want to be in a puppet show, see behind-the-scenes demonstrations, or check out the marionettes at the Swedish Marionette Theater in Central Park? Beyond the major productions that all families gravitate toward like current blockbusters *Mamma Mia, The Little Mermaid, Mary Poppins,* or the *Lion King,* there are kid-designed theaters offering kid-targeted shows like the *New Victory* or *Tada!* that even the littlest ones in your group will love. Quirky shows like *Blue Man Group* or *Stomp* will provide conversation for years to come. Then, of course, there are the perennial non-Broadway favorites that revolve around the holidays like the *Nutcracker* ballet at Lincoln Center or the *Christmas Spectacular* with the amazing Rockettes at Radio City Music Hall. All kids will be star-struck by these performances, an important not-to-miss part of any visit to New York City. The city is also a revolving door of spontaneity that's perfect for kids: in-the-park concerts and ad hoc street performers, mime troupes, and break-dancers in the subways, and roving Peruvian minstrels just to name just a few.

A fantastic and comprehensive reference for all arts programs for kids, including performing arts and museums, is the NYCkidsArts calendar published the Alliance for the Arts and available at the NYC & Co. visitors office or at NYCkidsARTS.org.

TICKETS 101

What do tickets sell for, anyway? Not counting the limited "premium seat" category, the top ticket price for Broadway musicals is now hovering just above $110, with a few venturing up to $120; the low end for musicals is in the $40–$60 range. Nonmusical comedies and dramas start at the same place as musicals and top out at about $90. Off-Broadway show tickets average $35–$70, while off-off-Broadway shows can run as low as $10. Tickets to an opera start at about $25 for nosebleed seats and can soar to well over $300 for prime locations. Classical music concerts go for $25 to $100, depending on the venue. Dance performances are usually in the $15 to $60 range,

TOP PERFORMING ARTS EXPERIENCES

Bounce, hop, sing, and scream along with the performers at the new Victory Theater, a theater especially designed for kids-oriented performances.

Marvel at the high-steppin' precision of the Rockettes at the *Christmas Spectacular* at Radio City Music Hall or the magic of the *Nutcracker* ballet at Lincoln Center.

Try to figure out whether Mary Poppins is actually levitating with her parasol as she rises to the top of the New Amsterdam Theater.

Put down the iPod and experience a close-up introduction to great music at the Philharmonic with the Very Young People's Concerts, Young People's Concerts, or Phil Teens.

but expect seats for the ballet to go higher. Scoring tickets is fairly easy, especially if you have some flexibility. But if timing or cost is critical, the only way to ensure you'll get the seats you want is to make your purchase in advance—and that might be months ahead for a hit show. In general, tickets for Saturday evenings and for weekend matinees are the toughest to secure.

Children's tickets can sometimes be less expensive. It's always best to have a student ID card, and ask whether discounts are offered. Discounted student (and adult) tickets are sometimes available on a "rush" basis on the day of a show. Consult Broadways news Web sites like www.playbill.com, call the box office ahead of time, or drop by the theater early during the day to see what's available. Prices for children-specific attractions are usually relatively inexpensive.

For opera, classical music, and dance performances, go to the box office or order tickets through the venue's Web site. For smaller performing-arts companies, including dance, music, and off-Broadway shows, also try **Ticket Central** (☎*212/279–4200* ⊕*www.ticketcentral.com*). For Broadway (and some other big-hall events), sure bets are the box office or either **Telecharge** (☎*212/239–6200* ⊕*www.telecharge.com*) or **Ticketmaster** (☎*212/307–4100* ⊕*www.ticketmaster.com*). Virtually all larger shows are listed with one service or the other, but never both; specifying "premium" will help you get elusive—and expensive (upward of $300–$400)—seats. A broker or your hotel concierge should be able to procure last-minute tickets, but be prepared to pay a steep surcharge.

■ TIP→ **Although most online ticket services provide seating maps to help you choose, the advantage of going to the box office is twofold: there are no add-on service fees, and a ticket seller can personally advise you about sight lines for the seat location you are considering, extremely useful if you're bringing your little ones with you. Some of the theaters may even offer booster seats to help.**

If you're in Midtown, inside the Times Square Visitors Center is the Broadway League's **Broadway Ticket Center** (✉*1560 Broadway, between W. 46th and W. 47th Sts., Midtown West* ☎*888/BROADWAY* ⊕*www.livebroadway.com* Ⓜ *1, 2, 3, 7, N, Q, R, W, S to 42nd St./Times Sq.; N, R, W to 49th St.*). Ticket hours are Monday–Saturday 9–7, Sunday 10–6. You can find a selection of discount vouchers here; it also serves as a one-stop shopping place for full-price tickets for most Broadway shows.

BROADWAY (AND OFF) AT A DISCOUNT

Some shows have front-row orchestra—or very rear balcony—"rush" seats available at a reduced price ($20–$25) on the day of the performance; you must go to the show's box office to buy them. The ⊕*www.broadwaybox.com* site provides a compilation of all discount codes available for a show. In some cases, as with all discount codes offered through the online subscriber services **TheaterMania** (⊕*www. theatermania.com*) and **Playbill** (⊕*www.playbill.com*), you must bring a printout of the offer to the box office, and make your purchase there.

For seats at 25%–50% off the usual price go to **TKTS** (✉*Duffy Sq., at W. 47th St. and Broadway, Midtown West* Ⓜ*1, 2, 3, 7, N, Q, R, W, S to 42nd St./Times Sq.; N, R, W to 49th St.; 1 to 50th St.* ✉*South St. Seaport, at Front and John Sts., Lower Manhattan* Ⓜ *2, 3, 4, 5, A, C, E, J, M, Z to Fulton St./Broadway-Nassau* ✉*Downtown Brooklyn, at the Myrtle St. Promenade and Jay St. Brooklyn* Ⓜ *A, C, F to Jay St.–Borough Hall; M, R, 2, 3, 4, 5 to Court St.- Borough Hall* ⊕*www.tdf.org*). While they do tack on a $4 per ticket service charge, and not all shows are predictably available, the broad choices and ease of selection—and of course, the solid discount—make TKTS the go-to source for the flexible theatergoer. Check the electronic listings board near the ticket windows to mull over your options while you're on line. At the snazzily updated Duffy Square

What's Playing Where

New York is rich with easily accessible and comprehensive listings resources in both print and online formats. The *New York Times'* (⊕*www.nytimes. com*) listings are concentrated in its Thursday, Friday, and Sunday papers, as well as on-line. *The New Yorker* (⊕*www. newyorker.com*) is highly selective but calls attention to performances with its succinct reviews. It hits the stands on Monday. In *New York* magazine (⊕*www.nymag.com*), also on newsstands on Monday, see "The Week" section for hot-ticket events. The freebie tabloid, the *Village Voice* (⊕*www. villagevoice.com*), comes out on Wednesday; it has extensive listings—especially for theater, music, and dance—as well.

Online-only venues ⊕*www. nytheatre.com*, ⊕*www.nyconstage.org*, ⊕*www.tdf.org*, and ⊕*www.broadway.com* provide synopses, schedules when theaters are dark, accessibility info, run times, seating charts, and links to ticket purchases. (Tip: most of these also cover nontheater performances, but they do Broadway and off-Broadway best.)

location (look for the bright red glass staircase), there is a separate *play only* window to further simplify, and speed, things. Duffy hours are Monday–Saturday 3–8 (for evening performances); for Wednesday and Saturday matinees 10–2; for Sunday matinees 11–3; Sunday evening shows, from 3 until ½ hour before curtain. Seaport hours are Monday–Saturday 11–6, Sunday 11–4. Brooklyn hours are Monday–Friday 11–6. With the exception of matinees at the Seaport and Brooklyn locations (they sell these for next-day performances only), all shows offered are same day. Credit cards, cash, or traveler's checks are accepted at all locations. ■TIP➔**Planning ahead? Their Web site lists what was available at the booths in the previous week, and for all current shows, notes whether they are "frequently," "occasionally," "rarely," or "never" available at their booths.** While you wait in line at the Times Square booth, your kids can visit the enormous Toys "R" Us nearby, accompanied by an adult, of course.

THEATER

BROADWAY

Nothing beats the thrill of a fabulous play on Broadway—walking through the flashing bright lights of Times Square en route to your show, there's an excitement that builds. Watch your kids' faces as the house lights dim, and the orchestra swells with the overture. And for clarification: although it's called Broadway, theaters are between 8th Avenue and 6th Avenue (which includes Broadway), roughly from 40th Street to 52nd Street (with some exceptions).

Usually held on four nights in February, Kids' Night on Broadway offers a wonderful opportunity for young people ages 6–18 to see a Broadway show free when accompanied by a full-paying adult. For specific dates and participating shows, refer to *www.kidsnightonbroadway.com*.

Some of Broadway's most kid-friendly theaters didn't start out that way. The **American Airlines Theatre** (originally the Selwyn Theatre) (⊠*227 W. 42nd St., between 7th and 8th Aves., Midtown West* ☎*212/719–1300* ⊕*www.round abouttheatre.org* Ⓜ *1, 2, 3, 7, N, Q, R, W, S to 42nd St./Times Sq.; A, C, E to 42nd St./Port Authority.* 5+up) had various incarnations as a burlesque hall and pornographic movie house before becoming the home to the Roundabout Theatre Company, which offers tickets half-price to kids under 17 for its musicals and plays. Disney refurbished the elaborate 1903 art nouveau **New Amsterdam Theater** (⊠*214 W. 42nd St., between 7th and 8th Aves., Midtown West* ☎*212/282–2907* Ⓜ *1, 2, 3, 7, N, Q, R, W, S to 42nd St./Times Sq.; A, C, E to 42nd St./Port Authority.* All ages), where Eddie Cantor, Will Rogers, Fanny Brice, and the Ziegfeld Follies once drew crowds. *The Lion King* ruled here for the first nine years of its run. The theater is operated by Disney, so shows here are great for kids of ages. Unfortunately, there are no student or family discounts. Don't be shy about asking about the child-appropriateness of any show at any of Broadway's 40 or so theaters.

OFF-BROADWAY THEATERS

Off-Broadway houses—defined by the size of the theater, not its proximity to Broadway—are where you can find showcases for emerging playwrights, unexpected stagings of classic plays, and perennial crowd-pleasers like *Blue*

Man Group that would not be appropriate for a larger space. The venues themselves are found throughout the city—clustering below 14th Street, in and around Times Square, and in parts of Brooklyn.

At the cozy 178-seat theater belonging to the Classic Stage Company (⊠*136 E. 13th St., between 3rd and 4th Aves., East Village* ☎*212/677–4210* ⊕*www.classicstage.org* Ⓜ*4, 5, 6, L, N, Q, R, W to Union Sq.* 5+up) you can see revivals of older works that still have relevance today. With the purchase of a $10 kid's ticket, parents get in free.

Playwrights Horizons (⊠*416 W. 42nd St., between 9th and 10th Aves., Midtown West* ☎*212/564–1235, 212/279–4200 tickets* ⊕*www.playwrightshorizons.org* Ⓜ *A, C, E to 42nd St./Port Authority.* 12+up) shows productions ranging from the debut of the acclaimed Broadway musical *Grey Gardens* to Pulitzer Prize winners such as Wendy Wasserstein's *The Heidi Chronicles.* Plays are oriented toward adults but mature kids may find some productions to be of interest. The **Public Theater** (⊠*425 Lafayette St., south of Astor Pl., East Village* ☎*212/260–2400* ⊕*www.publictheater.org* Ⓜ*6 to Astor Pl.; R, W to 8th St.* 12+up) presents fresh, often edgy theater. Many noted productions that began here (*A Chorus Line, Hair*) went on to Broadway. In summer you won't want to miss their incomparable—and free—Shakespeare in the Park performances. Most shows here tend toward the experimental and are largely inappropriate for children. If you have sophisticated tweens, teenagers, or young Shakespeare buffs, it's worth considering.

OFF-OFF BROADWAY & PERFORMANCE ART

The following theaters are all small—even tiny—but host works that are often startling in their originality. These may be too "strange" for most children, but some older students might appreciate the talent and innovation.

★ **P.S. 122** (⊠*150 1st Ave., at E. 9th St., East Village* ☎*212/ 477–5288, 212/352–3101 tickets* ⊕*www.ps122.org* Ⓜ*6 to Astor Pl.* 5+up), housed in a former public school, has nurtured talent like Karen Finley, Spalding Gray, and Eric Bogosian, and offers a dazzling repertoire of performance from the fringe. The new Avant-Garde Arama for the Family series offers experimental performance by and for kids. *Danceoff*, a showcase of emerging dance theater artists, will also appeal. **St. Ann's Warehouse** (⊠*38 Water St., between Main and Dock Sts., DUMBO, Brooklyn* ☎*718/254–8779*

⊕*stannswarehouse.org* Ⓜ *A, C to High St.; F to York St.*
9+up) hosts everything from puppet operas to the Tiger
Lillies. Call the theater for the appropriate age range for
a given performance. A four-theater cultural complex,
Theater for the New City (✉*155 1st Ave., between E. 9th
and E. 10th Sts., East Village* ☎*212/254–1109* ⊕*www.
theaterforthenewcity.net* Ⓜ *6 to Astor Pl.* 5+up) puts on
30–40 new American plays each year. The Bread and
Circus theater group's annual visit includes matinees that
are entertaining for older kids with their circus acts and
political comedy.

THEATER ESPECIALLY FOR CHILDREN

★ Fodor'sChoice **Just Kidding at Symphony Space** (✉*2537 Broadway, at W. 95th St., Upper West Side* ☎*212/864–5400*
⊕*www.symphonyspace.org* Ⓜ *1, 2, 3 to 96th St.* 7+up) is a
family series that has it all—musicals especially, but a non-
stop parade of plays, sing-alongs, and puppets as well.

★ Fodor'sChoice **The New Victory Theater** (✉*209 W. 42nd St.,
between 7th and 8th Aves., Midtown West* ☎*212/239–6200*
⊕*www.newvictory.org* Ⓜ *1, 2, 3, 7, N, Q, R, W, A, C,
E, S to 42nd St./Times Sq.* All ages) presents plays, music,
puppetry masterpieces, and dance performances, and even
minicircuses in a magnificently restored century-old theater.
The 500-seat theater bills itself as "the ultimate" for kids
and families with its programming that has something for
all ages and all maturity levels. The Web site indicates which
show is appropriate for which age group. Sloped ramps
allow clear viewing for kids of all heights, and booster
seats are available. VicTeens, for kids 11–18, offers special programs for teens with seats in a teens-only section
of the theater, free food, and time to hang out with the
cast. On weekends, **the Paper Bag Players** (☎*212/663–0390*
⊕*www.thepaperbagplayers.org.* 3+up), the country's oldest
children's theater group, stages original—and exuberant—
plays for youngsters under 10 at venues throughout the
city. Tickets are priced $10–$30. Shows are especially
geared for the 4 to 9 crowd. Using everyday objects like
cardboard boxes, plays reflect children's daily experiences.
Finely detailed wooden marionettes and hand puppets are
on the bill at **Puppetworks** (✉*338 6th Ave., at 4th St., Park
Slope, Brooklyn* ☎*718/965–3391* ⊕*www.puppetworks.org*
Ⓜ *F to 7th Ave.* 3+up). Familiar childhood tales like *Little
Red Riding Hood* and *Peter and the Wolf* come to life in
this 75-seat neighborhood theater. Shows are aimed at kids

3 to 7. Ticket prices are a friendly $7 for children and $8 for adults. Close to 100 marionettes are displayed on the theater walls. At the end of each performance, a puppeteer will bring out a puppet to show the kids.

The **Swedish Cottage Marionette Theater** (⊠*Swedish Cottage, W. Park Dr., north of W. 79th St., Central Park* ☎*212/988–9093* ⊕*www.centralparknyc.org* Ⓜ*B, C to 81st St.* 3+up) was brought here from Sweden in 1876. The charming wooden 100-seat (and now state-of-the-art) playhouse presents classics like *Hansel and Gretel* and *Cinderella.* Bring your younger kids here. Children 9 and up may find this a bit babyish. **TADA!** (⊠*15 W. 28th St., between Broadway and 5th Ave., Chelsea* ☎*212/252–1619* ⊕*www. tadatheater.com* Ⓜ *1, 6, R, W to 28th St.* All ages) presents vibrant musical theater pieces for children performed by children. Plays deal with topics of interest to kids. Children and teenagers can also take musical theater and acting classes here. Latino arts and culture are celebrated with a sly sense of humor at **Teatro SEA @ Los Kabayitos Puppet & Children's Theater** (⊠*Clemente Soto Vélez Cultural & Educational Center, 107 Suffolk St., between Delancey and Rivington Sts., Lower East Side* ☎*212/260–4080* ⊕*www. sea-ny.org* Ⓜ*F to Delancey St.; J, M, Z to Essex St.* All ages). All shows are presented in English and Spanish, and you may even see the *Three Little Pigs* dancing to salsa music. Check the schedule for special workshops as well.

Theatreworks/USA (⊠*Lucille Lortel Theatre, 121 Christopher St., between Hudson and Bleecker Sts., West Village* ☎*800/497–5007* ⊕*www.theatreworksusa.org* Ⓜ*1 to Christopher St.* 5+up) offers a Family Series for ages four and over. Its original productions are based on popular children's books like *Henry and Mudge* and *Junie B. Jones.* The theater's wide variety of programming includes puppet theater, storytelling, music, dance, and magic programs. Summer plays are free. At other times, seats are $25.

MUSIC

Classical music and jazz may bore some kids to death, so it's always best to do some research before you venture into this area. New York City has the best of the best when it comes to symphony, jazz, Latin bands, and more, so it would be a shame not to try out at least one concert on your family. But gently, gently. Perhaps start with a Young People's Concert at the Philharmonic, or have Inspector

Pulse of the Chamber Music Society teach them a bit about, music, rhythm, and instruments all in one highly amusing (and blissfully brief) concert.

CONCERT HALLS

The **Brooklyn Academy of Music (BAM)** (✉*Howard Gilman Opera House, Peter Jay Sharp Bldg., 30 Lafayette Ave., between Ashland Pl. and St. Felix St., Fort Greene, Brooklyn* ☎*718/636–4100* ⊕*www.bam.org* Ⓜ *2, 3, 4, 5, B, Q to Atlantic Ave.* 5+up) is the performing home of the **Brooklyn Philharmonic** (☎*718/488–5700* ⊕*www.brooklynphilharmonic.org*) and has some of the most adventurous symphonic programming to be found in the city. BAMfamily offers a program of music, workshops, and other family events. Children younger than 5 are not admitted.

★ Fodor'sChoice **Carnegie Hall** (✉*881 7th Ave., at W. 57th St., Midtown West* ☎*212/247–7800* ⊕*www.carnegiehall.org* Ⓜ*N, Q, R, W to 57th St.; B, D, E to 7th Ave.* 5+up) is one of the best venues—anywhere—to hear classical music. The world's top orchestras sound so good because of the incomparable acoustics of the fabulously steep Stern Auditorium. The subterranean **Zankel Hall,** also with excellent acoustics, attracts performers such as the Kronos Quartet, Alarm Will Sound, and Youssou N'Dour. Many young talents make their New York debuts in the **Weill Recital Hall.** Nonclassical musicians that your kids might recognize also play here. Check the Web site for the schedule and locations. The popular Family Concert Series, which began here in 1995, introduces children to classical, jazz, and folk music at affordable, family-friendly prices. Preconcert activities on the main stage and in other smaller Carnegie Hall spaces include storytelling, hands-on musical experiences, and instrument demonstrations. Concertgoers ages 5 to 12 will especially enjoy the KidsNotes program, with activities and information about each family concert. The McGraw-Hill Companies' CarnegieKIDS is designed to introduce music to preschool children; advance registration is required. One-hour guided tours are given. And if your kids want to get a close-up look at Benny Goodman's clarinet or catch a glimpse of Arturo Toscanini's baton, visit the free Rose Museum, open daily 11–4:30. ✉*881 7th Ave. , at W. 57th St., Midtown West* ☎ *212/247–7800* ⊕ *www.carnegiehall.org* 🎫 Family concerts $8; tour $10 adults, $7 students, $3 children 11 and under Ⓜ *N, Q, R, W to 57th St.; B, D, E to 7th.* 3+up (some 7+up)

★ **Lincoln Center for the Performing Arts** (✉ *W. 62nd to W. 66th Sts., Broadway to Amsterdam Ave., Upper West Side* ☎ *212/546–2656* ⊕ *www.lincolncenter.org* Ⓜ *1 to 66th St./Lincoln Center.* 5+up) is the city's musical nerve center, especially when it comes to classical music. Formal and U-shaped, the massive Avery Fisher Hall presents the world's great musicians and is home to the **New York Philharmonic** (☎ *212/875–5656* ⊕ *newyorkphilharmonic. org*), one of the world's finest symphony orchestras. Lorin Maazel conducts, from late September to early June. Bargain-price weeknight "rush hour" performances at 6:45 PM and Saturday matinee concerts at 2 PM are occasionally offered; orchestra rehearsals at 9:45 AM are open to the public on selected weekday mornings (usually Wednesday or Thursday) for $15. The **Chamber Music Society of Lincoln Center** (☎ *212/875–5788* ⊕ *www.chambermusic society.org*) performs in Alice Tully Hall, which—while updated for the 2008–09 season—is still considered to be as acoustically perfect as a concert hall can get. In August, Lincoln Center's longest-running classical series, the **Mostly Mozart Festival** (☎ *212/875–5399*), captures the crowds. Several of these resident organizations offer family-specific events and performances. The New York Philharmonic's Young People's concerts include Kidzone Live, an interactive music fair. The Chamber Music Society offers the wonderful Meet the Music! Series with concerts led by the amusing Inspector Pulse.

OPERA

MAJOR COMPANIES

★ FodorsChoice The titan of American opera companies, the **Metropolitan Opera** (✉ *W. 62nd to W. 66th Sts., Broadway to Amsterdam Ave., Upper West Side* ☎ *212/362–6000* ⊕ *www.metopera.org* Ⓜ *1 to 66th St./Lincoln Center.* 9+up), brings the world's leading singers to its vast stage at Lincoln Center from October to April. All performances, including those sung in English, are unobtrusively subtitled on small screens on the back of the seat in front of you. Watch the schedule for more children-friendly operas like *Hansel and Gretel* or a shortened version of Mozart's *Magic Flute,* offered during the Christmas season. A back stage tour will show older kids operatic wonders such as castle construction in the carpentry shop, ball gowns in the costume shop, or elaborate do's in the wigmaker's shop.

Perhaps not as famous as its next-door neighbor, the **New York City Opera** (✉ *W. 62nd to W. 66th Sts., Broadway to Amsterdam Ave., Upper West Side* ☎ *212/870–5570* ⊕ *www.nycopera.com* Ⓜ *1 to 66th St./Lincoln Center.* 12+up) draws a crowd to its performances at the New York State Theater. The company is known for its innovative and diverse repertory and its soft spot for American composers. City Opera performs September to November and March and April. All performances of foreign-language operas have supertitles—line-by-line English translations—displayed above the stage. ■TIP➔**For all performances, $16 same-day standing room tickets may be purchased during City Opera box office hours.** The New York City Opera Target Family Series is specially designed for kids 6–12, with tickets costing $15. The series includes a performance of a family-friendly opera plus an interactive hour-long pre-matinee workshop with City Opera musicians, singers, and teaching staff to introduce families to the exciting world of musical drama. Lunch is included. Advance reservations are required.

SMALLER COMPANIES

The **New York Gilbert & Sullivan Players** (☎ *212/769–1000* ⊕ *www.nygasp.org.* 7+up) stages lively productions of such G&S favorites as *The Pirates of Penzance* and *The Mikado*. Their New York performance season—usually throughout January—is spent primarily at City Center. For kids who are old enough to sit through a performance of opera or "light opera" as in the case of Gilbert & Sullivan, this can be a lot of fun, particularly with the zany police or the Major General in *The Pirates of Penzance*.

DANCE

Ballerinas-in-training and dance fans of all ages who can sit through an entire performance will find many choices including the beloved holiday Nutcracker ballet.

BALLET

The **American Ballet Theatre (ABT)** (☎ *212/477–3030* ⊕ *www. abt.org.* 9+up) is renowned for its gorgeous renditions of the 19th-century classics (*Swan Lake, Giselle, La Bayardère*) as well as its modern repertoire, including works by such 20th-century masters as George Balanchine, Jerome Robbins, and Agnes de Mille. Since its founding in 1940, the company has nurtured a stellar array of dancers, including Mikhail Baryshnikov, Natalia Makarova, Rudolf Nureyev, Gelsey Kirkland, and Cynthia Gregory. The ballet has two New York seasons—eight weeks beginning in May at its home in the Metropolitan Opera House and two weeks in fall (usually October) at City Center. ABT Kids schedules special one-hour performances for families with young children, which include an interactive pre-performance workshop. No children under age 5 admitted. With more than 90 dancers, the **New York City Ballet** (☎212/870–5570 ⊕*www.nycballet.com.* 9+up) has an unmatched repertoire of 20th-century works. Its fall season, which runs from mid-November through December, includes the beloved annual production of George Balanchine's *The Nutcracker.* Its spring season runs from April through June; an eight-week Winter Repertory program runs in January and February. The company performs in Lincoln Center's New York State Theater. Family-friendly Saturday matinees are offered throughout the regular season. Children enjoy the magic of the Nutcracker, particularly if they have been coached a bit ahead of time about the story. Other programs of interest to kids are the American Songs and Dances program, appropriate for all ages, with a behind-the-scenes tour before evening performances.

MODERN DANCE

★ Fodor\$Choice World-renowned dance troupes **Alvin Ailey American Dance Theater** (⊕www.alvinailey.org) and **Paul Taylor Dance Company** (⊕www.ptdc.org) present their primary New York seasons at **City Center** (✉*131 W. 55th St., between 6th and 7th Aves., Midtown West* ☎212/581–1212 ⊕*www.citycenter.org* Ⓜ*N, Q, R, W to 57th St./7th Ave.; F to 57th St./6th Ave.* 9+up). In December, family matinees are scheduled with discounted tickets. Check the Web site for programs that might be appropriate for older kids. **Dance Theater Workshop** (✉*219 W. 19th St., between 7th and 8th Aves., Chelsea* ☎212/924–0077 ⊕*www.dtw.org* Ⓜ*1 to 18th St., A, C, E, L to 14th St.–8th Ave.* 5+up) serves as a laboratory for new choreographers. They are also known for their multimedia and kid-friendly "Family Matters" series. The latter is designed to introduce even the youngest Madonna wannabes to the marvels of dance and music in a less formal setting.

In a former art deco movie house in Chelsea, the 500-seat **Joyce Theater** (✉*175 8th Ave., at W. 19th St., Chelsea*

☎*212/242–0800* ⊕*www.joyce.org* Ⓜ*A, C, E to 14th St.;
L to 8th Ave.* 7+up) has superb sight lines and presents a
full spectrum of contemporary dance. The buoyant **Pilobo-
lus** (⊕*www.pilobolus.org*) and the lively **Ballet Hispanico**
(⊕*www.ballethispanico.org*) are regulars on the lineup.
Their **Joyce SoHo** location (✉*155 Mercer St., between Houston and Prince Sts., SoHo* ☎*212/431–9233* ⊕*www.joyce.
org* Ⓜ*R, W to Prince St.; B, D, F, V to Broadway/Lafayette
St.*) showcases more experimental work. Another Joyce
regular, Elisa Monte Dance (⊕*www.elisamontedance.
org*) is a favorite among adults and children alike with the
company's athletic style. In spring and fall, family matinees
are offered at both locations. Petite ballerinas will get a
thrill from meeting the costumed members of the dance
companies at these special shows.

PERFORMING ARTS CENTERS

For Carnegie Hall, see the Music section.

★ **Fodor's**Choice America's oldest performing arts center, the
Brooklyn Academy of Music (BAM) (✉*Peter Jay Sharp Bldg.,
30 Lafayette Ave., between Ashland Pl. and St. Felix St.,
Fort Greene, Brooklyn* ☎*718/636–4100* ⊕*www.bam.org*
Ⓜ *2, 3, 4, 5, B, Q to Atlantic Ave.* 5+up), opened in 1859.
BAM has a much-deserved reputation for daring—and
spectacular—dance, music, opera, and theatrical productions, and its film programming. The main performance
spaces are the sublime 2,100-seat **Howard Gilman Opera
House,** a restored white-brick Renaissance Revival palace
built in 1908, and the 874-seat **Harvey Theater,** an updated
1904 theater a block away at 651 Fulton Street. Year-round
you can catch other live performances (including the **Brooklyn Philharmonic** [⊕*www.brooklynphilharmonic.org*]), a
movie at the **BAM Rose Cinemas,** or hit the glam **BAMcafé**
(☎*718/623–4139 reservations*), which becomes a cabaret
venue on Friday and Saturday nights. For a fare of $7 each
way, **BAMbus** provides round-trip transportation from Manhattan one hour prior to live performances. Pickup is at
the former Whitney Museum at Altria (✉*120 Park Ave.,
at E. 42nd St.*); drop-offs are at multiple locations around
the city. Call BAM's main number 24 hours ahead to make
reservations. BAMfamily Weekend offers great introduc-
tions to dance, music, and theater in beautiful theaters at
affordable prices. The springtime BAMkids Film Festival
includes animated shorts and international films (mostly

all have subtitles). Part of the fun are the BAMmies, where kids vote for their favorite films.

★ **City Center** (✉*131 W. 55th St., between 6th and 7th Aves., Midtown West* ☎*212/581–1212 CityTix* ⊕*www.citycenter. org* Ⓜ *N, Q, R, W to 57th St./7th Ave.; F to 57th St./6th Ave.* 12+up). The 2,750-seat main stage here showcases world-class dance troupes (including American Ballet Theatre) and special theatrical events including the hugely popular Encores! musicals-in-concert series. The smaller **City Center Stages** I and II present offerings by the Manhattan Theatre Club. Kids who love old Broadway musicals could find the intimate nature of Encores! entertaining.

Lincoln Center for the Performing Arts (✉*W. 62nd to W. 66th Sts., Broadway to Amsterdam Ave., Upper West Side* ☎*212/546–2656* ⊕*www.lincolncenter.org* Ⓜ*1 to 66th St./Lincoln Center* 5+up) is a 16-acre complex. As of this writing, construction geared to augmenting and expanding parts of the facility was at various stages of completion, but the grounds and most performance venues should remain open. Among the big boys comprising Lincoln Center are the **Metropolitan Opera House** (which also presents American Ballet Theatre), **New York State Theater** (home to New York City Opera and New York City Ballet), **Avery Fisher Hall** (the New York Philharmonic performs here), **Alice Tully Hall, Vivian Beaumont Theater, Mitzi E. Newhouse Theater, New York Public Library for the Performing Arts,** and **Walter Reade Theater. Jazz at Lincoln Center** (☎*212/258–9800* ⊕*www.jalc.org)* is in the Time Warner Building, a few blocks south in Rafael Viñoly's crisply modern **Frederick P. Rose Hall**. Seasonal festivals—music, theater, dance, film, and more—abound, and often take place in the huge open plaza surrounding the famous fountain on the main campus, and in adjacent Damrosch Park. The beloved Midsummer Night Swing outdoor dance festival is a favorite among adults and kids alike with lively music around the fountain. Kids are often dancing around on the sidelines to the music.

FILM

Theaters themselves run the gamut from sleek multiplexes with large screens and stadium seating to shoe-box-size screening rooms with room for less than a hundred people.

Movies are always a great choice for families overtired from sightseeing. Sold-out shows are common, so it's a good idea to purchase tickets in advance. For evening performances, especially for new releases, you'll need to get to the box office well ahead of showtime, even if you already have tickets so that you can get a good seat. Showings at the IMAX screen can be even harder to get so definitely order online beyond you arrive.

Tickets to most theaters in New York are $10 to $12. Discounts for children are usually available. For print listings, Friday's *New York Times* is comprehensive; *Time Out New York* (⊕*www.timeoutny.com*) splits out "Alternatives & Revivals" listings, which can be very helpful when you're not sure what you want to see.

Oddly enough, no one phone or online ticket service handles advance ticket purchase for all of the city's screens; you'll need to contact either Fandango or Moviefone to charge tickets ahead. There's usually a service fee of $1 to $2 for phone or online orders. **Fandango** (☎*800/326–3264 [FANDANGO] ⊕www.fandango.com*) handles AMC Loews and Regal theaters. AOL's **Moviefone** (☎*212/777–3456 [777–FILM] ⊕www.moviefone.com*) covers the remaining chains, including City Cinemas, Landmark, and Clearview.

Wherever you are in New York City, you usually don't have to walk far to find a movie theater showing recent releases.

Blockbusters are supersize at the **AMC Loews Lincoln Center Square 13 with IMAX** (✉*1998 Broadway, at 68th St., Upper West Side* ☎*212/336–5020* Ⓜ *1, 9 to 66th St.–Lincoln Center.* 5+up). Kids will appreciate the stadium seating for a clear view. The choices, while mainstream, usually include family films. Point out murals of classic movies like Lawrence of Arabia on your way to see the next Pixar film.

Adjacent to the Plaza Hotel sits the **Paris** (✉*4 W. 58th St., between 5th and 6th Aves., Midtown West* ☎*212/688–3800* Ⓜ*N, R, W to 5th Ave./59th St.; F to 57th St.* 12+up)—a rare stately remnant of the single-screen era. Opened in 1948, it retains its wide screen (and its balcony) and is a fine showcase for new movies, often foreign and with a limited release. Many films here are shown with subtitles and will not be suitable for kids with limited attention spans, but older girls with a crush on everything Parisian may enjoy it. (French films are the focus here.) Parents might recognize it as Carrie Bradshaw's cinema pick on *Sex and the City*. Movie lovers adore the **Quad Cinema** (⊠ *34 W. 13th St., between 5th and 6th Aves., Greenwich Village* ☎ *212/255–8800* ⊕ *www.quadcinema.com* Ⓜ *1, 2, 3, F, V to 14th St.; L to 6th Ave.* 5+up), probably because the four tiny theaters feel so much like private screening rooms. First-run art and foreign films are the fare here. Check the listings as some of these films will be of interest for kids and they offer discounted kids' tickets. Within a sleekly renovated space that was once a vaudeville theater, the **Sunshine Cinema** (⊠ *143 E. Houston St., between 1st and 2nd Aves., Lower East Side* ☎ *212/330–8182* ⊕ *www. landmarktheatres.com* Ⓜ *F, V to 2nd Ave.* 12+up) has five decent-size screens showing a mix of art-house and smaller-release mainstream films. These cinemas show a range of movies, some more appropriate for kids than others, like Napoleon Dynamite. Do your homework before you travel all the way downtown to see a movie here. The **Village East Cinemas** (⊠ *181–189 2nd Ave., at E. 12th St., East Village* ☎ *212/529–6799* Ⓜ *6 to Astor Pl.; L to 1st Ave.* 5+up) is housed in a former Yiddish theater that was restored and converted to a six-screen multiplex. Catch a film that's screening upstairs (you can call ahead to find out); sit in the balcony to best appreciate the Moorish-style decor and domed ceiling. Consult the magazine or newspaper listings to find an appropriate selection.

★ Its vintage is late 1960s, but the **Ziegfeld** (⊠ *141 W. 54th St., between 6th and 7th Aves., Midtown West* ☎ *212/765–7600* Ⓜ *F to 57th St./6th Ave.; N, Q, R, W to 57th St./7th Ave.* 12+up) is as close as you'll come to a movie-palace experience in New York today. Wide screen, chandeliers and crimson decor, good sight lines, and solid sound system make the Ziegfeld a special place to view the latest blockbusters as well as classics; grand-opening red-carpet galas often take place here as well. This truly is Cinema Paradiso, and if they're showing a movie that's appropriate for children, don't miss the chance to see it here.

FILM FOR CHILDREN

Several museums—notably the Museum of Modern Art and the American Museum of Natural History (don't miss their IMAX Theater)—sponsor special programs aimed at families and children. At the **Museum of the Moving Image** (☎718/784–0077 ⊕*www.movingimage.us*. All ages) in Queens, besides the hands-on behind-the-scenes stuff, the draw is Tut's Fever Movie Palace—the fab Red Grooms and Lysiane Luong–designed installation that screens classic movie serials (think Flash Gordon) every Saturday. The **Brooklyn Academy of Music (BAM)** (✉*Howard Gilman Opera House, Peter Jay Sharp Bldg., 30 Lafayette Ave., between Ashland Pl. and St. Felix St., Fort Greene, Brooklyn* ☎718/636–4100 ⊕*www.bam.org* Ⓜ*2, 3, 4, 5, B, Q to Atlantic Ave*. 3+up) presents the BAMkids Film Festival, which includes live performances and films from around the world (subtitled). Kids also vote for their favorite films from animated shorts to feature films. Each March the **New York International Children's Film Festival (NYICFF)** (☎212/349–0330 ⊕*www.gkids.com*. 3+up) screens 60 new films and videos for ages 3–18 at venues around the city. The **TriBeCa Family Film Festival** is a perennially popular feature of the TriBeCa Film Fest in late April and May (☎866/941–3378 ⊕*www.tribecafilmfestival.org*. 5+up). The festival offers selections appropriate for teens as well as some suitable for all ages.

★ **SonyWonder Technology Lab** (✉*550 Madison Ave., between E. 55th and E. 56th Sts., Midtown East* ☎212/833–7858 *weekdays* ⊕*www.sonywondertechlab.com* Ⓜ *E, V to 5th Ave./53rd St.* All ages), the kid-oriented hands-on extravaganza of high-tech how-to for moviemaking and more, also shows free films. Children under 18 must be accompanied by an adult. You may call ahead to reserve tickets. **Symphony Space**'s "Just Kidding" series is once again at the fore, with its fun Saturday film program (☎212/864–5400 ⊕*www.symphonyspace.org*. All ages). Musicals, puppets, and sing-alongs are highlights. Check the Web site for scheduled events.

Shopping

WORD OF MOUTH

"FAO [Schwarz] opens at 10am with a cute little ceremony where three men dressed as toy soldiers come out and roll out a red carpet onto the sidewalk. Then they play a song on the trumpet and then announce the store is open for business and open the doors. Inside every employee is lined up on both sides of the door and they all clap for you as you enter. It was a hoot! Since we are big fans of the movie BIG we went straight through the store and headed for the elevator to the piano."
—lisa_in_adirondacks

EVERYONE KNOWS THAT NEW YORK City is a shopping destination for high-fashion handbags, designer stilettos, and runway-ready dresses, but it's also a retail wonderland for the littlest browsers. From the razzle-dazzle high-tech temples of the Apple Store to mind-boggling toy emporiums like American Girl Place or FAO Schwarz, your kids will be tugging on you to buy, buy, buy. Clothes from the most Bohemian to the most couture for all ages, shoes right out of *Gossip Girl,* gadgets for their homework spaces, posters, and other souvenirs entice at every turn. The foremost American and international companies stake their flagships here; meanwhile, small neighborhood shops guarantee unexpected pleasures. Teens used to finding only a few choices from a favorite designer at home will find complete stores with exclusive Manhattan-only merchandise. Note especially stores like H&M, Zara, Miss Sixty, and Abercrombie & Fitch—your kids can have a complete wardrobe makeover, providing you set some realistic budget limits, and return looking every bit like a New Yorker.

Many specialty stores have several branches in the city; in these cases, we have listed the locations in the busier shopping neighborhoods. Happy hunting!

BOOKS

CHILDREN'S BOOKS

Books of Wonder. At this store completely dedicated to children's books, the friendly, knowledgeable staff can help select gifts for all reading levels from the extensive, beautiful selection. Oziana, a section all about Oz, is a specialty. An outpost of the Cupcake Café gives little browsers a second wind. You can also find a large selection of collectible and rare children's books that you'll recognize from your childhood, including retro Nancy Drew mysteries, the Bobbsey Twins, and the Hardy Boys stories. Story time is held every Sunday at noon. ⊠ *18 W. 18th St., between 5th and 6th Aves., Chelsea* ☎ *212/989–3270* Ⓜ *F, V to 14th St.*

Scholastic Store. An 11-foot orange dinosaur—with a cushioned tail doubling as a reading sofa—and a life-size Magic School Bus welcome kids to this truly fun emporium. With games, toys, DVDs, computers, arts and crafts workshops, and above all, books, this downtown spot is so family friendly, it has a separate entrance just for strollers (at 130 Mercer Street). ⊠ *557 Broadway, at Prince St., SoHo* ☎ *212/343–6166* Ⓜ *R, W to Prince St.*

TOP SHOPPING EXPERIENCES

Toe tap a musical tune on the larger-than-life-size keyboard on the floor, design your own Hot Wheels car, or outfit a Barbie and watch her perform in the fashion runaway show at FAO Schwarz.

Watch the gigantic pot of chocolate being stirred at Max Brenner and try a slice of chocolate pizza with melted marshmallows.

Compare your hands with the hand molds of NBA super-

stars at the NBA store or pick up a friendly competition with the electronic hoops.

Ride the gargantuan indoor Ferris wheel at Toys R Us in Times Square or test out a new video game on the plasma screens in the "R-Zone."

"Live" chat with the talking robot, B.B. Wonderbot, at the Sony Wonder Tech Lab or create your own racing game on one of the computers.

GENERAL INTEREST

Barnes & Noble. Without argument, this is the biggest bookstore presence in the city. The 86th Street store also has the busiest kids section in the country, with sections and sections of kids' favorites, and weekend story times. There's a stage for occasional events (check the Web site or signs posted in the window) or where kids can quietly play or read while their parents browse through the toddler, children, and teen sections. The upstairs Starbucks is great for a quick treat if your kids are getting hungry. All Barnes & Noble stores have decent restrooms. ✉ *240 E. 86th St., Upper East Side* ☎ *212/794–1962* Ⓜ *4, 5, 6 to 86th St.*

Borders. The smart, cheery flagship Columbus Circle branch of New York City's second-biggest bookstore chain is worth a browse. Various branches offer differing levels of kids' sections. Columbus Circle has story time, and music and crafts activities as well. ✉ *461 Park Ave., at E. 57th St., Midtown East* ☎ *212/980–6785* Ⓜ *N, R, W, 4, 5, 6 to 59th St./Lexington Ave.* ✉ *10 Columbus Circle, at 59th St., Upper West Side* ☎ *212/823–9775* Ⓜ *1, A, B, C, D to Columbus Circle.*

★ **McNally Robinson.** McNally makes a happy counterpart to the nearby Housing Works bookstore; both places have that welcoming vibe. Check the tables up front for hot-off-the-press novels, nonfiction, and manifestos. Upstairs you'll find fiction arranged by the authors' region of origin. The staff are by and large literary themselves, so ask for recommendations if you're browsing. There are separate sections for teens, preteens, and younger kids. ✉ *52 Prince St., between Lafayette and Mulberry Sts., SoHo* ☎*212/274–1160* Ⓜ*R, W to Prince St.*

Shakespeare & Co. Booksellers. The stock here represents what's happening in just about every field of publishing today: students can grab a last-minute Gertrude Stein for class, then rummage through the homages to cult pop-culture figures. The Upper East Side location invites kids to linger and read with comfortable child-size chairs. ✉*939 Lexington Ave., between E. 68th and E. 69th Sts., Upper East Side* ☎*212/570–0201* Ⓜ*6 to 68th St./Hunter College* ✉*137 E. 23rd St., at Lexington Ave., Gramercy* ☎*212/505–2021* Ⓜ*6 to 23rd St.* ✉*716 Broadway, at Washington Pl., Greenwich Village* ☎*212/529–1330* Ⓜ*R, W to 8th St.*

★ Fodor'sChoice **The Strand.** The Broadway branch—a downtown hangout—proudly claims to have "18 miles of books." Craning your neck among the tall-as-trees stacks is part of the experience. Rare books are next door, at 826 Broadway, on the third floor. (The buildings are connected inside.) The Fulton Street branch is near South Street Seaport; it's decidedly less overwhelming. Within this huge store is a huge children's section categorized very precisely: bedtime stories, Disney, monsters, space; and a Young Adults' section divided into groupings like adventure, horror, mystery, and romance. Books here are much discounted and you can score some amazing buys. The super-knowledgeable staff are happy to help you with your hunting. ✉*828 Broadway, at E. 12th St., East Village* ☎*212/473–1452* Ⓜ*L, N, Q, R, W, 4, 5, 6 to 14th St./Union Sq.*

CAMERAS & ELECTRONICS

★ **Apple Store.** After Apple's first store, in a former SoHo post office, hooked the e-mail generation, the brand took things a step further. The 5th Avenue location, topped by a giant plexiglass cube, is open 24 hours a day, every day, to satisfy those wee-hours computer cravings. At all stores you'll have to elbow through a crowd, but they're the best places to check out the latest gear. The tech-generation will be in heaven here. There are iPods to try, MacBooks where you can check your e-mail, every kind of headphone imaginable, iPhones to marvel at, and more. You could stay and play all day long—and that's just what some people do.

✉*103 Prince St., at Greene St., SoHo* ☎*212/226–3126* Ⓜ*R, W to Prince St.* ✉*767 5th Ave., between E. 58th and E. 59th Sts., Midtown East* ☎*212/336–1440* Ⓜ*R, W to 60th St.* ✉*401 W. 14th St., at 9th Ave., Meatpacking District* ☎*212/444–3400* Ⓜ*A, C, E to 14th St.*

SONY Style. This equipment and music store comes in a glossy package, with imaginative window displays and a downstairs demonstration area for the integrated systems. You'll find all the latest stereo and entertainment systems, digital cameras, and MP3 players on the shelves. Kids can try out the newest in computers and cameras if they can tear themselves away from the Playstation consoles. Wander behind the store to the fantastic Sony Wonder Technology Lab, a free interactive museum with gadgets and robots for hours and hours of wonderment. ✉*550 Madison Ave., at E. 55th St., Midtown East* ☎*212/833–8800* Ⓜ*E, V, 6 to 51st St./Lexington Ave.*

CHILDREN'S CLOTHING

PLAY CLOTHES

Oilily. Stylized flowers, stripes, and animal shapes splash across these brightly colored play and school clothes from the trippy Dutch brand. Note that the SoHo location doesn't stock the boys' line. Infants–12 year olds can buy matching mother–daughter outfits. The store also sells antique armoires and chests. ✉*820 Madison Ave., between E. 68th and E. 69th Sts., Upper East Side* ☎*212/772–8686* Ⓜ *6 to 68th St. /Hunter College* ✉*465 West Broadway, between Prince and Houston Sts., SoHo* ☎*212/871–0201* Ⓜ*6 to Spring St.*

Petit Bateau. Fine cotton is spun into comfortable underwear, play clothes, and pajamas; T-shirts come in dozens of colors and to every specification, with V-necks, round necks, snap-fronts, and more. Sizes go primarily from 0 to 12. Small adults can match their kids' styles with clothing for ages 14 and 16. ✉*1094 Madison Ave., at E. 82nd St., Upper East Side* ☎*212/988–8884* Ⓜ*4, 5, 6 to 86th St.*

★ **Space Kiddets.** The funky (Elvis-print rompers, onesies made from old concert tees) mixes with the old-school (retro cowboy-print pants, brightly colored clogs, New York borough-pride gear) at this casual, trendsetting store. The original space around the corner, at 46 East 21st Street, now stocks toys only. The main floor has girls' sizes from

0 to 6, and boys from 0 to 12. Upstairs are preteen styles like Juicy, Paul Frank, and Betsey Johnson. ✉ *26 E. 22nd St., between Broadway and Park Ave., Flatiron District* ☎*212/420–9878* Ⓜ*6 to 23rd St.*

PRECIOUS

Bonpoint. The sophistication here lies in the beautiful designs and impeccable workmanship—velvet-tipped coats with matching caps and hand-embroidered jumpers and blouses. The Parisian influence is unmistakable and your teens and preteens will be ready for their next tea party or cotillion. ✉ *1269 Madison Ave., at E. 91st St., Upper East Side* ☎*212/722–7720* Ⓜ*4, 5, 6 to 86th St.* ✉ *810 Madison Ave., at 68th St., Upper East Side* ☎*212/879–0900* Ⓜ*6 to 68th St. /Hunter College.*

Calypso Enfant et Bébé. Sailor-stripe tops, polka-dot PJs, lovely party dresses . . . you may find yourself dressing vicariously through your children. For ages infant–12. ✉ *407 Broome St., between Lafayette and Crosby Sts., NoLita* ☎*212/966–3234* Ⓜ*6 to Spring St.*

Flora and Henri. The padded twill coats, slate-blue pleated skirts, and pin-dot cotton dresses here are cute but not overly so. They'll stand up to wear and tear; witness the sturdy Italian-made shoes. Your little kids and preteens will look oh-so-sophisticated. ✉ *1023 Lexington Ave., between E. 73rd and E. 74th Sts., Upper East Side* ☎*212/249–1695* Ⓜ*6 to 77th St.*

Infinity. Mothers gossip near the dressing rooms as their daughters try on slinky Les Tout Petits dresses, Miss Sixty Jeans, and cheeky tees with slogans like "chicks ahoy." The aggressively trendy and the rather sweet meet in a welter of preteen accessories. Smaller moms will be able to dress just like their kids. Styles are both sophisticated as well as preteen "cool." ✉ *1116 Madison Ave., at E. 83rd St., Upper East Side* ☎*212/517–4232* Ⓜ*4, 5, 6 to 86th St.*

Les Petits Chapelais. Designed and made in France, these kids' clothes are adorable but also practical. Corduroy outfits have details like embroidered flowers and contrasting cuffs; soft fleecy jackets are reversible, and sweaters have easy-zip-up fronts and hoodies. If you're in need of formal wear for your 3 year old, you'll find it here as well. ✉ *86 Thompson St., between Spring and Prince Sts., SoHo* ☎*212/625–1023* Ⓜ*C, E to Spring St.*

Lilliput. At both locations, which face each other across the street, kids can up their coolness quotient with Paul Smith sweaters, sequined party dresses, and denim wear by Diesel. The difference is that the shop at No. 265 carries it all up to size 8, whereas the original shop goes up to teens. *240 Lafayette St., between Prince and Spring Sts., SoHo* 212/965–9201 *R, W to Prince St.* *265 Lafayette St., between Prince and Spring Sts., SoHo* 212/965–9567 *6 to Spring St.*

CHOCOLATE

★ **Jacques Torres Chocolate Haven.** Visit the café and shop here and you'll literally be surrounded by chocolate. The glass-walled space is in the heart of Torres's chocolate factory, so you can watch the goodies being made while you sip a richly spiced cocoa. ■TIP→**Signature taste: the "wicked" chocolate, laced with cinnamon and chili pepper.** Any kids who have seen Willie Wonka and the Chocolate Factory will adore this place and love devouring the chocolate covered Cheerios, raisins, and marshmallows. *350 Hudson St., at King St., SoHo* 212/414–2462 *1 to Houston St.*

★ **MarieBelle.** The handmade chocolates here are nothing less than works of art. Square truffles and bonbons—which come in such flavors as cappuccino and passion fruit—are painted with edible dyes so each resembles a miniature painting. Tins of aromatic tea leaves and Aztec hot chocolate are also available. Stop by the tearoom and cocoa bar in the back for MarieBelle's twist on a hot chocolate. *484 Broome St., between West Broadway and Wooster St., SoHo* 212/925–6999 *R, W to Prince St.*

Max Brenner: Chocolate by the Bald Man. The first U.S. outposts of this Australian arrival don't make a fuss about cocoa percentages or impeccable handcrafted bonbons; instead, they're all about the kid-in-a-candy-store sense of delight. The cafés encourage the messy enjoyment of gooey treats like chocolate fondues. Everything here is chocolate. There are chocolate pipes running along the ceiling, a big churning pot of chocolate, and huge jars of chocolates on display. In the café kids will go crazy over the chocolate pizzas, waffles, and parfaits, which you can also take out for snacking as you sightsee (take a pile of napkins, too). *841 Broadway, between E. 13th and E. 14th Sts., East Village* 212/388–0030 *L, N, Q, R, W, 4, 5, 6 to 14th*

St./Union Sq. ✉*142 2nd Ave., at E. 9th St., East Village* ☎*212/388–0030* Ⓜ*6 to Astor Pl.*

Vosges Haut Chocolat. This chandeliered salon takes chocolate couture to a new level. The creations are internationally themed: the Budapest bonbons combine dark chocolate and Hungarian paprika, the Black Pearls contain wasabi, and the Aboriginal collection uses such esoteric ingredients as wattleseed and ryeberry. Try the yummy chocolate flying pigs. Adventurous eaters (or kids who are triple-dog-dared) can try the bacon chocolate bars that many New Yorkers swear are the perfect combination of salty and sweet. ✉*132 Spring St., between Greene and Wooster Sts., SoHo* ☎*212/625–2929* Ⓜ*R, W to Prince St.* ✉*1100 Madison Ave., at 83rd St., Upper East Side* ☎*212/717–2929* Ⓜ*6 to 86th St.*

DEPARTMENT STORES

Most department stores keep regular hours on weekdays and are open late (until 8 or 9) at least one night a week. Many have personal shoppers who can walk you through the store at no charge, as well as concierges who will answer all manner of questions. Some have restaurants or cafés that offer decent meals and pick-me-up snacks.

★ **Fodor'sChoice** **Barneys New York.** Barneys continues to provide fashion-conscious and big-budget shoppers with irresistible, must-have items at its uptown flagship store. The extensive men's and women's departments showcase posh designers of all stripes. The shoe selection and cosmetics departments will keep you fashion-forward and looking your chicest. Trendy, less expensive items including shoes, leather bags, and clothing are sold in the store's famous Co-op department in Barneys' three Manhattan locations. Barneys carries clothes for your littlest fashionistas from birth through age 8, but it will be your teens and tweens who go crazy over Barneys Co-op. Be sure to check out the always-amusing store windows facing both Madison Avenue and 61st Street. ✉*660 Madison Ave., between E. 60th and E. 61st Sts., Upper East Side* ☎*212/826–8900* Ⓜ*N, R, W, 4, 5, 6 to 59th St./Lexington Ave.* ✉*Barneys Co-op, 236 W. 18th St., between 7th and 8th Aves., Chelsea* ☎*212/593–7800* Ⓜ*A, C, E to 14th St.* ✉*116 Wooster St., between Prince and Spring Sts., SoHo* ☎*212/965–9964* Ⓜ*R, W to Prince St.*

Bergdorf Goodman. Good taste reigns in an elegant and understated setting, but remember that elegant doesn't necessarily mean sedate. Bergdorf's carries some brilliant lines, such as John Galliano's sensational couture and Philip Treacy's dramatic hats. At any of the many make-up counters on the basement Level of Beauty, you can indulge in a quick makeover to complement your new wardrobe. Across the street is another entire store devoted to men. On the top floor, you'll find clothes for your youngest fashion plates, from size 0 to 14. 5F is the must-see floor for teen girls, with high-Manhattan style clothing and shoes. ⊠ *754 5th Ave., between W. 57th and W. 58th Sts., Midtown West* ⊠ *Men's store, 745 5th Ave., at 58th St., Midtown East* ☎ *212/753–7300* Ⓜ *N, R, W to 5th Ave./59th St.*

Bloomingdale's. Only a few stores in New York occupy an entire city block; the uptown branch of this New York institution is one of them. The main floor is a crazy, glittery maze of mirrored cosmetic counters and perfume-spraying salespeople. Once you get past this dizzying scene, you can find good buys on designer clothes, jewelry, and purses. The downtown location is smaller, and has a well-edited, higher-end selection. There are separate boys and girls clothing sections here, with selections from newborn to 16. The junior section has just about every popular label a girl could want. For fun, grab a bite upstairs at Le Train Bleu, a restaurant designed to look like a 1920s boxcar. ⊠ *1000 3rd Ave., main entrance at E. 59th St. and Lexington Ave., Midtown East* ☎ *212/705–2000* Ⓜ *N, R, W, 4, 5, 6 to 59th St./Lexington Ave.* ⊠ *504 Broadway, between Spring and Broome Sts., SoHo* ☎ *212/729–5900* Ⓜ *R, W to Prince St.*

★ FodorsChoice **Century 21.** For many New Yorkers, this downtown fixture—right across the street from the former World Trade Center site—remains the mother lode of discount shopping. Four floors are crammed with everything from Gucci sunglasses and half-price cashmere sweaters to Ralph Lauren towels, though you'll have to weed through racks of less-fabulous stuff to find that gem. The second floor is where you'll find European baby wear, boys' and girls' clothing, and juniors. Fortunately, the kids' fashions sections tend to be less crowded than some of the others in the store. Shoes are in a separate store next door. ⊠ *22 Cortlandt St., between Broadway and Church St., Lower Manhattan* ☎ *212/227–9092* Ⓜ *R, W to Cortlandt St.*

5

Macy's. Macy's headquarters store claims to be the largest retail store in America. Fashion-wise, there's a concentration on the mainstream rather than on the luxe. One strong suit is denim, with everything from Hilfiger and Calvin Klein to Earl Jeans and Paper Denim & Cloth. There's also a reliably good selection of American designs from Ralph Lauren, Tommy Hilfiger, and Nautica. The toy, babies, and kids departments are all relatively good sized. Your little ones can sit on Santa's lap if you're visiting during Christmas, or you come by to see the famous holiday windows. If too much shopping wears you down, Macy's famous Cellar has lots of goodies to snack on. ⊠*Herald Sq., 151 W. 34th St., between 6th and 7th Aves., Midtown West* ☎*212/695–4400* Ⓜ*B, D, F, N, Q, R, V, W to 34th St./Herald Sq.*

★ **Pearl River Mart.** This is the place for everything Asian, at excellent prices. Furnishings, housewares, and trinkets can be found here, from bamboo flutes and ceramic tea sets to paper lanterns and grinning Buddha statues. On the main floor, under a ceiling festooned with dragon kites and rice-paper parasols, you can buy kimono-style robes, pajamas, and embroidered satin slippers for the whole family. There's also a dry-goods section, where you can load up on packages of ginger candy, jasmine tea, and cellophane noodles. It's a great store for kids' exploration—everything is colorful and it's jam-packed with cool furnishings for teens' bedrooms. Girls will love the Chinese games and dolls, too. Hungry? Try some of the tinned Asian candies or other novelty foods. ⊠*477 Broadway, between Broome and Grand Sts., SoHo* ☎*212/431–4770* Ⓜ*N, R, Q, W to Canal St.*

Saks Fifth Avenue. A fashion- and beauty-only department store, Saks sells an astonishing array of clothing. The choice of American and European designers is impressive without being esoteric—the women's selection includes Gucci, Narciso Rodriguez, and Marc Jacobs, plus devastating ball gowns galore. The footwear collections are gratifyingly broad. In the men's department, sportswear stars such as John Varvatos counterbalance formal wear and current trends. The ground-floor beauty department stocks everything from the classic (Sisley, Lancôme) to the fun and edgy (Nars, Aussie-import Napolean Perdis). Kids of all ages can find great outfits here with an edge toward the upscale and elegant. The massive shoe department is known as the *Gossip Girls* and cohorts footwear-central.

Stop at one of the store's three restaurants for some revitalization after traversing the store's circular floors. ⊠611 5th Ave., between E. 49th and E. 50th Sts., Midtown East ☎212/753–4000 Ⓜ E, V to 5th Ave./53rd St.

GIFTS & HOME GOODS

Mxyplyzyk. Hard to pronounce (*mixy plit sick*) and hard to resist, this is a trove of impulse buys—creative riffs on household standbys such as dishes (covered in psychedelic patterns or made from old vinyl LPs), handbags (made to look like bocce balls), and toothbrush holders (shaped like giant teeth). There are lots of kooky things for kids, including talking gnomes and take-apart-puzzle cubes. ⊠125 Greenwich Ave., at W. 13th St., Greenwich Village ☎212/989–4300 Ⓜ A, C, E, L to 14th St./8th Ave.

Pylones. Even the most utilitarian items get a goofy, colorful makeover from this French company. Toasters and thermoses are coated in stripes or flowers, hairbrushes have pictures of frogs or ladybugs on their backs, and whisks are reimagined as squid. ■TIP→ There are plenty of fun gifts for less than $20, such as old-fashioned robot toys and candy-color boxes. No one can resist the cool pop-artish wallets, key chains, and iPod covers, all great gifts for friends and relatives. ⊠69 Spring St., between Crosby and Lafayette Sts., SoHo ☎212/431–3244 Ⓜ 6 to Spring St. ⊠183 Broadway, Lower Manhattan ☎212/227–9273 Ⓜ A, C to Broadway Nassau ⊠61 Grove St., Greenwich Village ☎212/727–2655 Ⓜ 1 to Christopher St. ⊠8 Grand Central Terminal, Grand Central, Midtown ☎212/867–0969 Ⓜ 4, 5, 6 to Grand Central ⊠842 Lexington Ave., Midtown ☎212/317–9822 Ⓜ F to Lexington Ave.–63rd St.

MUSEUM STORES

Metropolitan Museum of Art Shop. Of the three locations, the store in the museum has a phenomenal book selection, as well as posters, art videos, and computer programs. Reproductions of jewelry, statuettes, and other *objets* fill the gleaming cases in every branch. There are books about the museum mascot William and other kid-oriented treasures like enchanted paper dolls, an Egyptian pharaoh playset, puzzles, and costumes. All are fairly art-based or educational. ⊠5th Ave., at E. 82nd St., Upper East Side ☎212/879–5500 Ⓜ 4, 5, 6 to 86th St. ⊠12–14 Ful-

ton St., between Front and South Sts., Lower Manhattan
☎212/248–0954 Ⓜ4, 5, A, C to Fulton St./Broadway–
Nassau ✉15 W. 49th St., between 5th and 6th Aves., Rockefeller Center, Midtown West ☎212/332–1360 ⒨B, D, F,
V to 47th–50th Sts./Rockefeller Center.

★ **Museum of Modern Art Design and Book Store.** The redesigned
MoMA expanded its in-house shop with a huge selection of art posters and more than 2,000 titles on painting,
sculpture, film, and photography. Across the street is the
MoMA Design Store (✉44 W. 53rd St., between 5th and
6th Aves., Midtown West ☎212/767–1050 Ⓜ E, V to 5th
Ave./53rd St.), where you can find lots of clever trinkets.
The SoHo branch combines most of the virtues of the first
two, although its book selection is smaller. Here you can
find items with an educational slant, like animal flash cards,
subway map puzzles, graphic mobiles, funky bibs, and
other design-oriented toys. ✉11 W. 53rd St., between 5th
and 6th Aves., Midtown West ☎212/708–9700 ⒨E, V to
5th Ave./53rd St. ✉81 Spring St., between Broadway and
Crosby St., SoHo ☎646/613–1367 Ⓜ6 to Spring St.

Museum of the City of New York. Satisfy your curiosity about
New York City's past, present, or future with the terrific
selection of books, cards, toys, and photography posters. If
you've something classic in mind, look for the Tin Pan Alley
tunes and stickball sets. Besides Broadway memorabilia,
the store sells FDNY and NYPD figurines and other items,
plus magnets, toys, jigsaw puzzles, all having something to
do with New York City. ✉1220 5th Ave., at E. 103rd St.,
Upper East Side ☎212/534–1672 Ⓜ6 to 103rd St.

SPORTING GOODS

The NBA Store. Push through the bronze-armed door and
you'll find yourself in a basketball temple. Every imaginable item having to do with pro b-ball is here, from jerseys,
hats, and bags emblazoned with team logos to balls signed
by Yao Ming and Larry Bird. Players grin in the digital-
photo station, but they also make live appearances on the
store's half-court. It's always playoff time here with kids
competing in their own hoops tournaments amid posters
and hand molds of real NBA stars. There are video games
and an enormous screen showing great game footage. Kids
will like the circular ramp layout and the exhibit of historic
trading cards. ✉666 5th Ave., at W. 52nd St., Midtown
West ☎212/515–6221 Ⓜ E, V to 5th Ave./53rd St.

TOYS & GAMES

American Girl Place. No toy pink convertibles here; instead, the namesake dolls are historically themed, from Felicity of colonial Virginia to Kit of Depression-era Cincinnati. Each character has her own affiliated books, furniture, clothes, and accessories. There's a doll hair salon, a café (with seats for the dolls), a doll hospital, a photo studio, a theater with shows about the dolls, and, of course, lots of clothes shopping. The prix-fixe café is perfect for girls and their well-behaved dolls. Girls can enjoy a tea party here or throw their dolls a birthday party. Check out the online calendar for special events. If you have boys, think about letting the guys head to the NBA Store next door. ⊠*609 5th Ave., at E. 49th St., Midtown East* ☏*212/371–2220* Ⓜ*B, D, F, V to 47th–50th Sts./Rockefeller Center.*

Dinosaur Hill. These toys leave the run-of-the-mill far behind, with mini–bongo drums, craft kits, jack-in-the-boxes, and a throng of marionettes and hand puppets, from mermaids to farmers to demons. Priced from $2, the toys here include old favorites and cool imports. Look for favorites like Rubik's cubes, Slinkys, yo-yos, and wooden blocks that may be hard to find elsewhere. ⊠*306 E. 9th St., between 1st and 2nd Aves., East Village* ☏*212/473–5850* Ⓜ*R, W to 8th St.; 6 to Astor Pl.*

WORD OF MOUTH. "FAO Schwarz: Surely the world's most amazing collection of stuffed (as opposed to taxidermied) animals—just one delight after another. Check the schedule for the piano show in which a couple of young dancers (day job, I presume) hop, skip, and jump out recognizable tunes." —Marilyn

★ Fodor'sChoice **FAO Schwarz.** A New York classic that's better than ever, this children's paradise more than lives up to the hype. The ground floor is a zoo of extraordinary stuffed animals, from cuddly teddies to towering, life-size elephants and giraffes (with larger-than-life prices to match). FAO Schweets stocks M&Ms in every color of the rainbow; upstairs, you can dance on the giant musical floor keyboard (remember Tom Hanks in the movie Big?), browse through Barbies wearing Armani and Juicy Couture, shop for everything Harry Potter, and design your own custom-ized Hot Wheels car. The LEGO shop is reminiscent of their amusement parks. Everything in the store is hands-on (or feet-on!), so your kids will want to stay here for the entire day. After days of visiting museums and walking, this isn't a bad place to hang out or to enjoy a banana split at the ice-cream parlor in the back of the store. ✉*767 5th Ave., at E. 58th St., Midtown East* ☎*212/644–9400* Ⓜ*4, 5, 6 to E. 59th St.*

Forbidden Planet. This store is much more than science fiction: there's pretty much every kind of comic book you could think of including an entire floor dedicated to Eastern manga. Toys, action figures, shelves and shelves of sci-fi "stuff" line the store, which is open until midnight four nights a week and attracts an NYU and late-night fanboy (and fangirl) crowd. For a less overwhelming experience, bring your kids in the morning when revelers are still asleep and you can browse (and censor, if necessary). A student ID will get you 10% off. ✉*840 Broadway, at 13th St., Union Square* ☎*212/473–1576* Ⓜ*4,5, 6, L, N. R, Q, W to 14th St.*

Toys "R" Us. The Times Square megastore is so big that a three-story Ferris wheel revolves inside. With all the movie tie-in merchandise, video games, pogo sticks, stuffed animals, and what seems to be the entire Mattel oeuvre, this store has a lock on sheer volume. The 20-foot-high animatronic T-Rex, right out of Jurassic Park, is a favorite as is the two-story Barbie dollhouse. You can try new video games on the giant plasma screens in the gigantic "R" Zone, a clear sign of the times. ✉*1514 Broadway, at W. 44th St., Midtown West* ☎*646/366–8800* Ⓜ*1, N, Q, R, W to 42nd St./Times Sq.* ✉ *692 Broadway, at W. 4th St., Greenwich Village* ☎ *212/477–2051* Ⓜ *Q, R, W to W. 4th St.*

World of Disney New York. Expect to be flooded with merchandise relating to Disney films and characters—pajamas, toys, figurines, you name it. There's also the largest collection of Disney animation art in the country. You can spend hours in this three-story store as you would at a Disney theme park: have your picture taken with a Disney character, make your own potato head, stop at Goofy's Candy Company—it goes on and on. You'll be lucky to get out without having bought a new pair of Mickey ears. ✉*711 5th Ave., between E. 55th and E. 56th Sts., Midtown East* ☎*212/702–0702* Ⓜ*F to 57th St.*

Where to Eat

WORD OF MOUTH

"We always also eat at Carmine's on 200 West 44th St. in the theatre district. Carmine's is family style Italian and if you tell them you are going to the theater they are very good at making sure you get done with your meal in plenty of time. Reservations are a good idea . . . because they are very busy."

—hester

By Meryl
Pearlstein
& Nina
Callaway

YOU'LL FIND A LOT OF familiar dining chains in NYC, but try to save these as a last resort. Instead, take advantage of the fact that America's original melting pot remains the country's most diverse restaurant town.

Children used to eating macaroni and cheese, or peanut butter and jelly sandwiches will find those classic kid-friendly dishes with a hip, urban twist (just see Peanut Butter & Co.). You don't need to take them to the most high-brow of designer chef outposts either. Some of the more residential neighborhoods or funkier areas have smaller, ethnic cafes with lots of great choices. And, if your kids are truly resistant, you can usually find a simple pasta or chicken dish at pretty much all of them.

The recent mania for tapas or small plates is perfect for petite stomachs. Your whole brood can try out a variety of shareable dishes of Spanish, Italian, Mexican, and even French tapas without feeling that you've committed to a very expensive entrée that someone might not enjoy. Japanese and Chinese cuisine also lends itself to sharing. Sitting close to the action of an open kitchen or sushi bar is also a form of dinner theater for kids. Plus chefs in the city are switching gears from luxury to comfort, launching steak houses, burger joints, and neighborhood bistros, which are intrinsically more family-friendly.

HOURS, PRICES & DRESS

Plan ahead if you're determined to snag a sought-after reservation. But you can get lucky at the last minute if you're flexible—and friendly. Having kids who dine at early hours can be a real plus; there's less competition for those spots.

New Yorkers seem ready to eat at any hour. Many restaurants stay open between lunch and dinner, some offer early-morning breakfasts, and still others serve 'round-the-clock. If you have a child who wakes early or just can't sleep, you can often take them to a restaurant and pacify them with a midnight snack. Hotel concierges are good sources of information for where to find off-hours dining. Midtown has a tendency to open earlier (to accommodate the business crowd) while the downtown and Village areas stay open later. Unless otherwise noted, the restaurants listed in this guide are open daily for lunch and dinner.

If you're planning to do some fine dining, kick it up a notch and pull out your best clothing. As unfair as it seems, the way you look can influence how you're treated, whether your kids are welcome, and where you're seated. Generally speaking, jeans and a button-down shirt will suffice at most table-service restaurants in the $ to $$ range. Kids can dress more casually but leave the sweatpants and shorts at home unless everyone else is wearing them, too.

If you're watching your budget, be sure to ask the price of daily specials recited by the waiter. The charge for specials at some restaurants can be noticeably out of line with the other prices on the menu. Beware of the $10 bottle of water; ask for tap water instead.

If you eat early or late, you could catch a prix-fixe deal not offered at peak hours and you might be able to share your dinner quite affordably with smaller children. Most upscale restaurants offer great lunch deals with special menus at cut-rate prices designed to give customers a true taste of the place. No matter what meal, ask whether kids' menus are available or whether they can make simple kids favorites like pasta, chicken, hot dogs, or hamburgers if nothing else appeals to your brood.

Credit cards are widely accepted, but some smaller restaurants accept only cash. In most restaurants, tip the waiter 16%–20%. If your children have made a bit of a mess or been especially demanding, note that by giving an even larger tip. Your server will appreciate it and you'll be doing a favor for families to come. Bills for parties of six or more sometimes include the tip already.

WHAT IT COSTS				
¢	$	$$	$$$	$$$$
RESTAURANTS				
under $10	$10–$17	$18–$26	$27–$35	over $35

Price per person for a median main course or equivalent combination of smaller dishes. Note: if a restaurant offers only prix-fixe (set-price) meals, it has been given the price category that reflects the full prix-fixe price.

TOP DINING EXPERIENCES

Go for the classic New York hot dog experience at Papaya King (or Gray's Papaya). Do you agree with their claim that it's as good as filet mignon?

Dress your best and sit outside in the Secret Garden–like atmosphere at Tavern on the Green in Central Park, surrounded by topiary animals and hanging paper lanterns.

Venture way uptown for some of the sloppiest, most delectable barbeque around,

noting the array of decked-out motorcycles usually parked in front of mammoth, noisy Dinosaur Bar-B-Que.

Challenge your kids to join the secret society of the Burger Joint by finding its mysterious location at Le Parker Meridien hotel.

Steel yourself for the long waits and mountains of food at Carmine's where family-style really means family-style and where the Titanic dessert is aptly named.

LOWER MANHATTAN & DOWNTOWN

INCLUDING THE FINANCIAL DISTRICT, CHINATOWN, LITTLE ITALY & SOHO

$$ ✕**Arturo's.** *Pizza.* This is one of New York's classic pizzerias, with the star of the show the restaurant's acclaimed coal oven. The jam-packed room is filled with a pleasantly smoky scent. There's a full menu of Italian classics, but pizza is the main event. The thin-crust beauties cooked emerge sizzling from the oven with simple toppings like pepperoni, sausage, and eggplant. Monday to Thursday, you can call ahead to reserve a table; weekends, be prepared to wait and salivate. **Family Matters:** If your kids like pizza, this is the real deal. Larger families are welcome. ✉106 W. Houston St., near Thompson St., Greenwich Village ☎212/677–3820 ▭AE, MC, V ⊗No lunch Ⓜ1 to Houston St.; F, V to Broadway–Lafayette St.

$$ ✕**Balthazar.** *Brasserie.* Even with long waits and excruciating noise levels, most out-of-towners agree that it's worth making reservations to experience restaurateur Keith McNally's flagship, a painstakingly accurate reproduction of a Parisian brasserie. Like the decor, entrées re-create French classics: Gruyère-topped onion soup, steak-frites, and icy tiers of crab, oysters, and other shellfish. Brunch is one of the best in town—if you can get a table. The best strategy is to go at off-hours, or on weekdays for breakfast, to miss the crush of hungry New Yorkers. **Family Matters:** Well-traveled

older kids will feel like they're in France with crowded tables and a busy bar scene. Add to the illusion after you leave and buy a baguette to go at Balthazar's bakery next door. ⊠*80 Spring St., between Broadway and Crosby St., SoHo* ☎*212/965–1785* ⌂*Reservations essential* ⊟*AE, MC, V* Ⓜ*6 to Spring St.; N, R to Prince St.; B, D, F, V to Broadway–Lafayette.*

★ ✕**Blue Ribbon Bakery.** *Bistro.* When the owners renovated
$$ this space, they uncovered a 100-year-old wood-burning oven. They relined it with volcanic brick and let it dictate the destiny of their restaurant. The bakery-restaurant has an eclectic menu featuring substantial sandwiches on home-made bread (from the oven, of course), small plates, a legendary bread pudding, and entrées that span the globe, from hummus to grilled catfish with chorizo, and sweet potatoes. **Family Matters:** Less adventurous kids can enjoy small burgers, grilled cheese, and chicken fingers. Reservations are only taken for parties of five or more, so plan to dine very early. ⊠*35 Downing St., at Bedford St.* ☎*212/337–0404* ⊟*AE, DC, MC, V* Ⓜ*1 to Houston St.*

$ ✕**Bubby's.** *American.* Crowds clamoring for coffee and freshly squeezed juice line up for brunch at this TriBeCa mainstay, but Bubby's serves fine breakfasts, lunches, and dinners as well. The dining room is homey and comfortable with big windows; in summer neighbors sit at tables outside with their dogs. For brunch you can order almost anything, including homemade granola, sour-cream pancakes with bananas and strawberries, and *huevos rancheros* with guacamole and grits. Eclectic comfort food—macaroni 'n cheese, fried chicken—make up the lunch and dinner menus. **Family Matters:** The stroller set will love the early weekend dining, mobbed by families ordering alphabet soup and other kid faves. Later brunch times should be avoided due to the long waits. ⊠*120 Hudson St., at N. Moore St.,TriBeCa* ☎*212/219–0666* ⊟*D, DC, MC, V* Ⓜ*1 to Franklin St.*

$$ ✕**Chinatown Brasserie.** *Chinese.* This large, bi-level 175-seat dining room is thrillingly vibrant, featuring dark cherry banquettes and 10 stunning crimson pagoda silk lanterns suspended from two central columns. Chicken and pine nuts are wrapped in Bibb lettuce. Crispy Peking duck is roasted in a special barbecuing oven, then sliced and presented on a long platter with Mandarin pancakes, julienned scallions, and sweet, pungent hoisin sauce on hand. Dark chocolate

6

fortune cookies contain salient quotes from Albert Einstein and Ronald Reagan. **Family Matters:** Dumplings served dim-sum style are a kid pleaser, and large tables invite sharing family-style. ✉ *380 Lafayette St., at Great Jones St., East Village* ☎ *212/533–7000* ⊕ *www.chinatownbrasserie. com* ⊟ *AE, MC, V* Ⓜ *6 to Bleecker St.*

$$ ✕ **Do Hwa.** *Korean.* If anyone in New York is responsible for making Korean food cool and user-friendly, it is the mother-daughter team behind this perennially popular restaurant and its East Village sister, Dok Suni's. Jenny Kwak and her mother, Myung Ja, serve home cooking in the form of *kalbi jim* (braised short ribs), *bibimbop* (a spicy, mix-it-yourself vegetable-and-rice dish), and other favorites that may not be as pungent as they are in Little Korea, but they're satisfying nevertheless. **Family Matters:** Although the atmosphere is rather loungy, larger family groups are welcome. The restaurant will tone down the spice with basic rice dishes, potato and scallion pancakes, and noodles for younger customers. ✉ *55 Carmine St., between Bedford St. and 7th Ave., Greenwich Village* ☎ *212/414–1224* ⊟ *AE, D, MC, V* Ⓜ *1 to Houston St.*

¢ ✕ **Financier Patisserie.** *Café.* On the cobblestone pedestrian street that has become the financial district's restaurant row, this quaint patisserie serves up excellent pastries and delicious savory foods, like paninis, soup, salad, and quiches. After lunch, relax with a cappuccino and a *financier,* an almond tea cake, or an elegant French pastry. In warm weather, perch at an outdoor table and watch Manhattanites buzz by. **Family Matters:** To savor your muffins or croissants in peace, avoid lunchtime when the place is jammed with businesspeople. The colorful macaroons in flavors like lemon, pistachio, and strawberry are melt-in-your-mouth good. ✉ *62 Stone St., at William St.; 35 Cedar St., between Pearl and William Sts.; 3–4 World Financial Center, in Battery Park City, Lower Manhattan* ☎ *212/344–5600* ⊕ *www.financierpastries.com* ⊠ *Reservations not accepted* ⊟ *AE, DC, MC, V* ⊘ *Closed Sun.* Ⓜ *2, 3, to Wall St.; 4, 5 to Bowling Green.*

$ ✕ **Ghenet.** *Ethiopian.* A rotating exhibit of local, African-inspired art hangs on the walls of this mecca of African cuisine. Order one of the combination entrées mounded on a platter lined with spongy *injera* flat bread, which is your edible utensil. In addition to poultry and meat options, there's a good selection of vegetarian dishes such as collard greens with Ethiopian spices and carrots in an onion sauce. The service is warm, and the staff will help guide you through the menu. **Family Matters:** The kitchen will happily make nonspicy basic dishes of chicken, rice, and vegetables, served with spongy bread. Larger families will have to sit separately as the tables are small. ⊠*284 Mulberry St., between E. Houston and Prince Sts., NoLita* ☎*212/343–1888* ☐*AE, MC, V* ☉*Closed Mon. No dinner Sun.* Ⓜ*R, W to Prince St.; 6 to Spring St.; B, D, F, V to Broadway–Lafayette.*

¢ ✕**Great New York Noodletown.** *Chinese.* Although the soups and noodles are unbeatable at this no-frills restaurant, what you should order are the window decorations—the hanging lacquered ducks and roasted pork, which are superb served with pungent garlic-and-ginger sauce on the side. Seasonal specialties like duck with flowering chives and salt-baked soft-shell crabs are excellent. So is the *congee,* or rice porridge, available with any number of garnishes. **Family Matters:** The restaurant is always busy and may be too loud for younger kids. ⊠*28 Bowery, at Bayard St., Chinatown* ☎*212/349–0923* ☐*No credit cards* Ⓜ*6, J, M, Z to Canal St.; B, D to Grand St.*

$ ✕**Jing Fong.** *Chinese.* Come to this dim sum palace for a jolting taste of Hong Kong. On weekend mornings people pour into the escalator to Jing Fong's carnivalesque third-floor dining room. Servers push carts of steamed dumplings, barbecue pork buns, and shrimp balls. Arrive early for the best selection, and save room for mango pudding. **Family Matters:** Watching the carts rolling by is as fun as picking out what you want to eat before it's pushed along. Be prepared to share a table with other people when it's busy. ⊠*20 Elizabeth St., between Bayard and Canal Sts., Chinatown* ☎*212/964–5256* ☐*AE, MC, V* Ⓜ*6, J, M, N, Q, R, W, Z to Canal St.*

$ ✕**Joe's Shanghai.** *Chinese.* Joe opened his first Shanghai restaurant in Queens in 1995, but buoyed by the accolades accorded his soup dumplings—filled with a rich, fragrant broth and pork or a pork-crabmeat mixture—he soon opened in Manhattan's Chinatown and later in Midtown. There's always a wait, but the line moves fast. Try the homemade Shanghai noodles and rich pork meatballs braised in brown sauce. Other, more familiar Chinese dishes are also excellent. **Family Matters:** Try to go at an off-hour during the week so your kids can ask how these mysterious

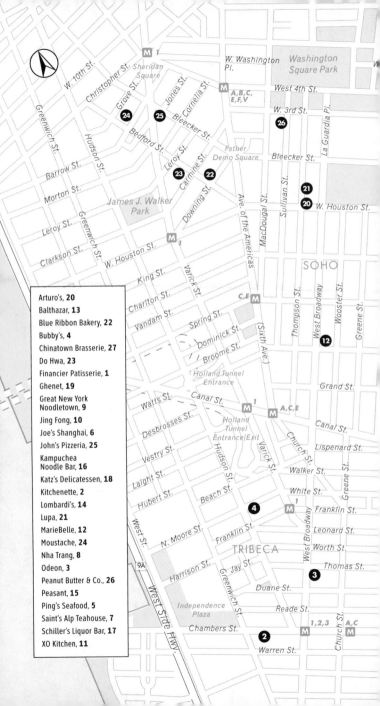

Arturo's, **20**
Balthazar, **13**
Blue Ribbon Bakery, **22**
Bubby's, **4**
Chinatown Brasserie, **27**
Do Hwa, **23**
Financier Patisserie, **1**
Ghenet, **19**
Great New York
Noodletown, **9**
Jing Fong, **10**
Joe's Shanghai, **6**
John's Pizzeria, **25**
Kampuchea
Noodle Bar, **16**
Katz's Delicatessen, **18**
Kitchenette, **2**
Lombardi's, **14**
Lupa, **21**
MarieBelle, **12**
Moustache, **24**
Nha Trang, **8**
Odeon, **3**
Peanut Butter & Co., **26**
Peasant, **15**
Ping's Seafood, **5**
Saint's Alp Teahouse, **7**
Schiller's Liquor Bar, **17**
XO Kitchen, **11**

dumplings are made. Bigger groups will have longer waits. Smaller groups will often need to share tables. The tables turn over quickly so loud or crying kids won't offend other diners for long. ✉9 Pell St., between the Bowery and Mott St., Chinatown ☎212/233–8888 ▤No credit cards Ⓜ6, J, M, N, Q, R, W, Z to Canal St.

$ ✕**John's Pizzeria.** *Pizza.* The original John's, an institution on Bleecker Street since 1929, is a perennial contender for best pizza pie in New York (as the famous sign on the window indicates, the place sells "no slices"). At peak times you'll find long lines on the sidewalk awaiting John's scalding thin-crust pies generously appointed with the usual toppings. Seated in a scuffed wood booth in the no-frills dining room, the only decisions you'll have to make are what toppings to order and whether you'd like an oversized shareable salad. **Family Matters:** John's has been catering to families for years. Try sneaking in some essence of garlic on your thin-crust pizza for a slight kick that won't overwhelm your kids. Kids can pretend they're adults with their own Shirley Temples. ✉278 Bleecker St., between 6th and 7th Aves., Greenwich Village ☎212/243–1680 ⚐Reservations not accepted ▤No credit cards Ⓜ1 to Christopher St./Sheridan Sq.

$ ✕**Kampuchea Restaurant.** *Cambodian.* This sophisticated Southeast Asian street-food spot is the most stylish noodle bar we've ever encountered with an eclectic menu that goes well beyond. Start with grilled corn lathered in coconut mayo, coconut flakes, and chili powder and move on to Cambodian savory crepes filled with Berkshire pork and chives or more familiar noodle dishes or steaming bowls of soup. **Family Matters:** Budding hipster teens will have a tough time deciding whether to pay attention to the food here or the very downtown crowd. Ask the server to suggest some of the less spicy and complex dishes, more suited for younger palates. ✉78 Rivington St., at Allen St., Lower East Side ☎212/529–3901 ⊕www.kampucheanyc.com ▤AE, D, DC, MC, V Ⓜ F to Delancey St.; J, M, Z to Essex St.

★ FodorsChoice ✕**Katz's Delicatessen.** *Deli.* Everything and noth-
$ ing has changed at Katz's since it first opened in 1888, when the neighborhood was dominated by Jewish immigrants. The rows of Formica tables, the long self-service counter, and such signs as "send a salami to your boy in the army" are all completely authentic. What's different

are the area's demographics, but all types still flock here for succulent hand-carved corned beef and pastrami sandwiches, soul-warming soups, and crisp half-sour pickles. **Family Matters**: The waiters are used to kids of all ages. This is a great place to introduce your family to Old New York. ⊠*205 E. Houston St., at Ludlow St., Lower East Side* ☎*212/254–2246* ⊕*www.katzdeli.com* ⊟*AE, MC, V* Ⓜ*F, V to 2nd Ave.*

$ ✕**Kitchenette.** *American.* This small, comfy restaurant lives up to its name with tables so close together you're likely to make new friends. The dining room feels like a breakfast nook, and the food tastes like your mom made it—provided she's a great cook. There are no frills, just solid cooking, friendly service, and a long line at peak times. For brunch don't miss the blackberry-cherry pancakes or the pear streusel French toast. **Family Matters**: Kids can chow down on biscuits with strawberry butter for breakfast and yummy finger-lickin' fried chicken from their own menu for dinner. ⊠*156 Chambers St., near Greenwich St., TriBeCa* ☎*212/267–6740* ⊟*AE, D, MC, V* Ⓜ*1, 2, 3, A, C to Chambers St.*

$ ✕**Lombardi's.** *Pizza.* Brick walls, red-and-white checkered tablecloths, and the aroma of thin-crust pies emerging from the coal oven set the mood for some of the best pizza in Manhattan. Lombardi's has served pizza since 1905 (though not in the same location), and business has not died down a bit. The mozzarella is always fresh, resulting in an almost greaseless slice, and the toppings, such as meatballs or pancetta are also top quality. Lombardi's is perhaps best known for its toothsome clam pizza, which features freshly shucked clams, garlic oil, pecorino-Romano cheese, and parsley. **Family Matters**: This is a no-slices pizzeria; if you have leftovers, you can take it to your hotel for a late-night bite. The busy, noisy rooms mean that kids of all ages will be comfortable here. ⊠*32 Spring St., between Mott and Mulberry Sts., Little Italy* ☎*212/941–7994* ⊕*www.first-pizza.com* ⊟*No credit cards* Ⓜ*6 to Spring St.; B, D, F, V to Broadway–Lafayette St.*

$$ ✕**Lupa.** *Italian.* Even the most hard-to-please connoisseurs have a soft spot for Lupa, Mario Batali, and Joseph Bastianich's "downscale" Roman trattoria. Rough-hewn wood and simple preparations with top-quality ingredients define the restaurant. People come repeatedly for dishes such as ricotta gnocchi with sweet-sausage ragù, house-made

salumi, and sardines with fennel and bulgar. The front of the restaurant is seated on a first-come, first-served basis; reservations are taken for the back. **Family Matters:** Weekend lunches are the best times for kids to enjoy gourmet helpings of buttered spaghetti. The down-home front room is boisterous and perfect for large families; the quieter back room is a place to teach manners and how to eat pasta with polish. ⊠*170 Thompson St., between Bleecker and W. Houston Sts., Greenwich Village* ☎*212/982–5089* ▤*AE, DC, MC, V* ⊕*www.luparestaurant.com* Ⓜ*A, B, C, D, E, F, V to W. 4th St.*

$ ✕**MarieBelle.** *Café.* Practically invisible from the front of the chocolate emporium, the back entry to the Cacao Bar opens into a sweet, high-ceiling, 12-table hot-chocolate shop. Most people order the Aztec, a rich but not too dense European-style version. The American-style, made with milk, is sweeter. Preface it with a salad or sandwich from the dainty lunch menu, or request one of the expensive but ravishing flavored chocolates sold out front, like passion fruit, or *dulce de leche.* **Family Matters:** Everyone loves the sweet crepes as well. The quiet atmosphere is less suitable for younger kids. ⊠*484 Broome St., between West Broadway and Wooster St., SoHo* ☎*212/925–6999* ⊕*www.mariebelle.com* ▵*Reservations not accepted* ▤*AE, D, MC, V* Ⓜ*A, C, E to Canal St.*

¢   ✕**Moustache.** *Middle Eastern.* There's typically a crowd waiting outside for one of the copper-topped tables at this appealing Middle Eastern neighborhood restaurant. The focal point is the perfect pita that accompanies tasty salads like lemony chickpea and spinach, and hearty lentil and bulgur. Also delicious is *lahambajin,* spicy ground lamb on a crispy flat crust. For entrées, try the leg of lamb or merguez sausage sandwiches. Service is slow but friendly. **Family Matters:** Go before 7 PM when it fills to capacity and the low-key feel shifts to loud and uncomfortable. ⊠*90 Bedford St., between Barrow and Grove Sts., Greenwich Village* ☎*212/229–2220* ▵*Reservations not accepted* ▤*No credit cards* Ⓜ*1 to Christopher St./Sheridan Sq.*

★ Fodor'sChoice ✕**Nha Trang.** *Vietnamese.* You can get a great
¢   meal for under $10 at this low-atmosphere Vietnamese restaurant in Chinatown. Start with crispy spring rolls, sweet-and-sour seafood soup, or shrimp grilled on sugarcane. For a follow-up, don't miss the thin pork chops, which are marinated in a sweet vinegary sauce and grilled until

charred. If the line is long, which it usually is, even with a second location around the corner, you may be asked to sit at a table with strangers. **Family Matters:** New Yorkers on jury duty love this place so try to avoid prime lunch break hours. ✉ 87 Baxter St., between Bayard and Canal Sts., Chinatown ☎ 212/233–5948 ⊟ No credit cards Ⓜ 6, J, M, N, Q, R, W, Z to Canal St. ✉ 148 Centre St., at Walker and White Sts., Chinatown ☎ 212/941–9292 ⊟ No credit cards Ⓜ 6, J, M, N, Q, R, W, Z to Canal St.

$$$ ✕ **Odeon.** Bistro. New Yorkers change hangouts faster than they can press speed-dial, but this spot has managed to maintain its quality and flair for more than 25 years. The neo–art deco room is still packed nightly with revelers. The pleasant service and well-chosen wine list are always in style. The bistro-menu highlights include frisée aux lardons and grilled sirloin steak. **Family Matters:** Families are also welcome here, and brunch is an especially popular time. Servers encourage kids to try out their creativity by drawing on the paper on the tables. ✉ 145 West Broadway, between Duane and Thomas Sts., TriBeCa ☎ 212/233–0507 ⊟ AE, D, DC, MC, V Ⓜ 1, 2, 3, A, C to Chambers St.

★ ✕ **Peanut Butter & Co.** American. It may feel a little strange to
ℭ be eating a peanut butter sandwich in the midst of sophisticated New York City, but don't question it. Just be happy indulging your inner child at this shrine to the joys of peanut butter. The menu starts with a basic PB&J, and if you ask, they'll even cut the crusts off for you. But they also branch out to sandwiches Moms never make, like Fluffernutters, white chocolate peanut butter and marmalade, or even spicy peanut butter and grilled chicken. **Family Matters:** For dessert, quiet your kids with a thick peanut butter milk shake or a waffle sundae. ✉ 240 Sullivan St., near 3rd St. ☎ 212/677–3995 ⊕ http://www.ilovepeanutbutter.com ⟨ Reservations not accepted ⊟ AE, D, MC, V Ⓜ A, C, E, E, F, V to W.4th St.

$$ ✕ **Peasant.** Italian. The crowd at this rustic restaurant is stylishly urban. Inspired by the proverbial "peasant" cuisine where meals were prepared in the kitchen hearth, chef-owner Frank DeCarlo cooks all of his wonderful food in a bank of wood- or charcoal-burning ovens. Don't fill up on the crusty bread and fresh ricotta, though, or you'll miss out on the other flavorful Italian fare. **Family Matters:** Kids will have fun watching the pizzas come out of the open brick ovens but most won't be able to read the menu: it's

in Italian. (Don't worry—spaghetti and lasagna are easy translations.) ✉*194 Elizabeth St., between Spring and Prince Sts., NoLita* ☎*212/965–9511* ⊕*www.peasantnyc. com* ≜*Reservations essential* ▤*AE, MC, V* ☉*Closed Mon. No lunch* Ⓜ*6 to Spring St.; R, W to Prince St.*

$$ ✗**Ping's Seafood.** *Chinese.* Although the original location in Queens still has the most elaborate menu with the most extensive selection of live seafood, the Manhattan location is more accessible both geographically and gastronomically. Helpful menus have pictures of most of the specialties. Among them are crisp fried tofu, silken braised *e-fu* noodles, and Peking duck. Pricier than some other Chinatown haunts, Ping's is also a notch above in setting and service. **Family Matters:** Waitstaff will accommodate kids' requests if nothing appeals from the fresher-than-fresh dim sum cart. Avoid the noon hour when locals on jury duty pack the place. ✉*22 Mott St., between Bayard and Pell Sts.,Chinatown* ☎*212/602–9988* ≜*Reservations essential* ▤*AE, MC, V* Ⓜ*6, J, M, N, Q, R, W, Z to Canal St.*

¢ ✗**Saint's Alp Teahouse.** *Vietnamese.* Join the hip Asian youth crowding the tables at Saint's Alp Teahouse. They're here for bubble tea—frothy, flavored, black, or green tea speckled with tapioca or sago, sucked through a jumbo straw. You can also order snacks like spring rolls and dumplings. **Family Matters:** Ask for a milk shake version of the bubble tea so you won't send your kids on a caffeine-induced high. ✉*51 Mott St., between Canal and Pell Sts., Chinatown* ☎*212/393–9009* ≜*Reservations not accepted* ▤*No credit cards* Ⓜ*6, J, M, N, Q, R, W, Z to Canal St.*

$ ✗**Schiller's Liquor Bar.** *Bistro.* It's the kind of hip Lower East Side hangout where you'd be equally comfortable as a celebrity or a parent with a stroller. The folks at Schiller's work hard to make it feel as if it's decades old. Vintage mirrored panels, subway tiles, a tin ceiling, and a checkered floor lend a Parisian feel. Cuban sandwiches and steak-frites reveal a steady hand in the kitchen. **Family Matters:** Kids will enjoy the burgers and fries, donuts, and filled baguettes. The chef is adept at accommodating changes to dishes on the menu for more finicky eaters. ✉*131 Rivington St., at Norfolk St., Lower East Side* ☎*212/260–4555* ▤*AE, MC, V* Ⓜ*F, J, M, Z to Delancey St.*

¢ ✗**XO Kitchen.** *Chinese.* Chinese students throng this Hong Kong–style eatery. The walls resemble bulletin boards— they're tacked with dozens of sheets announcing a mind-boggling variety of foods, from dim sum to Thai (there is also a menu). The food is some of Chinatown's finest. Try the delicate shrimp wonton soup, or the refreshingly light Hong Kong–style lo mein. **Family Matters:** You'll be in good company with other families and teenagers enjoying the no-frills service. If younger kids don't mind the noise, they certainly won't disturb anyone here. ✉*146 Hester St., between Elizabeth St. and Bowery, Chinatown* ☎*212/965–8645* 🍴*AE, MC, V* Ⓜ*B, D to Grand St.; 6, J, M, Z to Canal St.*

FROM THE VILLAGE TO THE THIRTIES

INCLUDING UNION SQUARE, CHELSEA & THE FLATIRON DISTRICT

★ Fodor'sChoice ✕ **Back Forty.** *American.* Pioneering chef Peter
$ Hoffman, a longtime leader in promoting local, sustainable food, attracts a devoted crowd at this casual restaurant that feels like a neighborhood joint. Prices on the short, rustic, greenmarket menu are extremely low and the homey decor features a pastoral mural behind the bar and rusty farm tools on the walls. The simple family-style dinner selections include a perfect grilled trout, a moist shareable whole rotisserie chicken, and a wide array of seasonal sides. **Family Matters:** Even more basic dishes like hamburgers and onion rings can be ordered for kids. ✉*190 Ave. B, at 12th St., East Village* ☎*212/388–1990* 🍴 *AE, MC, V* Ⓜ*L to 1st Ave.*

$$ ✕ **Blue Smoke.** *Barbecue.* Ever the pioneer, Danny Meyer led the way for barbecue in Manhattan with a "hands across America"–like approach representing regional 'cue styles. The menu features Texas salt-and-pepper beef ribs, saucy Kansas City–style ribs, and tangy North Carolina pulled pork on brioche buns. If mac 'n cheese is a weakness, many insist there's none better than Blue Smoke's. **Family Matters:** The loud, fun atmosphere is conducive to dining with kids. Tables are long so big family parties will have no problem. There's something for everyone on the menu, and the chocolate cake for dessert is a pièce de résistance. ✉*116 E. 27th St., between Lexington and Park Aves., Gramercy Park* ☎*212/447–7733* ⊕*www.bluesmoke.com* 🍴 *AE, DC, MC, V* Ⓜ*6 to 28th St.*

★ Fodor'sChoice ✕ **City Bakery.** *Café.* This self-service bakery-
$ restaurant has the urban aesthetic to match its name. The baked goods here—giant cookies, flaky croissants, elegant tarts—are unfailingly rich. A major draw is the salad bar

Where to Eat from the Village to the Thirties

CHELSEA

GREENWICH VILLAGE

Washington Square Park

W. 31st St.
Broadway
E. 28th St.
Franklin Terrace
W. 23rd St.
W. 21st St.
W. 20th St.
W. 19th St.
W. 18th St.
W. 17th St.
W. 16th St.
W. 15th St.
W. 14th St.
W. 13th St.
W. 12th St.
W. 11th St.
W. 10th St.
W. 9th St.
W. 8th St.
W. 4th St.
W. 3rd St.

Seventh Avenue
Ave. of the Americas
(6th Avenue)
Eighth Avenue
Ninth Avenue
Fifth Avenue

Gansevoort St.
Horatio St.
Greenwich Ave.
Waverly Pl.
W. 11th St.
W. 4th St.
Perry St.
Charles St.
W. 10th St.
Christopher St.
Grove St.
Jones St.
Cornelia St.
Gay St.
West Washington Pl.
Sheridan Square
West 4th St.

R,W
C,E
F,V
R,W
A,C,E,L
1,2,3
F,L,V
A,B,C, E,D,F,V

E. 31st St.

E. 30th St.

Kips
Bay
Plaza

**NYU
Medical
Center**

MURRAY HILL

E. 29th St.

Ⓜ 6

**Bellevue
Hospital**

E. 27th St.

**Madison
Square
Park**

⑩

⑪

E. 26th St.

Madison Avenue

Park Ave. South

Lexington Avenue

Second Avenue

First Avenue

**Worth
Square**

E. 25th St.

E. 24th St.

N ━ Ⓜ

Ⓜ 6

E. 23rd St.

E. 23rd St.

**Flatiron
Building**

GRAMERCY

E. 22nd St.

Broadway

E. 21st St.

E. 20st St.

Gramercy
Park

E. 19th St.

Irving Pl.

E. 18th St.

Stuyvesant
Square

Stuyvesant
Town

Fifth Avenue

Union
Square

E. 17th St.

⑤

E. 16th St.

Stuyvesant
Square

Union Sq.
Park

E. 15th St.

Third Avenue

Ⓜ L

Ⓜ L

Ⓜ
L,N,Q,R,W
4,5,6

E. 14th St.

Ⓜ

E. 13th St.

EAST
VILLAGE

E. 12th St.

Broadway

③

② →

E. 11th St.

University Pl.

Fourth Avenue

Third Avenue

①

E. 10th St.

Ⓜ

E. 9th St.

St. Marks Pl.

Greene St.

Ⓜ 6

Second Avenue

First Avenue

Astor Pl.

Cooper Union
Great Hall

E. 7th St.

Waverly Pl.

Lafayette St.

E. 6th St.

Cooper
Square

E. 5th St.

E. Washington
Pl.

**New York
University**

E. 4th St.

Great Jones St.

0   1,000 ft

0   300 m

that's worth every penny—a large selection of impeccably fresh food, including pressed sandwiches, roasted vegetables, and several Asian-accented dishes. Much of the produce comes from the nearby Union Square farmers' market. In winter the bakery hosts a hot-chocolate festival; in summer it's lemonade time. Weekend brunch includes limited table-side service. **Family Matters:** Shelter your family here on cold winter days and treat them to thicker-than-thick hot chocolate topped off with housemade marshmallows. ✉3 *W. 18th St., between 5th and 6th Aves., Flatiron District* ☎212/366–1414 ═AE, MC, V ⊘*No dinner* Ⓜ*L, N, Q, R, W, 4, 5, 6 to 14th St./Union Sq.; F, V to 14th St.*

¢ ✕**Eisenberg's Sandwich Shop.** *Café.* Since 1929 this narrow coffee shop with its timeworn counter and cramped tables has provided the city with some of the best tuna-, chicken-, and egg-salad sandwiches. The staff uses the cryptic language of soda jerks, in which "whiskey down" means rye toast and "Adam and Eve on a raft" means two eggs on toast. Considering the mayhem in the place, it's always a pleasant surprise when you actually get your sandwich, quickly and precisely as ordered. **Family Matters:** Kid favorites are the wonderful bacon and egg sandwich, or a real fountain coke, which means actual syrup mixed with seltzer in front of your eyes at the counter—it tastes just a bit sweeter than the can version. You can also introduce your kids to things that you loved as a child, like a wonderful lime rickey. ✉*174 5th Ave., between E. 22nd and E. 23rd Sts., Flatiron District* ☎212/675–5096 ⊕*www. eisenbergsnyc.com* ═AE, D, MC, V ⊘*No dinner* Ⓜ*R, W, 6 to 23rd St.*

$$ ✕**Gonzo.** *Italian.* Once you're seated in the cathedral-ceiling dining room, you'll swear you're in Florence. The restaurant is usually packed and can be noisy, but that's part of the scene. Start with Venetian bar snacks such as fried stuffed olives, marinated roasted peppers, or a salad of fava beans, pecorino, and walnuts. Then try one of the cracker-thin grilled pizzas or inventive entrées like fennel-crusted pork tenderloin with raspberry-onion marmalade. The praline ice-cream sandwich with Tahitian vanilla gelato is even better than it sounds. **Family Matters:** Kids have many choices, too, with lots of pizzas and pastas offered. Earlier in the evening you'll see lots of kids practicing their best menu Italian. ✉*140 W. 13th St., between 6th and 7th Aves., Greenwich Village* ☎212/645–4606 ⌖*Reservations essential* ═AE, MC, V Ⓜ*1, 2, 3 to 14th St.*

★ Fodor'sChoice ✕ **Hill Country.** *Barbecue.* This enormous barbe-
$$ cue joint is perfect for big groups and carnivorous appetites.
The beef-centric menu features meaty ribs and exceptionally
succulent slow-smoked brisket (check your diet at the door
and go for the moist, fatty option). Plump pork sausages,
in regular and jalapeño cheese versions, are flown in direct
from Texas. The market-style set-up can mean long lines.
Family Matters: The bar scene kicks in at 9 PM with live
music, too, so be sure to finish your meal well before. ⊠ *30
W. 26th St., between Broadway and 6th Ave., Flatiron*
☎ *212/255–4544* ⊟ *AE, D, MC, V* Ⓜ *N, R, W to 28th St.;
6 to 28th St.; F, V to 23rd St.*

$ ✕ **Piola.** *Pizza.* Festive rainbow lighting fills the spacious
dining room of Piola, which has 20 restaurants around
the world. But it couldn't feel less like a chain as it bursts
with character and Italian-Brazilian bonhomie. The entire
kitchen staff was trained in Treviso, and the menu lists
60 thin-crust pizzas, from a simple tomato-mozzarella-
Parmesan-arugula to the Brooklyn, which features broc-
coli, chicken, and Gorgonzola cheese. There are some fine
pastas and salads as well, and delicious profiteroles for
dessert. **Family Matters:** The servers know to bring the
basic margherita pizza for kids while suggesting more
interesting choices for the adults. Go for lunch or an early
dinner when it's not so packed. ⊠ *48 E. 12th St., between
Broadway and University Pl., East Village* ☎ *212/777–7781*
⊕ *www.piola.it* ⊟ *AE, DC, MC, V* Ⓜ *4, 5, 6, N, Q, R, W
to Union Sq./14th St.*

¢ ✕ **Republic.** *Asian.* Epicureans on a budget flock to this
Asian noodle emporium that looks like a cross between
a downtown art gallery and a Japanese school cafeteria.
The young waitstaff dressed in black T-shirts and jeans
hold remote-control ordering devices to accelerate the
already speedy service. Sit at the long, bluestone bar or at
the picnic-style tables and order appetizers such as smoky
grilled eggplant and luscious fried wontons. Entrées are
all based on noodles or rice. Spicy coconut chicken soup
and Vietnamese-style barbecued pork are particularly deli-
cious. **Family Matters:** There aren't many kids here, but the
price-friendly menu is definitely a kid-pleaser with dishes
like pad thai, chicken noodle soup, and bowls of chicken
udon. ⊠ *37 Union Sq. W, between E. 16th and E. 17th Sts.,
Flatiron District* ☎ *212/627–7172* ⊟ *AE, DC, MC, V* Ⓜ *L,
N, Q, R, W, 4, 5, 6 to 14th St./Union Sq.*

$ ⨉**R.U.B. BBQ.** *Barbecue.* Executive chef Paul Kirk's Kansas City dry rub has become legend on the growing New York City barbecue competition circuit. This is not a restaurant for the timid of appetite. Platters are so bountiful that even the side dishes come in overwhelming quantities. The shameless menu promises everything from beef, pork, ham, pastrami, and turkey to chicken, sausage, and of course ribs. Burned ends—delicious charred-crisp, rich edges of beef brisket—are highly prized, and they sell out every night. In fact, many items on the menu sell out by 8 PM, so it's wise to arrive fairly early. **Family Matters:** The enormous Frito pie is possibly even more popular among kids who get a charge out of the mountain of food served in a torn Frito bag. ✉*208 W. 23rd St., between 7th and 8th Aves., Chelsea* ☎*212/524–4300* ⌕*Reservations essential* ▭*AE, DC, MC, V* Ⓜ*1, C, E to 23rd St.*

$ ⨉**Turkish Kitchen.** *Turkish.* This striking multilevel room with crimson walls, chairs with red-skirted slipcovers, and colorful kilims is a favorite in Manhattan. For appetizers, choose from the likes of char-grilled eggplant, creamy hummus, or poached beef dumplings. The luscious stuffed cabbage is downright irresistible. The restaurant also hosts one of the most alluring Sunday brunch buffets in town, featuring 90 items, Turkish and American—all house-made, including a dozen breads. **Family Matters:** The menu offers lots for kids to like: chicken, pita bread, and rice pudding. The all-you-can-eat-brunch is a great way for everyone to experiment a bit with new tastes. ✉*386 3rd Ave., between E. 27th and E. 28th Sts., Murray Hill* ☎*212/679–6333* ⊕*www.turkishkitchen.com* ▭*AE, D, DC, MC, V* ☺*No lunch Sat.* Ⓜ*6 to 28th St.*

¢ ⨉**Veniero's Pasticceria.** *Café.* More than a century old, this bustling bakery-café sells every kind of Italian *dolci* (sweet), from cherry-topped cookies to creamy cannoli and flaky *sfogliatelle.* **Family Matters:** The displays of colorful pastries and gelati are well-admired by the throngs of families who have been coming here for decades. Be sure to buy some cookies to take back to your hotel for a bedtime treat. ✉*342 E. 11th St., near 1st Ave., East Village* ☎*212/674–7264* ⌕*Reservations not accepted* ▭*AE, D, DC, MC, V* Ⓜ*6 to Astor Pl.; L to 1st Ave.*

MIDTOWN

$$ ✕ **Beacon.** *American.* Pyromaniacs rejoice: open-fire cooking is the name of the game here at this 10-year-old Midtown staple. They make everything on the grill or the rotisserie of a wood-fired oven, including grilled pork chops and lamb, wood-oven thin crust pizza, and roasted duck cured with black pepper. Wood-roasted oysters might just be the most delicious thing on the menu. Even desserts are made over the hearth—like roasted strawberry and balsamic reduction served with cheesecake ice cream. Everything starts with good ingredients, prepared simply, with a few interesting twists here and there. On Sunday, a $44 family-style three-course prix fixe includes BYO wine with no corkage fee. (Other nights, it's $35.) Downstairs, a narrow counter overlooking the hearth seats six. At lunchtime, it serves as a burger bar showcasing hearth-grilled Niman Ranch beef. On Thursday nights, a 12-course tasting menu for $85 is so popular it's booked months in advance; all other nights feature an assortment of small plates. **Family Matters:** Though the dining room's often filled with Midtown suits, and the menu is expensive, it couldn't be more family friendly. There's a children's menu, those four and under eat *free*, and kids even get to help make cotton candy after their meal. ✉ *25 W. 56th St., near 5th Ave., Midtown* ☎ *212/332–0500* ⌂ *Reservations recommended* ▭ *AE, D, DC, MC, V* Ⓜ *E, V to Fifth Ave.*

★ **Fodor's**Choice ✕ **Burger Joint.** *Burger.* What's a college burger
¢ bar, done up in particleboard and rec room decor, doing hidden inside of a five-star Midtown hotel? This tongue-in-cheek spot buried in the Parker Meridien does such boisterous midweek business that lines often snake through the lobby. Stepping behind the beige curtain you can find baseball cap–wearing grease-spattered cooks dispensing paper-wrapped cheeseburgers and crisp thin fries. The burgers are straightforward, cheap, and delicious. **Family Matters:** Kids will get a kick out of trying to find this hidden spot—make it their mission to smell out the burgers. Pictures of celebrity guests, including sports favorites, adorn the walls along with kids' drawings. The brownies are awesome, too. ✉ *118 W. 57th St, between 6th and 7th Aves., Midtown West* ☎ *212/245–5000* ▭ *No credit cards* Ⓜ *F to 57th St.*

★ ✕ **Carmine's.** *Italian.* Savvy New Yorkers line up early for
$$ the affordable family-style meals at both branches of this large, busy eatery. There are no reservations taken for par-

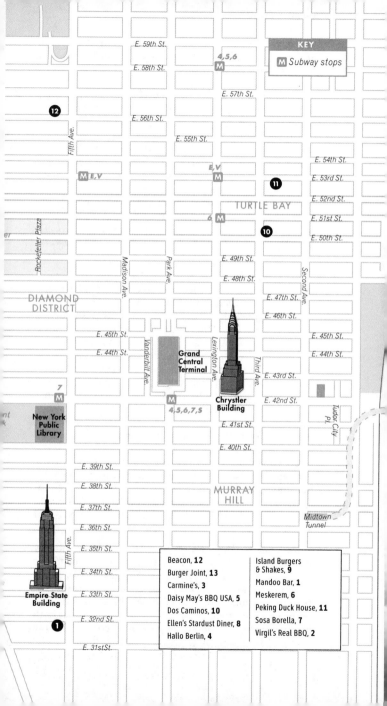

E. 59th St.

E. 58th St.

E. 57th St.

4,5,6 Ⓜ

E. 56th St.

❶❷

E. 55th St.

E. 54th St.

Fifth Ave.

Ⓜ E,V

E, V Ⓜ

E. 53rd St.

❶❶

E. 52nd St.

TURTLE BAY

6 Ⓜ

E. 51st St.

Rockefeller Plaza

❶⓿

E. 50th St.

E. 49th St.

Madison Ave.

Park Ave.

E. 48th St.

DIAMOND DISTRICT

E. 47th St.

E. 46th St.

E. 45th St.

E. 44th St.

Vanderbilt Ave.

Grand Central Terminal

Lexington Ave.

Chrystler Building

Second Ave.

E. 45th St.

E. 44th St.

Third Ave.

E. 43rd St.

7 Ⓜ

Ⓜ **4,5,6,7,S**

E. 42nd St.

Tudor City Pl.

New York Public Library

E. 41st St.

E. 40th St.

E. 39th St.

MURRAY HILL

E. 38th St.

E. 37th St.

Midtown Tunnel

E. 36th St.

Fifth Ave.

E. 35th St.

E. 34th St.

E. 33rd St.

Beacon, **12**	Island Burgers & Shakes, **9**
Burger Joint, **13**	Mandoo Bar, **1**
Carmine's, **3**	Meskerem, **6**
Daisy May's BBQ USA, **5**	Peking Duck House, **11**
Dos Caminos, **10**	Sosa Borella, **7**
Ellen's Stardust Diner, **8**	Virgil's Real BBQ, **2**
Hallo Berlin, **4**	

Empire State Building

❶

E. 32nd St.

E. 31st St.

ties of fewer than six people after 7 PM, but those who wait are rewarded with mountains of such popular, toothsome items as fried calamari, linguine with white clam sauce, chicken parmigiana, and veal saltimbocca. The Upper West Side dining room has dark woodwork and black-and-white tiles; outdoor seating is available in the front. The Times Square location can really be a zoo especially around theater time. **Family Matters:** There are families of all sizes here, and no one leaves without a to-go bag. Even so, don't ignore the awe-inspiring Titanic dessert with chocolate cake, five scoops of ice cream whipped cream, fruit, cookies, nuts and chocolate sauce—a bargain at $23.50. Find other Carmine's branches in the Upper West Side. ⊠ *200 W. 44th St., between Broadway and 8th Ave., Midtown West* ☎ *212/221–3800* ⊕ *www.carminesnyc.com* ☐ *AE, D, DC, MC, V* Ⓜ *A, C, E, N, Q, R, S, W, 1, 2, 3, 7 to 42nd St./Times Sq.*

$ ✕ **Daisy May's BBQ USA.** *Southern.* Doubting Southerners may question how a French-trained chef from Long Island could even *attempt* to make BBQ—much less how he would get it right. But Adam Perry Lang (who previously cooked at chi-chi spots like Daniel and Le Cirque) does down-home good here at his cafeteria-style restaurant and at pushcarts around the city. Order the Memphis-style ribs, where the dry rub forms an awesomely assertive crust, and the underlying meat is juicy and perfectly smoked. Though the pulled pork can occasionally be too dry, an authentic Carolina-style slaw and some decent sauce help. The baked beans are full of smoky bits of porky goodness and the creamed corn is overloaded with New York State cheddar, proving that sometimes adding a little New York to a Southern classic is a very good thing. (Are you listening, Southerners?) **Family Matters:** This is definitely a good spot to hit when you've got a hungry brood and you need a stick-to-your-ribs meal STAT. ⊠ *623 11th Ave., corner of 46th St. Hell's Kitchen, Midtown* ☎ *212/977–1500* ♨ *Reservations not accepted* ☐ *AE, D, MC, V* Ⓜ *A, C, E to 42nd St.*

$$ ✕ **Dos Caminos.** *Mexican.* Stephen Hanson, the visionary behind a dozen New York restaurants, has created a hit with the Dos Caminos brand. Start with guacamole, served in a granite mortar called a *molcajete.* Beef tacos studded with chilies, and slow-roasted pork ribs in chipotle barbecue sauce are solid choices. On weekend nights at both locations, the noise level can get out of control. **Family Matters:** Bring your older kids here early as the rooms are

tight but the tacos, tortillas, fondue, and ice creams are wonderful. SoHo and the Flatiron District also sport Dos Caminos branches. ⊠ *825 3rd Ave., at 50th St., Midtown East* ☎ *212/336–5400* ⊟ *AE, DC, MC* Ⓜ *6 to 51st St.*

$ ✕ **Ellen's Stardust Diner.** *Diner.* "Sing for your supper" takes on a new meaning here, where the waiters are all Broadway-bound babes. In between serving up burgers and fries, they hop up on the backs of the booths to sing show tunes. The waiter-singers are so energetic and charming that even skeptics and pouting kids will find themselves singing along and having a good time. **Family Matters:** You should know that the '50's style kitschy ambience is better than the food—standard diner fare with a Times Square markup. Still, it's better than most of the other family-friendly restaurants in the Theater District, and much more entertaining. ⊠ *1650 Broadway, at 51st St. Times Square, Midtown* ☎ *212/956–5151* ⊟ *AE, D, MC, V* Ⓜ *N, R to 49th St. or 1, 9 to 50th St.*

$ ✕ **Hallo Berlin.** *German.* When nothing but bratwurst will do, lunge for this Hell's Kitchen café. There are 10 varieties of wursts, accompanied by traditional German side dishes such as sauerkraut, spaetzle, or particularly addictive panfried potatoes. The atmosphere is low-budget and the low, low prices match the lack of pretension. **Family Matters:** Kids can order a more familiar American-style hot dog as well as potato pancakes and soups. ⊠ *626 10th Ave., at W. 44th St., Midtown West* ☎ *212/977–1944* ⊟ *AE, MC, V, $20 minimum* ⊗ *No lunch Sun.* Ⓜ *A, C, E to 42nd St.*

★ ✕ **Island Burgers and Shakes.** *American.* Toppings are king
¢ here at this solid Hell's Kitchen choice, where big, juicy burgers can be ordered with more than 60 different combinations of fixings. If their combinations—blackened, Thai, Cajun, Italian, Frog (Boursin, bacon, and onions), and dozens more—aren't enough, you can customize your own. The burgers themselves are definitely decent and properly cooked, although it can be hard to actually taste them underneath all of those toppings. Be prepared for things to get sloppy; the buns are not up to the daunting task of holding everything together neatly. **Family Matters:** The shakes are straw-stand-up thick, and come in classic flavors like black and white malted, a great old-fashioned treat for kids. The only bummer? No fries. There simply isn't room for a fryer in their tiny kitchen. ⊠ *766 9th Ave.,*

near 51st St., Midtown West ☎*212/307–7934* ⌂ ⊟*AE, MC, V* Ⓜ *C, E to 50th St.*

¢ ✕**Mandoo Bar.** *Korean.* At this appealing little dumpling shop on Little Korea's main drag, you can watch the ladies making the little oval treats in the window on your way to one of the blond-wood cafeterialike tables in the back. There are plenty of dumplings, or *mandoo,* to choose from, such as Korean kimchi, beef, pork, or leek. Rounding out the menu are noodle and rice dishes. **Family Matters:** Pretty much any favorite ingredients can be folded into the dumplings, a plus for picky eaters. Kids will get a kick out of the "show" while waiting for their meal. ⊠*2 W. 32nd St., between 5th Ave. and Broadway, Murray Hill* ☎*212/279–3075* ⊟*AE, MC, V* Ⓜ*6 to 33rd St.*

$ ✕**Meskerem.** *Ethiopian.* The tasty Ethiopian delicacies offered in this Hell's Kitchen storefront include *kitfo,* spiced ground steak and *yebeg alecha,* tender pieces of lamb marinated in butter flavored with curry, rosemary, and an herb called *kosart,* and then sautéed with fresh ginger and more curry. The vegetarian combination, served on injera, a yeasty and slightly porous flat bread used as a utensil to sop up the food, is a great deal. **Family Matters:** Even the pickiest of eaters will enjoy eating with their hands. Injera makes a great accompaniment to plain, nonspicy chicken, which the kitchen can offer if requested. ⊠*468 W. 47th St., near 10th Ave., Midtown West* ☎*212/664–0520* ⊟*AE, DC, MC, V* Ⓜ*C, E to 50th St.*

$$ ✕**Peking Duck House.** *Chinese.* This Chinatown institution is the place to go in New York for authentic Peking duck. Begin, as most tables do, with an order of Shanghai soup dumplings, then move onto the bird. It's carved up tableside with plenty of fanfare—crisp burnished skin separated from moist flesh. Roll up the duck, with hoisin and scallions, in tender steamed pancakes. **Family Matters:** For kids who can't understand why anyone would eat duck, there is a full Chinese menu here as well. If you're in Lower Manhattan, check out the Chinatown location on Mott Street. ⊠*236 E. 53rd St., between 2nd and 3rd Aves., Midtown East* Ⓜ *6 to 53rd St.–Lexington Ave.*

$$ ✕**Sosa Borella.** *Italian.* This is one of the theater district's top spots for reliable food at a reasonable cost. This bi-level, casual Italian eatery is an inviting and friendly space where diners choose from a wide range of options. The lunch menu features staples like warm sandwiches and

salads, while the dinner menu is slightly gussied up with meat, fish, and pasta dishes (the rich agnolotti with lamb Bolognese sauce, topped with a wedge of grilled pecorino cheese is a must-try). The warm bread served at the beginning of the meal with pesto dipping sauce is a nice touch as you wait for your meal. The service, at times, can be slow, so leave yourself plenty of time before the show. **Family Matters**: Pizzas and pastas here are perfect for younger theatergoers. ✉ *832 8th Ave., between 50th and 51st Sts., Midtown West* ☎*212/262–8282* ▭ *AE, MC, V* Ⓜ *C, E to 50th St.; 1 to 50th St.*

$$ ✕**Virgil's Real BBQ.** *Barbecue.* Neon, wood, and Formica set the scene at this massive roadhouse in the theater district. Start with the unbelievably succulent barbecued chicken wings. Go for the "Pig Out"—a rack of pork ribs, Texas hot links, pulled pork, rack of lamb, chicken, and, of course, more. It's that kind of place. This spot is absolutely mobbed pretheater, so if that's when you're going, arrive by 6 PM or you'll miss your curtain. **Family Matters**: The crayons and hot dogs called flatdogs are hits with kids. ✉ *152 W. 44th St., between 6th Ave. and Broadway, Midtown West* ☎*212/921–9494* ⌕*Reservations essential* ▭*AE, MC, V* Ⓜ*N, Q, R, S, W, 1, 2, 3, 7 to 42nd St./Times Sq.*

UPPER EAST SIDE

$ ✕ **Barking Dog.** *American.* Dog lovers love the Barking Dog. Not only is the decor an over-the-top celebration of all things canine, but the outdoor patio at the Midtown East location means that they can eat dinner with their pooches. Of course those pooches are treated royally, though service for humans can be a bit lax. **Family Matters**: Kids like to play treasure hunt, spotting all the doggy touches on the walls, and running around to pet the dogs. Be forewarned that the huge menu means the food can be inconsistent—stick to the reliable burgers and other comfort-food items. ✉ *1678 3rd Ave., at 94th St., Upper East Side* ☎*212/831–1800* ▭ *No credit cards* Ⓜ*6 to 96th St.*

★ ✕ **Le Pain Quotidien.** *Café.* This international Belgian chain **$** brings its homeland ingredients with it, treating New Yorkers to crusty organic breads, jams, chocolate, and other specialty products. You can grab a snack to go or stay and eat breakfast, lunch, or dinner at communal or private tables with waiter service. Come for soft-boiled eggs and croissants in the morning, a tartine (open-faced sandwich)

6

or salad at noon, and a Tuscan cheese-and-meat platter for a late afternoon snack. For a quick lunch or a refueling treat, this bakery-café can't be beat. **Family Matters:** Stroller-bound kids sit happily enjoying baguettes while older kids love the communal tables and their homemade lemonade and soups. Le Pain Quotidien also has several other branches around SoHo, the Flatiron District, and the Upper West Side. ✉ *252 E. 77th St., nr. 2nd Ave., Upper East Side* ☎ *212/249–8600* Ⓜ *6 to 77th St.*

¢ ✕ **Lexington Candy Shop.** *American.* Coming to NY without having an authentic egg cream or a thick malted should be a crime. And what better place to have one than, just blocks from the Metropolitan Museum, at this real old-fashioned diner where they make their own syrups. Just like its first customers in 1925, you can slide up to the counter, take a spin on a shiny aluminum bar stool, and place your order from the soda jerk. Though the diner still offers dishes popular during the depression, like grape-jelly omelets, there are also more-current omelets, BLTs, and even buffalo burgers. **Family Matters:** Just know that these aren't 1925 prices, or you may be a bit shocked when you get the bill. ✉ *1226 Lexington Ave., at 83rd St., Upper East Side* ☎ *212/288–0057* ⚠ *Reservations not accepted* ▭ *AE, MC, V* ⊗ *Mon.–Sat. 7 AM–7 PM, Sun. 9 AM–6 PM* Ⓜ *4, 5, 6 at 86th St.*

$$ ✕ **Sarabeth's.** *American.* Lining up for brunch here is a traditional Sunday afternoon event. Locals love the restaurant for sweet morning-time dishes like lemon ricotta pancakes, as well as for the comforting dinners. The afternoon tea includes buttery scones with Sarabeth's signature jams, savory nibbles, and outstanding baked goods. Dinner entrées include chicken potpie and truffle mac and cheese. **Family Matters:** Despite the crowds and long waits, kids and strollers abound with young ones enjoying porridge (Three Little Bears–style) and pumpkin waffles for breakfast and brunch, or very American burgers and pasta at other mealtimes. Keep an eye out for various other Sarabeth's on the Upper West Side and in Chelsea Market. ✉ *1295 Madison Ave., at 92nd St., Upper East Side* ☎ *212/410–7335* Ⓜ *6 to 96th St.*

$$ ✕ **Serafina.** *Pizza.* Mediterranean-hue friezes, a variety of indoor and outdoor rooms, and a steady stream of models and celebrities grace these very Italian cafés. Scene aside, the real draw here is some authentic Neapolitan pizza—

they even filter the water for the pizza dough to make it more closely resemble the water in Naples. Beyond the designer pizzas (Nutella, mascarpone, and robiola cheese; mozzarella, smoked salmon, and dill) are antipasti, salads, pastas including a number of ravioli dishes, and second courses like bass fillet pinot grigio. **Family Matters:** The individual pizzas are perfect for kids who will also enjoy the shareable Caesar salads, paillards, and pasta dishes. The Euro-vibe might be a bit too scene-y for the youngest guests, particularly at the shopper-heavy Madison Ave. location. (Other branches in the Upper East Side or Midtown can have slightly less traffic.) ✉ *1022 Madison Ave., at E. 79th St., Upper East Side* ☎ *212/734–2676* ▭ *AE, DC, MC, V* Ⓜ *6 to 77th St.*

$ ✕ **Two Boots.** *Pizza.* In NYC, pizza authenticity rules. Aficionados debate where to get that perfect crust, who uses coal-fired brick ovens, and who really is the "original" Ray. But Two Boots refreshingly shakes off that pretension, aiming instead for fun at their eight brightly colored locations. Named after the bootlike shapes of Italy and Louisiana, this pizzeria offers thin-crust pies with Cajun touches like andouille sausage, crayfish, tasso ham, and jalapeño along with more-traditional options. **Family Matters:** The Keith Haring–esque walls and casual vibe make it especially fun for kids. You'll find other branches in the East Village, Greenwich Village, the Lower East Side, Rockefeller Center, and Grand Central Station, so you're never that far from a slice. ✉ *1617 2nd Ave., Upper East Side* ☎ *212/734–0317* ⊕ *www.twoboots.com* Ⓜ *4, 5, 6 to 86th St.*

$ ✕ **Vynl.** *American.* Sometimes you just need a restaurant that knows how to have fun. At this kitschy pop-culture shrine, you'll find disco balls adorning the ceiling, menus made out of old record sleeves, creatively dressed Barbies mounting the wall, and best of all, each bathroom is a shrine to a different pop star, complete with piped-in music. Fortunately, in the midst of all that fun, the food is pretty decent, too. **Family Matters:** The menu is heavy with comfort food, but they've also got a whole selection of Thai specialties. Now if only you could tear your kids away from dancing to Dolly Parton in the little girl's room, and actually sit down to eat! There are other locations on the Upper West Side, Chelsea, and Hell's Kitchen. ✉ *1491 2nd Ave., at 78th St. Upper East Side* ☎ *212/249–6080* ⊕ *www.vynl-nyc.com* ▭ *AE, MC, V* Ⓜ *6 to 77th St.*

UPPER WEST SIDE

$ ✕ **Alice's Tea Cup.** *American.* Stumble down a rabbit hole and into Alice's Tea Cup for a fabulously feminine mid-afternoon break. Along with more than 100 different kinds of teas, fill up on dainty sandwiches, legendary scones, and crust-free sandwiches, all while you practice a proper pinky curl. A small shop sells loose teas and Alice-in-Wonderland-theme merchandise. **Family Matters:** They'll even loan you a pair of fairy wings and sprinkle you (or, more likely, your little one) with fairy dust to complete the transformation. The Upper East Side also has Alice locations. ✉ *102 W. 73rd St., Upper West Side* ☎ *212/799–3006* ⊕ *www.alicesteacup.com* ⚭ *Reservations not accepted* ▭ *AE, MC, V* ⊘ *8–8* Ⓜ *1, 2, 3, B, C to 72nd St.*

$ ✕ **Barney Greengrass.** *Deli.* At this New York Jewish landmark, brusque waiters send out stellar smoked salmon, sturgeon, and whitefish to a happy crowd packed to the gills at small Formica tables. Split a fish platter with bagels, cream cheese, and other fixings, or get your fish with scrambled eggs. If you're still hungry, go for a plate of cheese blintzes or the to-die-for chopped liver. Beware: the weekend brunch wait can exceed an hour. **Family Matters:** Finish your meal with an authentic black & white cookie, another "real New York" treat. ✉ *541 Amsterdam Ave., between W. 86th and W. 87th Sts., Upper West Side* ☎ *212/724–4707* ⊕ *www. barneygreengrass.com* ⚭ *Reservations not accepted* ▭ *No credit cards* ⊘ *Closed Mon. No dinner* Ⓜ *1 to 86th St.*

★ Fodor'sChoice ✕ **Gray's Papaya.** *Fast Food.* It's a stand-up, ¢ take-out dive. And, yes, limos do sometimes stop here for the legendary hot dogs. More often than not, though, it's neighbors or commuters who know how good the slim, traditional, juicy all-beef dogs are. Fresh-squeezed orange juice, a strangely tasty creamy banana drink, and the much-touted, healthful papaya juice are available along with more standard drinks. **Family Matters:** If your kids are adventurous, encourage them to be real New Yorkers and put some sauerkraut on their dogs. If you're in Midtown or Greenwich Village, you'll also find a local Gray's. ✉ *2090 Broadway, at 72nd St., Upper West Side* ☎ *212/799–0243* Ⓜ *1 to 72nd St.*

$ ✕ **Jackson Hole.** *American.* For those who love a huge juicy burger, Jackson Hole is place to come. Their baseball-size patties are steamed under a metal cup on the griddle, trapping in all that juice and flavor. You can order them plain,

Themed Dining

They're the restaurants that no childless New Yorker would be caught dead in, legendary for long lines, bad food, expensive prices, and gruff service. Parents' rewards here are limited to the huge smiles on their kids' faces. For those of you in the running for the parent-of-the-year award, here's a quick survival guide:

At the strangely B-movie-like **Mars 2112** (✉ *1633 Broadway, at 51st St., Midtown* ☎ *212/582–2112* ⊕ *www. mars2112.com*), a simulated space flight takes you to your table, surrounded by red, craterous walls. The food is nothing special, but your kids won't mind when they're chatting with a costumed alien. After all, who ever claimed that astronauts ate well? When all this gets to be too much, relax with a Mars-tini.

The American Girl phenomenon isn't as big as Barbie, but Barbie never had a dream house like the **American Girl Place** (at 49th Street (✉ *609 5th Ave, at 49th Str.,Midtown* ☎ *877/247–5223* ⊕ *www.amer icangirl.com* ⚷ *Reservations essential*). Along with a doll beauty salon and photo studio, there's a fancy café where your girl and her doll can sit side-by-side to eat like grownups. Be sure to keep your kids' expectations, and your wallet, in check, as no opportunity is missed to market new accessories. One other tip: the teatime menu is a few dollars cheaper and the food more reliable.

Both the food and the service at **Jekyll and Hyde** (✉ *91 7th Ave. S, Greenwich Village* ☎ *212/541–9505* ⊕ *www. jekyllpub.com*) (✉ *1409 6th Ave., Midtown* ☎ *212/541–9517* ⊕ *www.jekyllandhydeclub.com*) can be downright ghoulish. But kids old enough to enjoy the haunted-house atmosphere, and young enough not to find it cheesy (generally ages 5–12) will love it. Flickering lights, talking statues, and skeleton decor create the scene. Be aware that the food is expensive even for Manhattan ($16 for a hamburger without fries), and there's a $2.75 entertainment charge to boot.

Since 1954, **Serendipity 3** (✉ *225 E. 60th St., Upper East Side* ☎ *212/838–3531* ⊕ *www. serendipity3.com*) has found fans in celebs like the cast of *High School Musical 3*. Unfortunately, that popularity means the rest of us have to wait in gargantuan lines for their legendary Frozen Haute Chocolate, especially without reservations. Since the savory part of the menu is not worth the tired feet, put your name down on the list, slip around the corner for a light lunch, then return for desserts. —*Nina Callaway*

or with a number of different topping combinations—
the Texas burger, with a fried egg on top, is particularly
good. **Family Matters:** The service couldn't be friendlier,
and they're happy to host both large groups and small
children. Three more locations are on the Upper East
Side. ⊠ *517 Columbus Ave., at 85th St. Upper West Side*
☎ *212/362–5177* ⊕ *www.jacksonholeburgers.com* ⚘*Reservations not accepted* ⊟*AE, MC, V* Ⓜ*1, B, C to 86th St.*

$ ✕**Kefi.** *Greek.* Michael Psilakis's homage to his grand-
mother's Greek cooking is showcased at this wonderful
restaurant, now occupying a larger space and accepting
reservations. Among the mezes, the meatballs with roasted
garlic, olives, and tomato is a standout, and the flavorful
roast chicken, potatoes, red peppers, garlic, and thyme
makes for a winning entrée. Reasonable prices make it
easy to stick around for a piece of traditional walnut cake
with walnut ice cream. **Family Matters:** Family-style sharing is great for kids, and the noise level means that no one
will worry about crying or fussing kids. ⊠ *505 Columbus Ave., between 84th and 85th Sts., Upper West Side*
☎ *212/873–0200* ⊟*No credit cards* Ⓜ*1 to 79th St.*

¢ ✕**Ollie's Noodle Shop.** *Chinese.* This local chain offers Chinese fare in a no-frills setting. Fans rave about the Canton-
ese-style barbecued meats (duck, pork, chicken), steamed
dumplings and buns, and Mandarin noodle soups. The
portions are generous, but don't expect any culinary rev-
elations. If you order a noodle bowl, you can get out of
here for under $10. But if you want to splurge a little,
try the fried fillet of sea bass with spicy salt, spicy egg-
plant in garlic sauce, steamed little juicy buns, and BBQ
spare ribs. **Family Matters:** Staff will put a rubber band
around two chopsticks (with the paper cover rolled up in
between) and help your kids get in the groove fork-free
as they share your dishes. You'll find a few other Ollie's
around the Upper West Side, Midtown, and Morningside
Heights. ⊠ *1991 Broadway, at W. 67th St., Upper West
Side* ☎ *212/595–8181* ⚘*Reservations not accepted* ⊟*AE,
MC, V* Ⓜ*1 to 66th St./Lincoln Center*

★ ✕**Tavern on the Green.** *American.* As you might expect, given
$$$ the kitchen's near-impossible task of accommodating more
than 500 guests at once, food and service vary wildly here.
Nonetheless, people throng (by foot, by taxi, even by horse
and carriage) to this fantastical maze of dining rooms and
outdoor topiary patio in Central Park. In good weather

try for a spot in the lovely garden area under a canopy of lighted trees. Think of the place as an elaborately catered wedding party with beautiful lights strung outdoors and stick to simpler menu choices. **Family Matters:** This is a wonderful dress-up place for kids who will appreciate how glitzy and special the experience is. The extensive children's menu offers the likes of chicken fingers, pasta, chicken soup, hot dogs, French toast, and scrambled eggs. Wandering photographers will make your kids feel like celebrities, and the gorgeous setting will remind them of scenes from *Stuart Little.* ⊠*In Central Park at W. 67th St., Upper West Side* ☎*212/873–3200* ⊕*www.tavernon thegreen.com* ⌲*Reservations essential* ⊟*AE, D, DC, MC, V* Ⓜ*1 to 66th St.–Lincoln Center.*

HARLEM

★ **Fodor'sChoice** ✕**Dinosaur Bar-B-Que.** *Barbecue.* New York's
$ reputation for inferior barbecue improved instantly when John Stage opened the third outpost of his Syracuse-based joint in 2004, installing it in a riverside meatpacking ware-house in Harlem. Here, the city's friendliest waitstaff serves piled-high plates of pulled pork, ribs, chicken, brisket, and knockout wings. **Family Matters:** Reserve well in advance and in time to exit before the live music starts on weekend nights. The motorcycles parked in front will amuse kids, although the inappropriate graffiti in some of the restrooms won't amuse parents. The portions are huge, so stick to ordering side dishes for kids and let them eat off your plates. High chairs and booster seats are available. ⊠*646 W. 131st St., at 12th Ave., Harlem* ☎*212/694–1777* ⊕*www.dinosaur barbque.com* ⌲*Reservations not accepted* ⊟*AE, D, DC, MC, V* ⊗*Closed Mon.* Ⓜ*1 to 125th St.*

¢ ✕ **Joy Burger Bar.** *American.* With many new young residents movin' on up to Spanish Harlem, Tommy Tavakoli and Roy Ben Jacob knew there'd be a market for a fresh, hip place. Joy Burger Bar is their answer: Retro-style decor, a choice of three different sizes of juicy burgers, and a huge array of toppings, so you can be sure to have it your way. Here's what your way should be: Though the 8 -ounce. Maxi burger is overwhelmingly huge (kids may want to split this!), it is the juiciest and has the best outside sear. Since the flimsy bun is not up to the task of handling all those toppings, get the spicy mayo on the side, and use it as dip for your fries. Speaking of fries, a standard order here is something more like thick potato chips, which tend to be limp and less-than-crisp. So make sure to ask

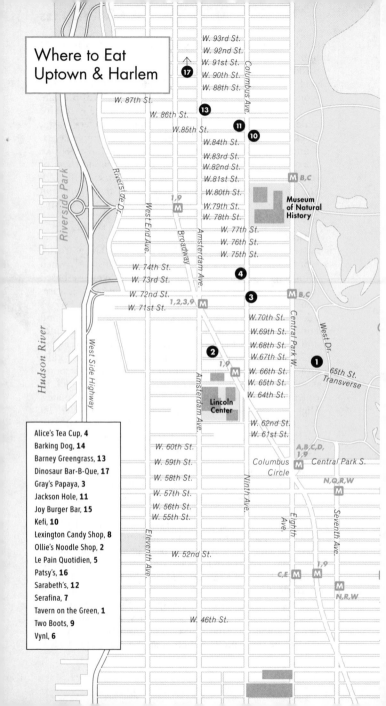

Where to Eat
Uptown & Harlem

Alice's Tea Cup, **4**
Barking Dog, **14**
Barney Greengrass, **13**
Dinosaur Bar-B-Que, **17**
Gray's Papaya, **3**
Jackson Hole, **11**
Joy Burger Bar, **15**
Kefi, **10**
Lexington Candy Shop, **8**
Ollie's Noodle Shop, **2**
Le Pain Quotidien, **5**
Patsy's, **16**
Sarabeth's, **12**
Serafina, **7**
Tavern on the Green, **1**
Two Boots, **9**
Vynl, **6**

for "classic-cut fries," which are well salted and delicious. **Family Matters**: You'll definitely want to wash it all down with mint lemonade or a thick milk shake you can share with your kids. Now that's fresh and hip. ✉ 1567 Lexington Ave., *at 100th St., Spanish Harlem* ☎212/289–6222 ▤ *AE, MC, V* Ⓜ6 *to 103rd St.*

$ ✕**Patsy's.** *Pizza.* The granddaddy of NY pizzerias, Patsy's first started turning out pies in East Harlem in 1932, and now has become a mini-chain serving old-fashioned pizza and family-style pastas all over the city. Pizza snobs should head only for the original location, a favorite of Sinatra's. The pies here are thin and crisp, yet doughy inside and they don't skimp on the cheese. The other franchised locations still serve a decent slice, with the exception of the two locations without coal ovens, and thus lacks that trademark NYC slightly charred, crispy crust. **Family Matters**: To balance out all that melted cheese, all locations make surprisingly great green salad, full of roasted peppers and artichokes, and served with homemade dressing, something most moms heartily approve. ✉ *2287 1st Ave., between 117th and 118th Sts., Harlem* ☎212/534–9783 ⊕ *www.patsyspizzeriany.com* ⊲ *Reservations recommended* ▤*No credit cards* Ⓜ *6 to 116th St.*

Where to Stay

WORD OF MOUTH

"If any of your occupants are children, different hotels have different policies. The policies can range from free to a per-person charge determined by age."

—Claire_bluesky

THE DREAM: A PLACE WITH fluffy duvets, hot chocolate from room service, and big beds the kids can jump on. The reality: in New York space is at a premium, high prices are dictated by high demand, and often rooms are sized small, smaller, smallest. While kids find it fun to watch the urban crowds and traffic from your room, noise can be a problem, especially for little ones who sleep early. And scoring rooms large enough for the whole family or even connecting rooms poses another challenge. Still there's nothing like staying in this energy-packed city and waking up like a true urban family to the swirling yellow cabs and NYC skyline right outside your door.

Before you consider squeezing in a cot or foldout couch for your child, ask just how large your hotel room is—there's a chance you can upgrade to a suite for little or no upcharge. Desirable family amenities like kitchenettes can be found, but they are the exception. Ask if your room has a minibar or small refrigerator if you need to store baby bottles and other necessities. Most hotels in New York allow children under a certain age to stay in their parents' room at no extra charge, but others charge for them as extra adults; be sure to find out the cutoff age for children's discounts and the number of people allowed per room.

Bear in mind that you'll pay prime prices depending where you stay. Many visitors to New York City cram themselves into hotels in the hectic Midtown area with its business-y "Master of the Universe" vibe. That's not always the best choice for parents. If you prefer parks over skyscrapers, neighborhoods like Murray Hill, the Upper West Side, or the Upper East Side are often just as convenient. (Another bonus: they're less touristy and more residential so you'll see a slice of day-to-day city living.)

Deals do exist so don't fret. But you'll have to do a little homework to find them, and flexibility with dates will help. Consider the month of your visit: the least expensive time to book rooms in the city is during January and February, so February school vacation could be a good option if you want to save money.

TOP HOTEL EXPERIENCES

Indulge your preteens' and teens' fascination with Gossip Girl by ordering Serena's grilled cheese sandwich at Gilt at the New York Palace Hotel.

Give them a rubber-ducky arranged by a bath butler at the Ritz-Carlton New York, Battery Park, followed by cookies, milk, and a teddy bear at bedtime.

Take your family to swim in the rooftop pool, watch cartoons in the elevators, and find the elusive Burger Joint at Le Parker Meridien.

Show off the results of your kids' etiquette lessons at the Waldorf=Astoria's afternoon tea while decorating cookies and listening to stories about tea's origins.

Treat your kids to a "mocktail" at the Fireside restaurant at Omni Berkshire Place after they've rummaged through the Omni Sensational Kids Package filled with toys and activities.

WHAT IT COSTS

¢	$	$$	$$$	$$$$
HOTELS				
Under $150	$150–$299	$300–$449	$450–$600	Over $600

Prices are for a standard double room, excluding 13.625% city and state taxes.

7

DOWNTOWN, CHELSEA & MURRAY HILL

$$ Duane Street Hotel. Amid TriBeCa's historic warehouses and trendy art galleries sits the Duane Street Hotel, a fashionable addition to the neighborhood. Comfortable rooms are painted in shades of soft lilac or green apple, and light pours in loftlike windows. Hardwood floors, flat-screen TVs, and fold-up desks give rooms a modern, playful feel. Sophisticated bathrooms have slate floors, showers with half-glass doors, and "We Live Like This" brand amenities. You can use complimentary passes to work out at a nearby Equinox fitness club. **Pros:** great location; in-room spa treatments available through Euphoria Spa TriBeCa; turndown service with Jacques Torres Chocolates. **Cons:** no DVD players in rooms. **Family Matters:** lots of families; four people fit in a double double; older teens can use health club; kids stay

free. ⊠ *130 Duane St., TriBeCa* ☎*212/964–4600* ⊕*www.*
duanestreethotel.com ⤹*45 rooms* ⌂*In-room: safe, Wi-Fi*
(no fee). In-hotel: restaurant, room service, bar, business
center, public Wi-Fi, no-smoking rooms ⊟ *AE, DC, MC,*
V Ⓜ*A, C, J, M, Z, 1, 2, 3 to Chambers St.*

$$ Embassy Suites Hotel New York. With an attractive downtown
location directly across from the World Trade Center site
on one side, and a waterfront park on the other, this flashy
Embassy Suites has a lot to offer. The hotel is part of a com-
plex with a six-screen movie theater and a 20,000-square-
foot health club. As the name suggests, every one of the
modern rooms here is at least a one-bedroom suite, with a
living area that includes a pull-out sofa, dining table, and
microwave oven. The hotel has an attractive lobby, with
a 14-story center atrium with a colorful mural running
down its entire length. You'll have a relatively long walk
to the subway, but a complimentary breakfast bonanza
will make up for it. **Pros:** good for families; movie theater
downstairs. **Cons:** long walk to subway; far from midtown
tourist sights. **Family Matters:** suites can fit a family of
six; cribs; short walk to riverside esplanade, playground;
reasonably priced dining; kids under 18 stay free; near
Statue of Liberty and Ellis Island ferries. ⊠*102 North End*
Ave., at Murray St., Lower Manhattan ☎*212/945–0100*
or 800/362–2779 ⊕*www.newyorkcity.embassysuites.com*
⤹*463 suites* ⌂*In-room: safe, refrigerator, Wi-Fi. In-hotel:*
restaurant, room service, bar, concierge, laundry service,
public Internet, public Wi-Fi, parking (fee), no-smoking
rooms ⊟*AE, D, DC, MC, V* Ⓜ *R, W to Cortlandt St.; A,*
C, E to Chambers St.

$$ Holiday Inn SoHo. Guests here are the hippest you'll find at
any Holiday Inn and the rates are the cheapest in SoHo.
Historical features in this former bank building include
oversize windows and high ceilings. Rooms are standard-
issue, but clean and well maintained, with in-room cof-
feemakers and CD players. Bustling Canal Street is on the
corner for bargain shopping. **Pros:** cheap SoHo solution,
well-trained staff. **Cons:** nothing stylish; standard-issue
rooms. **Family Matters:** quieter in evening; busy location
by day; kids menu; cribs and rollaway beds in some rooms;
connecting double rooms; kids under 17 stay free. ⊠*138*
Lafayette St., near Canal St., Little Italy ☎*212/966–8898*
or 800/465–4329 ⊕*www.ichotelsgroup.com* ⤹*215 rooms,*
12 suites ⌂*In-room: safe, Wi-Fi. In-hotel: restaurant, room*
service, bar, gym, laundry service, concierge, public Inter-

net, public Wi-Fi, parking (fee), no-smoking rooms ☐*AE, D, DC, MC, V* Ⓜ*6, M, N, Q, R, W to Canal St.*

$$ **Hotel on Rivington.** The rooms here have something completely original and breathtaking—when you hit a button on a remote control, your curtains slowly open to reveal floor-to-ceiling glass windows. Seen that trick before? Well, this is the only tall building around, and the views of the Lower East Side and Midtown are unadulterated New York. The bathrooms don't shy away from the scene either, and privacy curtains can be requested. The mezzanine bar–art library–billiard room is a hangout you can call your own. **Pros:** superhip location and vibe; huge windows with wonderful New York views; happening bar and restaurant. **Cons:** feels like a club on weekends; noisy; small rooms and suites. **Family Matters:** high trendiness factor and pulsing bar scene not a family attraction; restaurant can make kid dishes; family suite with two full bedrooms, two full baths, bunk beds and toy bins; across from Economy Candy; kids stay free. ☒*107 Rivington St., between Ludlow and Essex Sts., Lower East Side* ☎*212/475–2600 or 800/915–1537* ⊕*www.hotelonrivington.com* ⬅*110 rooms* ⬙*In-room: safe, refrigerator, Ethernet, Wi-Fi. In-hotel: restaurant, room service, bar, laundry service, concierge, parking (fee), some pets allowed* ☐*AE, D, DC, MC, V* Ⓜ *F, J, M, Z to Delancey/Essex Sts.*

★ **Inn on 23rd.** Charming and friendly innkeepers Annette
$$ and Barry Fisherman will welcome you to this five-floor, 19th-century building in the heart of Chelsea. They took care to make each guest rooms spacious and unique. One exotic and elegant room is outfitted in bamboo, another in the art moderne style of the 1940s. Although it's small and homey, the inn provides private baths and satellite TV in all rooms. Dorothy, the house cat, is very friendly, and has an endearing quirk: she loves to ride the elevator. A big Continental breakfast is cooked daily by famous-chefs-to-be: members of the New School's culinary program, who use the kitchen in the mornings as a laboratory. If you're a B&B person, you've found your New York retreat. **Pros:** charming innkeepers; comfy and relaxed library; affordable for location. **Cons:** few services for businesspeople; some older amenities; beware if you have cat allergies. **Family Matters:** cribs in king and queen rooms only; homelike environment; kids under 18 stay free. ☒*131 W. 23rd St., between 6th and 7th Aves., Chelsea* ☎*212/463–0330* ⊕*www.innon23rd.com* ⬅*13 rooms, 1 suite* ⬙*In-room:*

Where to Stay Downtown, Chelsea & Murray Hill

Duane Street Hotel, **3**
Embassy Suites, **2**
Holiday Inn SoHo, **5**
Hotel on Rivington, **6**
Inn on 23rd, **8**
Ritz-Carlton Battery Park, **1**
Roger Willams Hotel, **9**
TriBeCa Grand, **4**
Washington Square Hotel, **7**

0   1/4 mile
0   400 meters

Bryant Park
E. 40th St.
E. 38th St.
E. 36th St.
E. 34th St.
W. 34th St.
Madison Ave.
Park Ave.
Lexington Ave.
9th Ave.
8th Ave.
7th Ave.
Broadway
Ave. of the Americas
5th Ave.
W. 31st St.
E. 31st St.
E. 29th St.
E. 27th St.
Madison Sq.
W. 23rd St.
E. 23rd St.
W. 20th St.
W. 18th St.
E. 21st St.
E. 19th St.
Gramercy Park
W. 16th St.
W. 15th St.
Union Sq.
Irving Pl.
Stuyvesant Sq.
2nd Ave.
W. 14th St.
E. 14th St.
E. 13th St.
Abingdon Sq.
E. 12th St.
E. 11th St.
Ave. A
Ave. B
Ave. C
Ave. D
Hudson St.
Greenwich St.
Christopher St.
Varick St.
W. Houston St.
E. 9th St.
E. 8th St.
Waverly Pl.
Washington Sq.
E. 7th St.
E. 5th St.
E. 3rd St.
1st Ave.
MacDougal St.
Broadway
E. Houston St.
West Side Highway
Prince St.
Spring St.
Church St.
W. Broadway
Wooster
Greene
Mercer
Lafayette St.
Bowery
Chrystie St.
Allen St.
Essex St.
Rivington St.
Delancey St.
Grand St.
Broome St.
Canal St.
Holland Tunnel
West St.
Walker St.
White St.
Worth St.
Duane St.
Reade St.
Chambers St.
Manhattan Bridge
FDR Drive
Brooklyn Bridge
Vesey St.
Liberty St.
Fulton St.
Pearl St.
South St.
Wall St.
Hudson River
East River
Battery Park
Brooklyn-Battery Tunnel

DVD (some), Ethernet, Wi-Fi. In-hotel: laundry service, public Internet, public Wi-Fi, no-smoking rooms ⊟AE, D, DC, MC, V ⊚CP Ⓜ F, V to 23rd St.

★ Fodor'sChoice **Ritz-Carlton New York, Battery Park.** If you're stay-
$$ ing downtown, this is your top luxury choice. The hotel provides the expected personalized service—you'll be greeted by at least one staffer each time you walk into the hotel or enter the lobby from your room—and big rooms with sweeping views of the Statue of Liberty and Ellis Island. West-facing rooms all come with telescopes. The hotel is an oasis of fine living; the luxurious, large rooms and suites with plush fabrics and furnishings seem more like expensive living rooms than hotel rooms. The superlative staff includes a bath butler who can fill your deep soaking tub with anything from rose petals to rubber duckies. There's steak-house fare at 2 West. **Pros:** NYC's only waterfront luxury hotel; best base for downtown exploring; pet- and kid-friendly; Statue of Liberty views. **Cons:** removed from Midtown tourist sights; limited nighttime activities and few neighborhood options for dining and entertainment.**Family Matters**: quiet at night; long walk from subway; board games and movies; teddy bear turndown with cookies and milk; kids in harborview 14th-floor Rise Bar until 6 PM; pullout sofas; rollaways; some rooms with Nintendo; kids' room-service menu; kids under 12 stay free. ⊠*2 West St., at Battery Park, Lower Manhattan* ☎*212/344–0800 or 800/241–3333* ⊕*www.ritzcarlton.com* ⤷*254 rooms, 44 suites* ⌂*In-room: refrigerator (some), DVD (some), Ethernet, Wi-Fi. In-hotel: 2 restaurants, room service, bars, laundry service, concierge, executive floor, public Internet, public Wi-Fi, parking (fee), some pets allowed, no-smoking rooms* ⊟*AE, D, DC, MC, V* Ⓜ *1, R, W to Rector St.*

$$ **Roger Williams Hotel.** Vibrant colors, bold architecture, and an informal, residential vibe are keystones of this Murray Hill neighborhood hotel. The hotel lobby's "living room" features 20-foot-high windows and a comfortable seating area stocked with newspapers. Rooms are comfortably appointed with playfully colored down comforters, robes, and Aveda bath products, as well as candles, books, and flat-screen plasma TVs. The $14 breakfast buffet features local delicacies like croissants from Balthazar, smoked salmon from Petrossian, and bagels from H&H. It's served in the comfortable "breakfast pantry." Fifteen rooms have private, landscaped terraces facing Midtown. **Pros:** colorful room decor, easygoing vibe; good value. **Cons:** no

room service. **Family Matters:** quiet neighborhood; mostly business people; kids lounge menu; cribs; rollaways; maximum of four per room; charge for fourth person. ⊠*131 Madison Ave., at E. 31st St., Murray Hill* ☎*212/448–7000 or 877/847–4444* ⊕*www.rogerwilliamshotel.com* ⚟*193 rooms, 2 suites* ⏅*In-room: Wi-Fi. In-hotel: restaurant, room service, bar, gym, concierge, parking (fee), public Internet, public Wi-Fi, no-smoking rooms* ⊟*AE, D, MC, V* ⦿*CP* Ⓜ*6 to 33rd St.*

$$$ TriBeCa Grand. A fabulous, suburban-style eight-story atrium in the middle of one of New York's hippest hotels? It's all part of the wild fun. Movie- and music-industry celebs hang out at the Church Lounge—a bar, café, and dining room at the base of the atrium—well into the night, sometimes to the dismay of serenity-seeking guests (a white noise filter in rooms helps keep the peace). It's a great place to meet friends and have meetings without straying too far from the twin glass elevators that whisk you up and away. Comfortable and stylish rooms with a retro nod have low platform beds, large work spaces, and podlike bathrooms with aluminum consoles reminiscent of those in airplanes. **Pros:** great dining; celeb sightings; fun social atrium; pet-friendly (you can even request goldfish brought to your room). **Cons:** rooms get noise from restaurant below; bathroom has slightly cold design. **Family Matters:** kids' travel aids including pacifiers, baby bathrobes and baby bath; kids 3–12 welcome package and a kids' NYC guide; noisy bar scene and no pullout beds are minuses; two-bedroom suites can fit crib; kids stay free. ⊠*2 Ave. of the Americas (6th Ave.), between Walker and White Sts., TriBeCa* ☎*212/519–6600 or 800/965–3000* ⊕*www.tribecagrand. com* ⚟*197 rooms, 6 suites* ⏅*In-room: safe, refrigerator, Wi-Fi. In-hotel: restaurant, room service, bar, gym, laundry service, concierge, parking (fee), public Wi-Fi, public Internet, some pets allowed, no-smoking rooms* ⊟*AE, D, DC, MC, V* Ⓜ*A, C, E to Canal St.*

$ Washington Square Hotel. Across from Washington Square Park's magnificent arch and right in the heart of New York University and Greenwich Village, this low-key European-style hotel is convenient for parents visiting NYU and close to just about everything else downtown, since it's one block from the very central West 4th Street subway station. Rooms are small but cheerfully decorated—deluxe rooms in a Hollywood art deco style and standard rooms in pastel florals. Deluxe rooms come with pillowtop mattresses and complimentary high-speed Internet access. The North Square restaurant has a jazz brunch and offers surprisingly sophisticated fare. **Pros:** park-front location; smoke-free hotel; convenient to nearly every subway. **Cons:** NYU students everywhere; small rooms. **Family Matters:** on-the-park location; Super Quad or Deluxe Quad rooms for two double beds; rollaways; cribs; no connecting doubles; Continental breakfast included; kids stay free in same room. ⊠ *103 Waverly Pl., at MacDougal St., Greenwich Village* ☎ *212/777–9515 or 800/222–0418* ⊕ *www.washington-squarehotel.com* ⌖ *160 rooms* ⌂ *In-room: safe, dial-up. In-hotel: restaurant, bar, gym, Wi-Fi* ⊟ *AE, MC, V* ⏆ *CP* ⓜ *A, B, C, D, E, F, V to W. 4th St./Washington Sq.*

MIDTOWN

★ **Affinia 50.** This extremely popular hotel has a distinctly
$$ businesslike mood, but it's also supremely comfortable for families or other leisure travelers. Most studios and all suites come with full kitchens and a clean, modern design with oversize chairs and couches, and plenty of space to stretch out. The second-floor club lounge has board games for guest use. There's no restaurant in the hotel, but a restaurant next door provides room service and there's unlimited complimentary fruit and iced tea at reception. All rooms have a mini-refrigerator and microwave, and suites have countertop stoves. **Pros:** apartment-style living; good value; kid and pet friendly. **Cons:** outdated lobby décor; unattractive room color scheme. **Family Matters:** many families; spacious rooms; junior suites can fit up to 6; children 18 and under can use gym with parent; creative family packages; books and board games; kids stay free. ⊠ *155 E. 50th St., at 3rd Ave., Midtown East* ☎ *212/751–5710 or 800/637–8483* ⊕ *www.affinia.com* ⌖ *56 rooms, 151 suites* ⌂ *In-room: safe, kitchen (some), refrigerator, Ethernet. In-hotel: room service, gym, laundry facilities, laundry service, concierge, public Internet, public Wi-Fi, parking (fee), some pets allowed, no-smoking rooms* ⊟ *AE, D, DC, MC, V* ⓜ *6 to 51st St./Lexington Ave.; E, V to Lexington–3rd Aves./53rd St.*

$$$ **The Alex.** The goal of the David Rockwell–designed Alex is to create a soothing environment for travelers, enhanced by impeccable service. What remains is a clean, calm space where you can truly appreciate details such as kitchenettes and flat-screen bathroom TVs. Comfortable beds feature Frette linens. Award-winning chef Marcus Samuelsson runs

Asian-influenced Riingo restaurant, which also provides room service. **Pros:** most rooms have kitchens; good service; on-site fitness facilities. **Cons:** cramped lobby; small bathrooms; no in-room Wi-Fi. **Family Matters:** connecting rooms; two-bedroom suites; staff knowledgeable about kid activities; near United Nations; kids under 12 stay free. ✉ *205 E. 45th St., between 2nd and 3rd Aves., Midtown East* ☎ *212/867–5100* ⊕ *www.thealexhotel.com* ✍ *73 rooms, 130 suites* ⚭ *In-room: kitchen (some), refrigerator (some), DVD, Ethernet. In-hotel: restaurant, room service, bar, gym, laundry service, public Internet, public Wi-Fi, parking, some pets allowed, no-smoking rooms, concierge* ⊟ *AE, MC, V* Ⓜ *4, 5, 6, 7, S to 42nd St./Grand Central.*

$ Casablanca Hotel. When entering the hushed Casablanca, it's hard to believe you're a stone's throw from all the Times Square hoopla. Evocative of a locale straight out of its namesake film with Humphrey Bogart, the sultry Mediterranean feel permeates throughout the hotel, with mirrors and mosaic in public spaces to the room's ceiling fans, wooden blinds and dainty little bistro tables. Huge tiled bathrooms, many with windows, feature Baronessa Cali amenities. On the second floor, classical music plays while guests linger in the spacious librarylike Rick's Café for the complimentary breakfast buffet. **Pros:** great access to the theater district; all rooms are smoke-free. **Cons:** exercise facilities at nearby New York Sports Club, not on premises; heavy tourist foot traffic. **Family Matters:** double can fit crib; no rollaways; near Theater District and 42nd Street attractions; 24-hour café; DVD library; lots of teens; kids stay free. ✉ *147 W. 43rd St., Midtown West* ☎ *212/869–1212* ⊕ *www.casablancahotel.com* ✍ *48 rooms* ⚭ *In-room: safe, DVD player, Wi-Fi (no fee). In-hotel: restaurant, room service, bar, laundry, concierge, public Wi-Fi, no-smoking rooms* ⊟ *AE, MC, V* Ⓜ *1, 2, 3, 7, N, Q, R, S, W to Times Sq.–42nd St.*

$$$$ Four Seasons Hotel. Want to see what ascending to modernist heaven is like? Just walk up the towering lobby steps from 57th Street—past the rigid refinement of austere limestone, the legion of polished blond wood. The much-revered Four Seasons service, at this hotel the epitome of professionalism, begins here. Indeed, everything at this hotel comes in biblical proportions—including rooms starting at 600 square feet, and a cost of $915 in high season. They all have 10-foot-high ceilings, silk-covered walls, large plasma TVs, English sycamore walk-in closets, and blond-marble bathrooms with tubs that fill in 60 seconds. **Pros:** spacious and comfortable rooms; perfect concierge and staff service; afternoon tea in the lobby lounge. **Cons:** rooms are spare, unexciting. **Family Matters:** suites; a few connecting doubles; Beanie Babies' Ty Warner lounge for breakfast and afternoon tea; kids robes; baby toiletries and equipment; babysitting available; kids restaurant menu; "teen concierge" during school vacations; toys, videos, DVDs; kids stay free. ⊠ *57 E. 57th St., between Park and Madison Aves., Midtown East* ☎ *212/758–5700 or 800/487–3769* ⊕ *www.fourseasons.com* ⇨ *300 rooms, 68 suites* ♿ *In-room: safe, DVD, Ethernet, Wi-Fi. In-hotel: restaurant, room service, bar, gym, spa, laundry service, concierge, parking (fee), public Internet, public Wi-Fi, some pets allowed, no-smoking rooms* ☰ *AE, D, DC, MC, V* Ⓜ *4, 5, 6, N, Q, R, W to 59th St./Lexington Ave.*

$$$ Hilton Times Square. The Hilton Times Square sits atop a 335,000-square-foot retail and entertainment complex that includes a 25-theater movie megaplex and Madame Tussauds Wax Museum, on bustling and renewed 42nd Street. The building has a handsome Mondrian-inspired facade, but room decor is chain-hotel bland. Nonetheless, the rooms are comfortable and larger than at many chains, with amenities such as in-room coffeemakers and bathrobes. The hotel is efficiently run and the staff is pleasant. Because all guest rooms are above the 21st floor, many afford excellent views of Times Square and Midtown. Restaurant Above is off the "sky lobby" on the 21st floor. **Pros:** lovely views from restaurant; immediate access to entertainment; convenient to public transportation. **Cons:** impersonal feel; many annoying small charges; overpriced food and drink. **Family Matters:** high chairs; kids' DVDs; spacious rooms; pullout beds; cribs; kids menus; many families; kids under 18 stay free. ⊠ *234 W. 42nd St., between 7th and 8th Aves., Midtown West* ☎ *212/642–2500 or 800/445–8667* ⊕ *www.hilton.com* ⇨ *444 rooms, 15 suites* ♿ *In-room: safe, refrigerator, Wi-Fi, Ethernet. In-hotel: restaurant, room service, bar, gym, laundry service, concierge, parking (fee), some pets allowed, no-smoking rooms* ☰ *AE, D, DC, MC, V* Ⓜ *1, 2, 3, 7, S, N, Q, R, W to 42nd St./Times Sq.*

$$$$ The Iroquois. Built in 1923, this once-prosaic hotel is now among the neighborhood's better properties, and significantly more modern than its traditional exterior would lead you to suspect. Service is friendly and top-notch, and rooms are a quiet retreat from the frenetic neighborhood.

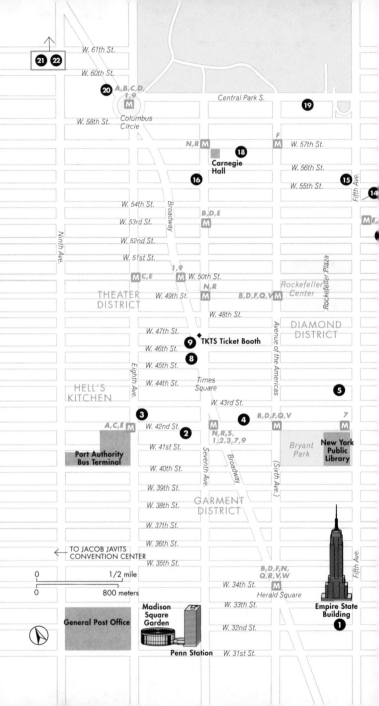

21 **22**

W. 61st St.

W. 60th St.

20 A,B,C,D, 1,9

Central Park S.

19

W. 58th St.

Columbus Circle

N,R **M** **18**

W. 57th St.

Carnegie Hall

16

W. 56th St.

W. 55th St.

15

Fifth Ave.

14

M E,

W. 54th St.

W. 53rd St.

B,D,E

W. 52nd St.

W. 51st St.

Broadway

M C,E

1,9 **M** W. 50th St.

THEATER DISTRICT

W. 49th St.

N,R **M**

B,D,F,Q,V **M**

Rockefeller Center

Rockefeller Plaza

W. 48th St.

DIAMOND DISTRICT

W. 47th St.

9 ◆ TKTS Ticket Booth

Avenue of the Americas

W. 46th St.

8

W. 45th St.

HELL'S KITCHEN

Eighth Ave.

W. 44th St.

Times Square

W. 43rd St.

5

3 **M**

W. 42nd St.

2

4

B,D,F,Q,V **M**

7

M

A,C,E

W. 41st St.

N,R,5, 1,2,3,7,9

Bryant Park

(Sixth Ave.)

New York Public Library

Port Authority Bus Terminal

W. 40th St.

W. 39th St.

Seventh Ave.

Broadway

W. 38th St.

GARMENT DISTRICT

W. 37th St.

W. 36th St.

← TO JACOB JAVITS CONVENTION CENTER

W. 35th St.

0   1/2 mile

0   800 meters

B,D,F,N, Q,R,V,W **M**

W. 34th St.

Herald Square

Empire State Building

Fifth Ave.

W. 33rd St.

General Post Office

Madison Square Garden

W. 32nd St.

1

Penn Station   W. 31st St.

Ninth Ave.

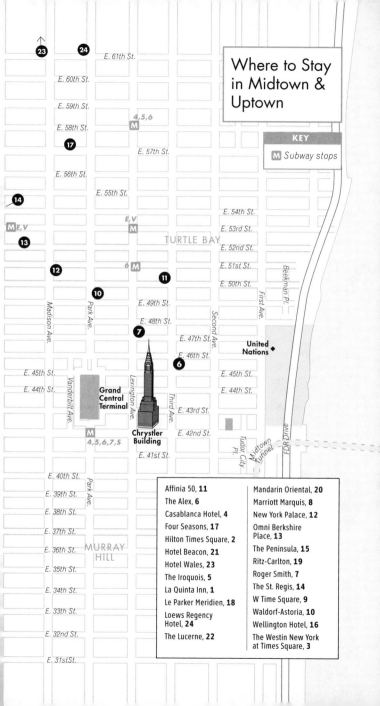

Where to Stay in Midtown & Uptown

TURTLE BAY

MURRAY HILL

Grand Central Terminal

Chrysler Building

United Nations

E. 61st St.
E. 60th St.
E. 59th St.
E. 58th St.
E. 57th St.
E. 56th St.
E. 55th St.
E. 54th St.
E. 53rd St.
E. 52nd St.
E. 51st St.
E. 50th St.
E. 49th St.
E. 48th St.
E. 47th St.
E. 46th St.
E. 45th St.
E. 44th St.
E. 43rd St.
E. 42nd St.
E. 41st St.
E. 40th St.
E. 39th St.
E. 38th St.
E. 37th St.
E. 36th St.
E. 35th St.
E. 34th St.
E. 33rd St.
E. 32nd St.
E. 31st St.

Madison Ave.
Park Ave.
Vanderbilt Ave.
Lexington Ave.
Third Ave.
Second Ave.
First Ave.
Beekman Pl.
Tudor City Pl.
Midtown Tunnel
FDR Drive

Affinia 50, **11**	Mandarin Oriental, **20**
The Alex, **6**	Marriott Marquis, **8**
Casablanca Hotel, **4**	New York Palace, **12**
Four Seasons, **17**	Omni Berkshire Place, **13**
Hilton Times Square, **2**	The Peninsula, **15**
Hotel Beacon, **21**	Ritz-Carlton, **19**
Hotel Wales, **23**	Roger Smith, **7**
The Iroquois, **5**	The St. Regis, **14**
La Quinta Inn, **1**	W Time Square, **9**
Le Parker Meridien, **18**	Waldorf-Astoria, **10**
Loews Regency Hotel, **24**	Wellington Hotel, **16**
The Lucerne, **22**	The Westin New York at Times Square, **3**

Children can enjoy in-room Nintendo systems, pint-size Frette bathrobes, and other specialized services. The large, restful chocolate-color standard rooms have ultracomfortable beds, and the marble-and-brass bathrooms contain phones and pedestal sinks. Off the tiny lobby are a homey reading area and the intimate Triomphe restaurant. Suites are significantly brighter than their basic counterparts. **Pros:** 24-hour gym; free wireless; turndown service. **Cons:** dark rooms. **Family Matters:** welcome gifts for kids; coloring books; cookies; list of kids' activities; babysitting; mini-bath bubbles and soaps; rooms sleep four; no pullout beds; 2 adults and 1 kids under 12 allowed per room. ⊠*49 W. 44th St., between 5th and 6th Aves., Midtown West* ☎*212/840–3080 or 800/332–7220* ⊕*www.iroquoisny. com* ⇆*105 rooms, 9 suites* ♿*In-room: safe, DVD, Wi-Fi. In-hotel: restaurant, room service, bar, gym, laundry service, concierge, public Internet, public Wi-Fi, parking (fee), no-smoking rooms* ⊟*AE, D, DC, MC, V* Ⓜ *B, D, F, V to 42nd St.; 7 to 5th Ave.*

¢ **La Quinta Inn.** Smack in the middle of Koreatown and close to Penn Station, this friendly hotel in a beautiful old beaux arts building may be one of the best deals in town. Never mind the drab decor when your room features treats like free Wi-Fi, an iPod plug-in, and a bathtub. In the mornings, the free Continental breakfast goes beyond the usual fare with granola and oatmeal. **Pros:** self check-in machines; gift shop on the premises for necessities. **Cons:** no room service; no frills. **Family Matters:** not kid-oriented; no cribs or cots; Nintendo games; kids under 15 stay free. ⊠*17 W. 32nd St., Midtown West* ☎*212/736–1600* ⊕*www.lq.com* ⇆*182* ♿*In-room: safe, Wi-Fi (no fee). In-hotel: bar, gym, laundry, public Wi-Fi, parking (fee), no-smoking rooms* ⊟*AE, D, DC, MC, V* Ⓜ *B, D, F, N, Q, R, V, W to 34th St.–Herald Sq.*

★ Fodor'sChoice **Le Parker Meridien.** No hotel in New York is as
$$$ lighthearted as the Parker. Despite the Meridien marketing affiliation, this is the largest privately owned hotel in the city, which means the hotel freely uses a refreshingly wry approach, and takes chances: Tom & Jerry cartoons in the elevators, a $1,000 omelet on the breakfast menu, and door privacy signs that read FUHGETTABOUDIT. Simultaneously it's sleek. The lobby's striking atrium combines cherry paneling, hand-painted columns, and contemporary art. Crisp, modern rooms include low platform beds, super-cool rotating ceiling-to-floor entertainment units,

and Central Park or skyline views (ask for the Park rooms). Gravity, a 15,000-square-foot health club with a glass-enclosed rooftop pool and spa services, is, by far, the best hotel gym facility in New York. Norma's serves the morning meal from 6:30 AM to 3 PM, with a famous brunch. The wonderful, discreetly hidden Burger Joint has—if you haven't heard—possibly the best burger in the city. **Pros:** lively, animated spirit; best hotel gym in the city; fun eating options; tech-friendly rooms. **Cons:** lobby is a public space; building heat sometimes does not come on in fall months. **Family Matters:** strollers on request; lots of families; kid-friendly restaurants; near theaters and Carnegie Hall; coloring books; cartoons and movies in elevators; kids stay free. ✉*118 W. 57th St., between 6th and 7th Aves., Midtown West* ☎*212/245–5000 or 800/543–4300* ⊕*www.parkermeridien.com* ⮑*484 rooms, 249 suites* ⌂*In-room: safe, refrigerator, DVD, VCR, Ethernet. In-hotel: 3 restaurants, room service, bar, pool, gym, spa, concierge, laundry service, parking (fee), no-smoking rooms* ▭*AE, D, DC, MC, V* Ⓜ*B, D, E, N, Q, R, W to 57th St.*

$$$$ Marriott Marquis. With its own little city of restaurants, a sushi bar, shops, meeting rooms, and ballrooms—there's even a Broadway theater—this brash behemoth in the heart of the theater district virtually defines over-the-top. Of course, as at other Marriotts, all of the nearly 2,000 rooms here look alike, with New York–scene artwork, plasma screens with HDTV in all rooms; they're pleasant and functional. But you won't find another hotel with a fun circle of 16 glass elevators shooting you to your room. Some have more dramatic urban views than others. The View, the only revolving restaurant in NYC, is on the 47th floor. **Pros:** fantastic and fun elevators rides; NYC's only revolving restaurant; good package deals. **Cons:** noisy and crowded in public spaces; massive scale may seem unwelcoming. **Family Matters:** confusing elevator operation; very busy; children's check-in packet; American Girl doll packages; concierges knowledgeable about kids' activities; by theaters and 42nd Street attractions; kids under 13 stay free. ✉*1535 Broadway, at W. 45th St., Midtown West* ☎*212/398–1900 or 800/843–4898* ⊕*www.marriott.com* ⮑*1,891 rooms, 58 suites* ⌂*In-room: safe, Ethernet. In-hotel: 3 restaurants, room service, bars, gym, laundry service, concierge, parking (fee), public Internet, public Wi-Fi, no-smoking rooms* ▭*AE, D, DC, MC, V* Ⓜ*1, 2, 3, 7, S, N, Q, R, W to 42nd St./Times Sq.*

$$$ **New York Palace Hotel.** Connected mansions built in the 1880s create the base of this palatial hotel. The lobby, with its sweeping staircases, golden chandeliers, and arched colonnades fit for royalty, is host to the acclaimed New American restaurant Gilt. Standard rooms in the main section of the hotel are traditional in style and quite large, but a bit worn around the edges. Better options are rooms in the tower. These are either modern or classic, depending on the floor, and have more luxe decor and bathrooms, separate check-in, and more attentive service. Many hotel rooms, as well as the 7,000-square-foot health club, have terrific views of St. Patrick's Cathedral. **Pros:** gorgeous courtyard with 15th Italian-style motifs; great service; unmatched views of St. Patrick's Cathedral. **Cons:** expensive restaurant and room service; inconsistent room cleanliness. **Family Matters:** recognizable as Serena's home in *Gossip Girl*; Serena's grilled cheese sandwich offered at Gilt; kids restaurant menu; near Fifth Avenue and Madison Avenue shopping; babysitting; "American Girl" package with doll bed; kids under 11 stay free. ⊠*455 Madison Ave., at E. 50th St., Midtown East* ☎*212/888–7000 or 800/697–2522* ⊕*www.newyorkpalace. com* ⇌*804 rooms, 88 suites* ⌂*In-room: safe, refrigerator (some), dial-up. In-hotel: 2 restaurants, room service, bars, gym, spa, laundry service, concierge, public Internet, public Wi-Fi, parking (fee), some pets allowed, no-smoking rooms* ▭*AE, D, DC, MC, V* Ⓜ *6 to 51st St./Lexington Ave.; E, V to Lexington–3rd Aves./53rd St.*

★ **Fodor'sChoice** **Omni Berkshire Place.** Omni Berkshire's East
$$$ Coast flagship hotel brings sophistication to the Omni name. Old-world maps hang in the reception area, which leads to a dramatic, two-story atrium lounge with a fireplace, an elaborately stained dark-wood floor, and a piano. The spacious guest rooms have a contemporary simplicity as well as plush bedding, tasteful furnishings, spacious bathrooms, and Web TV. The hotel offers an Ideal Living program that supplies guests with healthy meals and private workout programs. Kids receive their own welcome bag of treats. **Pros:** in the heart of a see-it-all New York location; one of city's most kid-friendly hotels. **Cons:** bland luxury decor. **Family Matters:** "Omni Sensational" kids receive jacks, kazoo, kaleidoscope, bracelet; omnikidsrule.com Web site; "suitcase of fun" with books and games; video games in most rooms; fun Fireside restaurant; special cup for free drink refills; kids' menu with "mocktails"; kids stay free. ⊠*21 E. 52nd St., between 5th and Madison Aves.,*

Midtown East ☎212/753–5800 *or* 800/843–6664 ⊕*www. omnihotels.com* ⌖*352 rooms, 44 suites* ⌂*In-room: safe, Ethernet, Wi-Fi. In-hotel: restaurant, room service, bar, gym, laundry facilities, concierge, laundry service, parking (fee), public Internet, public Wi-Fi, some pets allowed, no-smoking rooms* ☰*AE, D, DC, MC, V* Ⓜ*E, V to 5th Ave.*

$$$$ **The Peninsula.** Everything is completely stunning about this beautiful hotel with its beaux arts facade, grand staircase overhung with a monumental chandelier, and world-class service. Rooms have the latest touches in luxury comfort. The views are stunning: see the northward sweep up 5th Avenue to Central Park past church steeples; or look east toward the beautiful St. Regis across the street. The high-tech amenities are excellent, from a bedside console that controls the lighting, sound, and thermostat for the room to a TV mounted over the tub for bath-time viewing (in all but standard rooms). The rooftop health club, with indoor pool, is monumental. **Pros:** brilliant service; fabulous rooms; unforgettable rooftop bar. **Cons:** expensive. **Family Matters:** buzzy bar scene; bar line in lobby for roof; grand luxe rooms sleep five; kids stay free; there is a charge for rollaways. ✉*700 5th Ave., at 55th St., Midtown East* ☎*212/956–2888 or 800/262–9467* ⊕*www.peninsula.com* ⌖*185 rooms, 54 suites* ⌂*In-room: safe, refrigerator, dial-up, Wi-Fi. In-hotel: restaurant, room service, bars, pool, gym, spa, laundry service, concierge, parking (fee), some pets allowed, no-smoking rooms* ☰*AE, D, DC, MC, V* Ⓜ*E, V to 5th Ave.*

★ **Fodor'sChoice Ritz-Carlton New York, Central Park South.** A luxuri-
$$$$ ous retreat with stellar views of Central Park, the former St. Moritz is one of the top properties in the city. No request is too difficult for the superlative staff, one reason the hotel is a favorite of celebrities and royalty. Quietly elegant rooms and suites are sumptuous without feeling stuffy, with high-thread-count sheets and rich, plush fabrics throughout. Chef Laurent Tourondel's BLT Market features a monthly menu based on local purveyors. For getting around town in style, luxury car service is available upon request. The club levels features six food servings a day, including an hors d'oeuvres reception overlooking the park from the second floor Club Lounge. **Pros:** great concierge and personalized service, stellar location and views. **Cons:** pricey, limited common areas. **Family Matters:** Star Bar/lounge not family-friendly; pets are welcome; can accommodate kids' dining requests; afternoon tea; across from park and

carriage rides; maximum of 4 people per room; no charge for kids in room. ✉*50 Central Park S, at 6th Ave., Midtown West ☎212/308–9100 or 800/241–3333 🌐www.ritzcarlton.com ⇨259 rooms, 47 suites ♨In-room: safe, DVD (some), Ethernet, Wi-Fi. In-hotel: restaurant, room service, bar, gym, spa, laundry service, concierge, executive floor, no-smoking rooms, parking (fee), some pets allowed ▭AE, D, DC, MC, V Ⓜ F, V to 57th St.*

$ Roger Smith. Riotous murals fill this colorful boutique hotel. The art-filled rooms are homey and comfortable. Some have stocked bookshelves and fireplaces. Suites have kitchenettes and minibars. Bathrooms are small but do have tubs. An eclectic mix of room service is provided by five local restaurants. Guests have access to the nearby New York Sports Club ($10 fee). A complimentary Continental breakfast is included. **Pros:** good location; intimate atmosphere; free Wi-Fi. **Cons:** can hear street noise; small bathrooms. **Family Matters:** cool "artist-in-residence" lobby and bar; kids' bistro menu; suites with pantry and refrigerator; rollaways; cribs; kids under 14 stay free; Continental breakfast included. ✉*501 Lexington Ave., between E. 47th and E. 48th Sts., Midtown East ☎212/755–1400 or 800/445–0277 🌐www.rogersmith.com ⇨102 rooms, 28 suites ♨In-room: kitchen (some), refrigerator, dial-up, Wi-Fi. In-hotel: restaurant, room service, bar, laundry service, parking (fee), some pets allowed, no-smoking rooms ▭AE, D, DC, MC, V 🍽CP Ⓜ 6 to 51st St./Lexington Ave.; E, V to Lexington–3rd Aves./53rd St.*

★ Fodor'sChoice **The St. Regis.** World-class from head to toe, the **$$$$** St. Regis is a 5th Avenue beaux arts landmark that ranks near the top of any best-of list. Guest rooms feature the best technology in the city, including easy-to-use bedside consoles (developed by an in-house R&D team) that control lighting, audio, and climate; and huge flat-screen TVs that rise via remote control from the foot of your bed. Each floor is serviced by its own butler. Rooms have high ceilings, crystal chandeliers, silk wall coverings, and Louis XVI antiques. If you require the best, the St. Regis delivers. **Pros:** rooms combine true luxury with helpful technology; easy-access butler service; superb in-house dining; prestigious location. **Cons:** expensive; can feel too serious for families seeking fun. **Family Matters:** afternoon tea; kids restaurant menu; teddy bears dressed as butlers upon request; child-proofing amenities; concierge has lists of kids activities; kids stay free. ✉*2 E. 55th St., at 5th Ave., Midtown East*

☎212/753–4500 or 877/787–3447 ⊕www.stregis.com
➡164 rooms, 65 suites �In-room: safe, refrigerator, DVD,
Ethernet. In-hotel: restaurant, room service, gym, laundry
service, concierge, parking (fee), no-smoking rooms ▭AE,
D, DC, MC, V Ⓜ E, V to 5th Ave.

$$$$ W Times Square. Times Square turned hip when the W
opened there in 2002. This super-sleek 57-floor mono-
lith isn't shy about its presence, with a neon exterior and
an entrance that shoots you up a glass-enclosed elevator
through cascading water. You emerge onto the seventh-floor
lobby where Michael Kors–clad "welcome ambassadors"
await. The contemporary Jetsons experience continues in
the space-age, white-on-white lobby backed with a huge,
hot-pink wall. Rooms are sleek with multiple shades of
gray. The bi-level Blue Fin restaurant with its sushi bar
and floor-to-ceiling windows caps the architectural wonderment. **Pros:** bustling nightlife and happy-hour scene;
brash design. **Cons:** if you want quiet, head elsewhere.
Family Matters: more night-clubby than kid-friendly; kids'
menu; kids' packages contain fun stuff like Dylan's candy,
kids' camera, Paul Frank book, and ugly dolls; suites can
fit five; no rollaways; maximum of 4 people per room; no
charge for kids in room. ✉1567 Broadway, at W. 47th
St., Midtown West ☎212/930–7400 or 877/946–8357
⊕www.whotels.com ➡464 rooms, 43 suites �In-room:
safe, DVD, VCR, Ethernet. In-hotel: restaurant, room
service, bar, gym, spa, laundry service, concierge, public
Internet, public Wi-Fi, some pets allowed, no-smoking
rooms ▭AE, D, DC, MC, V Ⓜ1, 2, 3, 7, S, N, Q, R, W
to 42nd St./Times Sq.

★ Fodor'sChoice **Waldorf=Astoria.** The lobby of this landmark
$$$ 1931 art deco masterpiece, full of murals, mosaics, and
elaborate plaster ornamentation, features a grand piano
once owned by Cole Porter and still played daily. Astoria-
level rooms have the added advantages of great views, fax
machines, and access to the Astoria lounge, where a lovely,
free afternoon tea is served. The ultra-exclusive Waldorf
Towers (the 28th floor and above) has a separate entrance
and management. The Waldorf is famous for its überfa-
mous former residents including Brad Pitt and Angelina
Jolie. **Pros:** historic art-deco building filled with NYC's
aristocratic, gangster, and jazz histories; best Waldorf salad
in town; knowledgeable doormen; dreams of Brangelina
sighting. **Cons:** rooms not contemporary; very public lobby
includes loads of tourists. **Family Matters:** Saturday kids'

afternoon tea with storytellers, gift bags, and cookies to decorate (except in summer); near tourist sites; constant lobby and sidewalk traffic can be tricky to negotiate with little ones; fun star and politician sightings; classic grand lobby; some suites with kitchenettes; connecting doubles; kids under 18 stay free; rollaways and cribs depending on room type. ⊠*301 Park Ave., between E. 49th and E. 50th Sts., Midtown East* ☎*212/355–3000 or 800/925–3673* ⊕*www.waldorfastoria.com* ☜*1,176 rooms, 276 suites* ⚐*In-room: safe, Ethernet. In-hotel: 4 restaurants, room service, bars, gym, laundry service, concierge, executive floor, parking (fee), public Wi-Fi, public Internet, some pets allowed, no-smoking rooms* ▤*AE, D, DC, MC, V* Ⓜ *6 to 51st St./Lexington Ave.; E, V to Lexington–3rd Aves./53rd St.*

$ **Wellington Hotel.** This large, old-fashioned property's main advantages are reasonable prices and its proximity to Central Park and Carnegie Hall. From the lighted red awning outside to the chandeliers and ornate artwork inside, the lobby has an aura of faded glamour. The hotel appeals to families, groups, and those traveling on a budget. Rooms are small, baths are serviceable, and the staff is helpful. **Pros:** affordable, centrally located. **Cons:** clunky wood furniture; dated linens. **Family Matters:** maximum of 4 people per room; no charge for kids in room. ⊠*871 7th Ave., at W. 55th St., Midtown West* ☎*212/247–3900 or 800/652–1212* ⊕*www.wellingtonhotel.com* ☜*500 rooms, 100 suites* ⚐*In-room: Wi-Fi. In-hotel: restaurant, bar, laundry facilities, laundry service, public Internet, public Wi-Fi, parking (fee), no-smoking rooms* ▤*AE, D, DC, MC, V* Ⓜ*N, Q, R, W to 57th St.*

★ **Westin New York at Times Square.** The Westin changed the
$ skyline of Midtown with this soaring skyscraper that subtly mimics the flow of the city—look for subway patterns in the carpets and the city reflected on the building's exterior. A thoughtful staff helps make the cavernous lobby and throngs of guests tolerable. Exceptionally large rooms are blissfully quiet and built to give optimal views. Try especially for the light-filled corner rooms. Decor is sleek and amenities like flat-screen TVs are up to the latest standards. Bathrooms are stylish and have fun double showerheads. **Pros:** busy Times Square location; big and stylish rooms and baths. **Cons:** busy Times Square location; small bathroom sinks. **Family Matters:** Westin Kids Club packet on arrival with kids' room key and make-your-own postcard;

telephone to hear bedtime stories; coloring books; toys; puzzles; lots of families; kids menus; babysitting; suites can fit four or more; kids stay free. ✉*270 W. 43rd St., at 8th Ave., Midtown West* ☎*212/201–2700 or 866/837–4183* ⊕*www.westinny.com* ⟲*737 rooms, 126 suites* ♿*In-room: safe, refrigerator, Wi-Fi. In-hotel: restaurant, room service, bars, gym, spa, laundry service, concierge, public Internet, public Wi-Fi, parking (fee), some pets allowed, no-smoking rooms* ▭*AE, D, DC, MC, V* Ⓜ*A, C, E to 42nd St./Times Sq.*

UPTOWN

$ **Hotel Beacon.** The Upper West Side's best buy for the price is three blocks from Central Park and Lincoln Center, and footsteps from Zabar's gourmet bazaar. All of the generously sized rooms and suites include marble bathrooms, kitchenettes with coffeemakers, pots and pans, stoves, and microwaves. Closets are huge, and some of the bathrooms have Hollywood dressing room–style mirrors. High floors have views of Central Park, the Hudson River, or the Midtown skyline; the staff here is especially friendly and helpful. The Hotel Beacon makes a nice choice to explore a different corner of New York in a safe, exciting residential neighborhood. **Pros:** kitchenettes in all rooms; heart of UWS location; affordable. **Cons:** slightly outdated rooms. **Family Matters:** quiet neighborhood; cribs; rollaways; extra charge for more than four people per room; children under 12 stay free. ✉*2130 Broadway, at W. 75th St., Upper West Side* ☎*212/787–1100 or 800/572–4969* ⊕*www.beaconhotel.com* ⟲*120 rooms, 110 suites* ♿*In-room: safe, kitchen, refrigerator. In-hotel: laundry facilities, parking (fee), no-smoking rooms* ▭*AE, D, DC, MC, V* Ⓜ*1, 2, 3 to 72nd St.*

$$ **Hotel Wales.** Every effort has been made to retain the turn-of-the-20th-century mood of this 1901 Carnegie Hill landmark—from the cavernous lobby to the Pied Piper parlor, where vintage children's illustrations cover the walls. A complimentary European-style breakfast is served in the parlor; on a nice day head up to the rooftop terrace with your treats. Guest rooms are cozy if small, but they do have fine oak woodwork, and all are equipped with CD players. Most of the suites face Madison Avenue; unfortunately, soundproof windows are not de rigueur. The lovely Sarabeth's Restaurant, a local favorite for brunch, is in the hotel. **Pros:** on-site fitness facilities; good restaurant; charm-

ing decor. **Cons:** can be noisy; expensive Internet access; small rooms. **Family Matters:** kids' menu from Sarabeth's; playpens; kids' videos; suites with pullout sofa; residential area; near museums, Central Park, and playgrounds; continental breakfast included; kids stay free. ✉ *1295 Madison Ave., between E. 92nd and E. 93rd Sts., Upper East Side* ☎*212/876–6000 or 877/847–4444* ⊕*www.waleshotel.com* ⊷*46 rooms, 42 suites* ⊸*In-room: safe, kitchen (some), refrigerator (some), DVD (some), VCR (some), Wi-Fi. In-hotel: restaurant, room service, bar, gym, laundry service, concierge, parking (fee), some pets allowed, no-smoking rooms* ▭*AE, D, DC, MC, V* ◎*CP* Ⓜ *4, 5, 6 to 86th St.*

$$$–$$$$ **Loews Regency Hotel.** Regency-style furnishings, potted palms, and gold sconces line an understated lobby perfect for VIPs and heads-of-state. The modern guest rooms have silk wallpaper, velvet throw pillows, and polished Honduran mahogany, but the smallish bathrooms with their marble countertops are unspectacular. The Loews Regency accepts pets. **Pros:** friendly and helpful staff; relatively quiet; good for pets. **Cons:** tired appearance could use updating; overpriced room service; expensive. **Family Matters:** kids under 18 stay free; suites can sleep five with rollaway; connecting rooms; welcome gifts for kids 12 and under; "Fisher Price Little People" gift; cribs with Fisher Price baby gear; night lights; coloring books; Nintendo games; toys. ✉ *540 Park Ave., at E. 61st St., Midtown East 10021* ☎*212/759–4100 or 800/233-2356* ⊕*www.loewshotel.com* ⊷*266 rooms, 87 suites* ⊸*In-room: safe, kitchen (some), refrigerator, VCR, Internet. In-hotel: restaurant, room service, bar, gym, laundry service, concierge, parking (fee), some pets allowed, no-smoking rooms* ▭ *AE, D, DC, MC, V* Ⓜ*4, 5, 6, N, Q, R, W to 59th St./Lexington Ave.*

$ **The Lucerne.** The landmark facade of this exquisite building has more pizzazz than the predictable guest rooms. Health-conscious adults might like the gym on the top floor, with its city views, and children may be glued to the in-room Nintendo games. Service is the hotel's strong suit, and their popular Mediterranean restaurant Nice Matin is one of the better ones on the Upper West Side. The affluent residential neighborhood is filled with an impressive array of boutiques and gourmet food shops, and the American Museum of Natural History is a short walk away. **Pros:** free wireless; clean; close to Central Park. **Cons:** inconsistent room size; some report uncomfortable pillows. **Family Matters:** rollaways not available in doubles; suites good for larger families; lots of other families staying. ✉*201 W. 79th St., at Amsterdam Ave., Upper West Side* ☎*212/875–1000 or 800/492–8122* ⊕*www.thelucernehotel.com* ⤳*142 rooms, 42 suites* ✆*In-room: kitchen (some), refrigerator (some), Wi-Fi. In-hotel: restaurant, room service, bar, gym, laundry service, concierge, parking (fee), public Internet, public Wi-Fi, no-smoking rooms* ☐*AE, D, DC, MC, V* Ⓜ*1 to 79th St.*

$$$$ **Mandarin Oriental.** The Mandarin is the most exciting of the city's top-tier luxury hotels. Its cavernous lobby sizzles with energy on the 35th floor of the Time Warner Center. Here you'll find a wonderful lounge and the restaurant Asiate, from which to soak in the dramatic views above Columbus Circle and Central Park. On the higher floors, silk-encased throw pillows nearly cover plush beds, and the marble-ensconced bathrooms showcase Mandarin's mastery of luxury touches. That said, contrasted with the monumental frame created by floor-to-ceiling glass, and the view it presents, regular rooms feel small. Suites are really what set this hotel apart, by creating enough stage space to make the hotel's Asian-influenced decor, and the views, really kindle. The swimming pool has panoramic Hudson River vistas. **Pros:** a vibrant urban hotel; luxury all the way; fantastic pool with views; best spa in the city. **Cons:** Trump International Hotel blocks portion of park views; expensive; Time Warner Center can feel like a mall. **Family Matters:** connecting rooms for four or more; babysitting; pool; baby equipment; video games; toys; kids room service menu; welcome bags for kids; near Central Park and Lincoln Center; kids stay free. ✉*80 Columbus Circle, at 60th St., Midtown West* ☎*212/805–8800* ⊕*www.mandarinoriental. com* ⤳*203 rooms, 46 suite s* ✆*In-room: DVD, refrigerator, Ethernet. In-hotel: restaurant, room service, bar, pool, gym, spa, laundry service, concierge* ☐*AE, D, DC, MC, V* Ⓜ*A, B, C, D, 1 to 59th St./Columbus Circle.*

01.	American Museum at Natural History	*Night at the Museum* exteriors
02.	Metropolitan Museum of Art	Famous steps used in *Hitch*, Temple of Dendur used in *When Harry Met Sally*
03.	Bethesda Terrace's Angel Fountain, Central Park	*Stuart Little II*, *One Fine Day*, *Godspell*, many others
04.	The Mall, Central Park	*Big Daddy*, *Kramer vs. Kramer* and, of course, *Maid in Manhattan*
05.	Sheep Meadow, Central Park	*Wall Street*, *Fisher King*, and (extra credit) *Ants*
06.	55 Central Park West	aka "The *Ghostbusters*' building," aka "Spook Central"
07.	Revson Fountain, Lincoln Center	*Ghostbusters*, *Moonstruck*

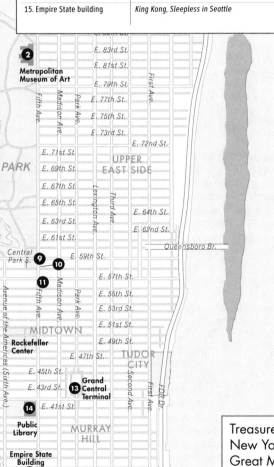

08.	Columbus Circle subway station	*Enchanted*
09.	The Plaza	*Home Alone* II, *Crocodile Dundee* I & II, other greats
10.	FAO Schwartz	Piano from *Big*, second floor. Take off your shoes, first
11.	Tiffany's	Famous exterior for a movie about breakfast; ask your parents
12.	Sardi's Restaurant	*Muppets Take Manhattan*; see Kermit's mug on the wall
13.	Grand Central Terminal	Has the clock Mellman wears on his head in *Madagascar*
14.	NY Public Library, Main branch	*Spider-Man, Day After Tomorrow* exteriors
15.	Empire State building	*King Kong, Sleepless in Seattle*

Treasure Map of New York City's Great Movie Close Ups

THE CLASSICS

"I'm thinking of an animal . . ."

With older kids you can play 20 Questions: Have your leader think of an animal, vegetable, or mineral (or, alternatively, a person, place, or thing) and let everybody else try to guess what it is. The correct guesser takes over as leader. If no one figures out the secret within 20 questions, the first person goes again. With younger children, limit the guessing to animals and don't put a ceiling on how many questions can be asked. With rivalrous siblings, just take turns being leader. Make the game's theme things you expect to see at your day's destination.

"I see something you don't see and it is blue."

Stuck for a way to get your youngsters to settle down in a museum? Sit them down on a bench in the middle of a room and play this vintage favorite. The leader gives just one clue—the color—and everybody guesses away.

FUN WITH THE ALPHABET

Family Ark

Noah had his ark—here's your chance to build your own. It's easy: Just start naming animals and work your way through the alphabet, from antelope to zebra.

"I'm going to the grocery . . ."

The first player begins, "I'm going to the grocery and I'm going to buy . . ." and finishes the sentence with the name of an object, found in grocery stores, that begins with the letter "A". The second player repeats what the first player has said, and adds the name of another item that starts with "B". The third player repeats everything that has been said so far and adds something that begins with "C" and so on through the alphabet. Anyone who skips or misremembers an item is out (or decide up front that you'll give hints to all who need 'em). You can modify the theme depending on where you're going that day, as "I'm going to X and I'm going to see . . ."

"I'm going to Asia on an ant to act up."

Working their way through the alphabet, players concoct silly sentences stating where they're going, how they're traveling, and what they'll do.

What I See, from A to Z

In this game, kids look for objects in alphabetical order—first something whose name begins with "A", next an item whose name begins with "B", and so on. If you're in the car, have children do their spotting through their own window. Whoever gets to Z first wins. Or have each child play to beat his own time. Try this one as you make your way through zoos and museums, too.

JUMP-START A CONVERSATION

What if . . .?

Riding in the car and waiting in a restaurant are great times to get to know your youngsters better. Begin with imaginative questions to prime the pump.

• If you were the tallest man on earth, what would your life be like? The shortest?

• If you had a magic carpet, where would you go? Why? What would you do there?

• If your parents gave you three wishes, what would they be?

• If you were elected president, what changes would you make?

• What animal would you like to be and what would your life be like?

• What's a friend? Who are your best friends? What do you like to do together?

• Describe a day in your life 10 years from now.

Druthers

How do your kids really feel about things? Just ask. "Would you rather eat worms or hamburgers? Hamburgers or candy?" Choose serious and silly topics—and have fun!

Faker, Faker

Reveal three facts about yourself. The catch: One of the facts is a fake. Have your kids ferret out the fiction. Take turns being the faker. Fakers who stump everyone win.

KEEP A STRAIGHT FACE

"Ha!"

Work your way around the car. First person says "Ha." Second person says "Ha, ha." Third person says "Ha" three times. And so on. Just try to keep a straight face. Or substitute "Here, kitty, kitty, kitty!"

Wiggle & Giggle

Give your kids a chance to stick out their tongues at you. Start by making a face, then have the next person imitate you and add a gesture of his own—snapping fingers, winking, clapping, sneezing, or the like. The next person mimics the first two and adds a third gesture, and so on.

Junior Opera

During a designated period of time, have your kids sing everything they want to say.

Igpay Atinlay

Proclaim the next 30 minutes Pig Latin time, and everybody has to talk in this fun code. To speak it, move the first consonant of every word to the end of the word and add "ay." "Pig" becomes "igpay," and "Latin" becomes "atinlay." To words that being with a vowel, just add "ay" as a suffix.

MORE GOOD TIMES

Build a Story

"Once upon a time there lived . . ." Finish the sentence and ask the rest of your family, one at a time, to add another sentence or two. Bring a tape recorder along to record the narrative—and you can enjoy your creation again and again.

Not the Goofy Game

Have one child name a category. (Some ideas: first names, last names, animals, countries, friends, feelings, foods, hot or cold things, clothing.) Then take turns naming things that fall into that category. You're out if you name something that doesn't belong in the category—or if you can't think of another item to name. When only one person remains, start again. Choose categories depending on where you're going or where you've been—historic topics if you've seen a historic sight, animal topics before or after the zoo, upside-down things if you've been to the circus, and so on. Make the game harder by choosing category items in A-B-C order.

Color of the Day

Choose a color at the beginning of your outing and have your kids be on the lookout for things that are that color, calling out what they've seen when they spot it. If you want to keep score, keep a running list or use a pen to mark points on your kids' hands for every item they spot.

Click

If Cam Jansen, the heroine of a popular series of early-reader books, says "Click" as she looks at something, she can remember every detail of what she sees, like a camera (that's how she got her nickname). Say "Click!" Then give each one of your kids a full minute to study a page of a magazine. After everyone has had a turn, go around the car naming items from the page. Players who can't name an item or who make a mistake are out.

The Quiet Game

Need a good giggle—or a moment of calm to figure out your route? The driver sets a time limit and everybody must be silent. The last person to make a sound wins.

Travel Smart
New York City
with Kids

WORD OF MOUTH

"If you are traveling with kids just make sure a parent goes through the [subway] turnstile first and last in case one of the metro cards doesn't work and one of you is stuck on the wrong side from the others."

—richbutnot

GETTING HERE & AROUND

▌ BY AIR

Generally, more international flights go in and out of Kennedy Airport, more domestic flights go in and out of LaGuardia Airport, and Newark Airport serves both domestic and international travelers.

Airlines & Airports Airline and Airport Links.com (⊕www.airlineandairportlinks.com) has links to many of the world's airlines and airports.

Airline Security Issues Transportation Security Administration (⊕www.tsa.gov) has answers for almost every question that might come up.

AIRPORTS

The major air gateways to New York City are LaGuardia Airport (LGA) and JFK International Airport (JFK) in the borough of Queens, and Newark Liberty International Airport (EWR) in New Jersey. Cab fares are generally higher to and from Newark. LaGuardia is closer to Manhattan and easier to navigate than JFK. The AirTrain link between Newark Airport and New Jersey Transit makes the journey in less than 15 minutes; then you must transfer to a NJ Transit train to Penn Station.

Airport Information JFK International Airport (☎718/244–4444 ⊕www.panynj.gov). **LaGuardia Airport** (☎718/533–3400 ⊕www.laguardiaairport.com). **Newark**

Liberty International Airport (☎973/961–6000 or 888/397–4636 ⊕www.newarkairport.com).

TRANSFERS—CAR SERVICES

Car services can be a great deal because the driver will often meet you on the concourse or in the baggage-claim area and help you with your luggage. The flat rates and tolls are often comparable to taxi fares, but some car services will charge for parking and waiting time at the airport. To eliminate these expenses, other car services require that you telephone their dispatcher when you land so they can send the next available car to pick you up. New York City Taxi and Limousine Commission rules require that all car services be licensed and pick up riders only by prior arrangement; if possible, call 24 hours in advance for reservations, or at least a half day before your flight's departure. This is a great boon for families carrying strollers and kid gear, as you can often request a minivan with more span than a traditional yellow taxi or a black Town Car. Drivers of nonlicensed vehicles ("gypsy cabs") often solicit fares outside the terminal in baggage-claim areas. Don't take them: even if you do have a safe ride you'll pay more than the going rate.

For phone numbers, see By Taxi.

TRANSFERS—TAXIS & SHUTTLES

Outside the baggage-claim area at each of New York's major airports are taxi stands where a uniformed dispatcher helps passengers find taxis *(⇨By Taxi)*. Cabs are not permitted to pick up fares anywhere else in the arrivals area, so if you want a taxi, take your place in line. Shuttle services generally pick up passengers from a designated spot along the curb.

New York Airport Service runs buses between JFK and LaGuardia airports, and buses from those airports to Grand Central Terminal, Port Authority Bus Terminal, Penn Station, Bryant Park, and hotels between 31st and 60th streets in Manhattan. Fares cost between $12 and $15. Buses operate from 6:15 AM to 11:10 PM from the airport; between 5 AM and 10 PM going to the airport.

SuperShuttle vans travel to and from Manhattan to JFK, LaGuardia, and Newark. These blue vans will stop at your home, office, or hotel. There are courtesy phones at the airports. For travel to the airport, the company recommends you make your requests 24 hours in advance. Fares range from $13 to $22 per person.

Shuttle Service New York Airport Service (☎718/875–8200 ⊕www. nyairportservice.com). **SuperShuttle** (☎212/258–3826 ⊕www.super-shuttle.com).

TRANSFERS FROM JFK INTERNATIONAL AIRPORT

Taxis charge a flat fee of $45 plus tolls (which may be as much as $6)

to Manhattan only, and take 35–60 minutes. Prices are roughly $20–$55 for trips to most other locations in New York City. You should also tip the driver.

AirTrain JFK links to the A subway line's Howard Beach station, and to Long Island Railroad's (LIRR) Jamaica Station, which is adjacent to the Sutphin Boulevard/Archer Avenue E/J/Z subway station, with connections to Manhattan. The light rail system runs 24 hours, leaving from the Howard Beach and the LIRR stations every 4–8 minutes during peak times and every 12 minutes during low traffic times. From Midtown Manhattan, the longest trip to JFK is via the A train, a trip of less than an hour that costs $2 in subway fare in addition to $5 for the AirTrain. The quickest trip is with the Long Island Railroad (about 30 minutes), for a total cost of about $12. When traveling to the Howard Beach station, be sure to take the A train marked FAR ROCKAWAY or ROCKAWAY PARK, not LEFFERTS BOULEVARD.

JFK Transfer Information AirTrain JFK (⊕www.airtrainjfk.com). **Long Island Railroad** (Jamaica Station ✉146 Archer Ave., at Sutphin Ave. ☎718/217–5477 ⊕www.mta.info/lirr).

TRANSFERS FROM LAGUARDIA AIRPORT

Taxis cost $21–$30 plus tip and tolls (which may be as high as $6) to most destinations in New York City, and take at least 20–40 minutes.

For $2 you can ride the M-60 public bus (there are no luggage facilities on this bus) to 116th Street and Broadway, across from Columbia University on Manhattan's Upper West Side. From there, you can transfer to the 1 train to Midtown. Alternatively, you can take Bus Q-48 to the Main Street subway station in Flushing, where you can transfer to the 7 train. Allow at least 90 minutes for the entire trip to Midtown.

TRANSFERS FROM NEWARK AIRPORT

Taxis to Manhattan cost $40–$65 plus tolls ($5) and take 20 to 45 minutes. "Share and Save" group rates are available for up to four passengers between 8 AM and midnight—make arrangements with the airport's taxi dispatcher. If you're heading to the airport from Manhattan, a $15 surcharge applies to the normal taxi rates and the $5 toll.

AirTrain Newark is an elevated light rail system that connects to New Jersey Transit and Amtrak trains at the Newark Liberty International Airport Station. Total travel time to Penn Station in Manhattan is approximately 20 minutes and costs $14. AirTrain runs every three minutes from 5 AM to midnight and every 15 minutes from midnight to 5 AM.

The AirTrain to Newark's Penn Station takes 5 minutes. From Newark Penn Station you can catch PATH trains, which run to Manhattan 24 hours a day. PATH trains run every 10 minutes on weekdays, every 15 to 30 minutes on weeknights and weekends. After stopping at Christopher Street, one line travels along 6th Avenue, making stops at West 9th Street, West 14th Street, West 23rd Street, and West 33rd Street. Other PATH trains connect Newark Penn Station with the World Trade Center site. PATH train fare is $1.50.

Coach USA with Olympia Trails buses leave for Grand Central Terminal and Penn Station in Manhattan about every 15 to 30 minutes until midnight. The trip takes roughly 45 minutes, and the fare is $14. Between the Port Authority or Grand Central Terminal and Newark, buses run every 20 to 30 minutes. The trip takes 55 to 65 minutes. Another route travels to downtown Manhattan. The fare is $13.

Newark Airport Information **AirTrain Newark** (☎888/397–4636 ⊕www.airtrainnewark.com). **Coach USA** (☎ 877/894–9155 ⊕www.coachusa.com). **PATH Trains** (☎800/234–7284 ⊕www.pathrail.com).

▌ BY BUS

Most long-haul and commuter bus lines feed into the Port Authority Bus Terminal, on 8th Avenue between West 40th and 42nd streets. You must purchase your ticket at a ticket counter, not from the bus driver, so give yourself enough time to wait in a line. Several bus lines, serving northern New Jersey and Rockland County, New York, make daily stops at the George Washington Bridge Bus Station from 5 AM to 1 AM. The station is connected to the 175th Street Station on the A line of the subway, which travels down the West Side of Manhattan.

Most city buses follow easy-to-understand routes along the Manhattan street grid. Routes go up or down the north–south avenues, or east and west on the major two-way crosstown streets: 96th, 86th, 79th, 72nd, 57th, 42nd, 34th, 23rd, and 14th. Usually bus routes operate 24 hours, but service is infrequent late at night. Traffic jams can make rides maddeningly slow, especially along 5th Avenue in Midtown and the Upper East Side. Certain bus routes provide "Limited-Stop Service" during weekday rush hours, which saves travel time by stopping only at major cross streets and transfer points. A sign posted at the front of the bus indicates it has limited service; ask the driver whether the bus stops near where you want to go before boarding.

To find a bus stop, look for a light-blue sign (green for a limited bus) on a green pole; bus numbers and routes are listed, with the stop's name underneath.

Bus fare is the same as subway fare: $2. Kids under 44 inches ride free. MetroCards *(⇨By Public Transportation)* allow you one free transfer between buses or from bus to subway; when using coins on the bus, you can ask the driver for a free transfer coupon, good for one change to an intersecting route. Legal transfer points are listed on the back of the slip. Transfers generally have time limits of two hours. You cannot use the transfer to enter the subway system.

Route maps and schedules are posted at many bus stops in Manhattan and at major stops throughout the other boroughs. Each of the five boroughs of New York has a separate bus map; they're available from some station booths, but rarely on buses. The best places to obtain them are the MTA booth in the Times Square Information Center, or the information kiosks in Grand Central Terminal and Penn Station.

Pay your bus fare when you board, with exact change in coins (no pennies, and no change is given) or with a MetroCard.

Buses in New York Metropolitan Transit Authority (MTA) Travel Information Line (☎718/330–1234, 718/330–4847 for non-English speakers ⊕www.mta.nyc.ny.us). **MTA Status information hotline** (☎718/243–7777), updated hourly.

Buses to New York Adirondack, Pine Hill & New York Trailways (☎800/225–6815 ⊕www.trailways.com). **Greyhound Lines Inc.** (☎800/231–2222 ⊕www.greyhound.com). **New Jersey Transit** (☎800/772–2222 ⊕www.njtransit.com). **Peter Pan Trailways** (☎413/781–2900 or 800/237–8747 ⊕www.peterpanbus.com). **Shortline** (☎800/631–8405 ⊕www.shortlinebus.com). **Vermont Transit** (☎800/552–8737 ⊕www.vermonttransit.com).

Bus Stations George Washington Bridge Bus Station (✉4211 Broadway, between 178th and 179th Sts., Washington Heights ☎800/221–9903 ⊕www.panynj.gov). **Port Authority Bus Termi-**

nal (✉625 8th Ave., at 42nd St., Midtown West ☏212/564–8484 ⊕www.panynj.gov).

▌ GETTING AROUND NEW YORK

BY BOAT

The Staten Island Ferry runs across New York Harbor between Whitehall Street next to Battery Park in Lower Manhattan and St. George terminal in Staten Island. The free 25-minute ride gives you a view of the financial district skyscrapers, the Statue of Liberty, and Ellis Island.

New York Water Taxi, in addition to serving commuters, shuttles tourists to the city's many waterfront attractions between the West and East sides and Lower Manhattan, the South Street Seaport, and Brooklyn's waterfront parks. The hop-on, hop-off one-day pass ticket is $20; the two-day pass is $25 (for adults). Both passes cost $15 for kids.

Information **New York Water Taxi** (NYWT ☏212/742–1969 ⊕ newyorkwatertaxi.com). **Staten Island Ferry** (⊕ nyc.gov).

BY CAR

If you plan to drive into Manhattan, try to avoid the morning and evening rush hours and lunch hour. Repairs to bridges to Manhattan as well as construction along 2nd Avenue on the Upper East Side will be ongoing for the next few years. Listen to traffic reports on the radio before you set off, and don't be surprised if a bridge is partially or entirely closed.

Driving within Manhattan can be a nightmare of gridlocked streets, obnoxious drivers and bicyclists, and seemingly suicidal jaywalkers. Narrow and one-way streets are common, particularly downtown, and can make driving even more difficult. The most congested streets of the city lie between 14th and 59th streets and 3rd and 8th avenues.

GASOLINE

Gas stations are few and far between in Manhattan. If you can, fill up at stations outside the city, where prices are anywhere from 10¢ to 50¢ cheaper per gallon. The average price of a gallon of regular unleaded gas is a whopping $4.50, at this writing. In Manhattan, you can refuel at stations along the West Side Highway and 11th Avenue south of West 57th Street and along East Houston Street. There are also a few stations on the East side in the 40s and 90s. Some gas stations in New York require you to pump your own gas; others provide attendants.

PARKING

Free parking is difficult to find in Midtown and on weekday evenings and weekends in other neighborhoods. All over town, parking lots charge exorbitant rates—as much as $23 for two hours (this includes an impressive sales tax of 18.625%). If you do drive, use your car sparingly in Manhattan. Instead, park it in a guarded parking garage for at least several hours; hourly rates decrease somewhat if a car is left for a significant amount of time. If you find a spot on the street, check parking signs carefully. Parking meters have varying limits and some streets employ a Muni-Meter system. Before leaving your car, scour the curb for that bane of every motorist's existence, the painted yellow line that's so faded you had better look twice to ascertain both its existence and range.

RULES OF THE ROAD

On city streets the speed limit is 30 MPH, unless otherwise posted. No right turns on red are allowed within city limits, unless otherwise posted. Be alert for one-way streets and "no left turn" intersections.

The law requires that front-seat passengers wear seat belts at all times. Children under 16 must wear seat belts in both the front and back seats. Always strap children under age four into approved child-safety seats.

There is a certain Zen about driving in the city—it's a nebulous and seamless mix of aggressiveness and passivity. Unless you're really comfortable about driving, it's best to leave that role to someone else. Manhattan drivers (particularly taxi drivers) are more aggressive than those in other cities, even if they aren't driving quickly.

BY LIMOUSINE

You can rent a chauffeur-driven car from one of many limousine services. Companies usually charge by the hour or a flat fee for sightseeing excursions.

Limousine Services Carey Limousines (☎212/599–1122 or 800/336–0646 ⊕www.carey.

com). **Concord Limousines, Inc.** (☎718/965–6100 ⊕www.concordlimo.com). **London Towncars** (☎212/988–9700 or 800/221–4009 ⊕ www.londontowncars.com).

BY PUBLIC TRANSPORTATION

When it comes to getting around New York, you have your pick of transportation in almost every neighborhood. The subway and bus networks are extensive, especially in Manhattan, although getting across town can take some extra maneuvering. If you're not pressed for time, take a public bus (⇨By Bus); they generally are slower than subways, but you can also see the city as you travel and it's easier to bring your fold-up stroller on-board. If you're on one of the city's giant flex buses, sitting in the middle (where the bus folds) is also amusing for kids. Yellow cabs (⇨By Taxi) are abundant, except during the evening rush hour, when many drivers' shifts change. Like a taxi ride, the subway (⇨By Subway) is a true New York City experience; it's also often the quickest way to get around. But New York is really a walking town, and depending on the time of day and your destination, hoofing it could be the easiest and most enjoyable option.

During weekday rush hours (from 7:30 AM to 9:30 AM and 4:30 PM to 7 PM) avoid the jammed Midtown area, both in the subways and on the streets—travel time on buses and taxis can easily double.

Subway and bus fares are $2, although reduced fares are available for senior citizens and people with disabilities during nonrush hours. Children under 44 inches tall ride free when traveling with an adult.

You pay for mass transit with a MetroCard, a plastic card with a magnetic strip. After you swipe the card through a subway turnstile or insert it in a bus's card reader, the cost of the fare is automatically deducted. If you're pushing a stroller, don't struggle through a subway turnstile; ask the station agent to buzz you through the gate (the attendant will ask you to swipe your MetroCard through the turnstile nearest the gate). With the MetroCard, you can transfer free from bus to subway, subway to bus, or bus to bus. You must start with the MetroCard and use it again within two hours to complete your trip.

MetroCards are sold at all subway stations and at some stores—look for an "Authorized Sales Agent" sign. The MTA sells two kinds of MetroCards: unlimited-ride and pay-per-ride. Seven-day unlimited-ride MetroCards ($25) allow bus and subway travel for a week. If you will ride more than 13 times, this is the card to get.

The one-day unlimited-ride Fun Pass ($7.50) is good from the day of purchase through 3 AM the following day. It's sold only by neighborhood MetroCard merchants and MetroCard vending machines at stations (not through the station agent).

When you purchase a pay-per-ride card worth $7 or more, you get a 15% bonus. Unlike unlimited-ride

cards, pay-per-ride MetroCards can be shared between riders. (Unlimited-ride MetroCards can be used only once at the same station or bus route in an 18-minute period.)

You can buy a new MetroCard valued from $4 to $80 or add money to an existing MetroCard at a MetroCard vending machine, available at most subway station entrances (usually near the station booth). The machines accept major credit cards and ATM or debit cards. Many also accept cash, but note that the maximum amount of change they will return is $6.

Keep a sharp eye on your young ones while on the subway. At some stations there is a gap between the train doors and the platform. Don't assume that you'll automatically get a seat if you're traveling with a child, but a beseeching look can sometimes land you a spot. Strollers are common on the subway and should be folded up on buses. If your child is still very small, it is easier to use a Snugli or other baby carrier.

Schedule & Route Information

Metropolitan Transit Authority (MTA) Travel Information Line (☎718/330–1234, 718/596–8585 travelers with disabilities ⊕www. mta.info).

BY SUBWAY

The 714-mi subway system operates 24 hours a day and serves nearly all the places you're likely to visit. It's cheaper than a cab, and during the workweek it's often faster than either taxis or buses. The trains are well lit and air-conditioned. Still, the New York subway is hardly problem-free. Many trains are crowded, the older ones are noisy, and platforms can be dingy and damp. Homeless people sometimes take refuge from the elements by riding the trains, and panhandlers head there for a captive audience. Hold on to your little ones' hands, as doors close quickly and crowds can be scary. With older kids, it's always best to have a plan should you find yourself separated from your family. In general, it's a good idea to get off at the next stop and look for a subway official for assistance. Cell phones don't generally work in the subways, so you'll need some walkie-talkie help. Although trains usually run frequently, especially during rush hours, you never know when some incident somewhere on the line may stall traffic. In addition, subway construction sometimes causes delays or limitation of service, especially on weekends.

Most subway entrances are at street corners and are marked by lamp-posts with an illuminated Metropolitan Transit Authority (MTA) logo or globe-shaped green or red lights—green means the station is open 24 hours and red means the station closes at night. Subway lines are designated by numbers and letters, such as the 3 line or the A line. Some lines run "express" and skip stops, and others are "locals" and make all stops. Each station entrance has a sign indicating the lines that run through the station. Some entrances are also marked "uptown only" or "downtown only." Before entering subway stations, read the signs carefully.

One of the most frequent mistakes visitors make is taking the train in the wrong direction. Maps of the full subway system are posted in every train car and on the subway platform in most stations. You can usually pick up free maps at station booths.

For the most up-to-date information on subway lines, call the MTA's Travel Information Center or visit its Web site. The Web site www.HopStop.com is a good source for figuring out the best line to take to reach your destination. (You can also call or text HopStop for directions.) Alternatively, ask a station agent.

Subway fare is the same as bus fare: $2. You can transfer between subway lines an unlimited number of times at any of the numerous stations where lines intersect. If you use a MetroCard (⇨ *By Public Transportation*) to pay your fare, you can also transfer to intersecting MTA bus routes for free. Such transfers generally have time limits of two hours.

Pay your subway fare at the turnstile, using a MetroCard bought at the station booth or from a vending machine.

There are very few elevators and you'll also have to contend with some escalators. If you have a stroller, don't be shy about asking someone to help you carry it (with your child strapped in) up or down the stairs. Practice your best escalator balancing prior to using the subways if possible.

Subway Information HopStop
(☎1-888-2-HOPSTOP ⊕www.hop
stop.com). **Metropolitan Transit
Authority (MTA) Travel Information Line** (☎718/330–1234,
718/330–4847 for non-English
speakers ⊕www.mta.info). **MTA Lost
Property Office** (☎212/712–4500).
MTA Status information hotline
(☎718/243–7777), updated hourly.

BY TAXI

Yellow cabs are in abundance
almost everywhere in Manhattan,
cruising the streets looking for
fares. They are usually easy to hail
on the street or from a cabstand in
front of major hotels, though finding one at rush hour in the morning or late afternoon, or in the rain
can take some time. Another tough
time to find a cab is 4–4:30 in the
afternoon when many cabbies go
off-duty. The rooftop light on the
sides of the taxi number will be
turned on and will say "Off Duty."
A good strategy at this time is to
try to find the ones coming into the
city via the 59th Street bridge, near
63rd Street on the East side.

Even if you're stuck in a downpour
or at the airport, do not accept a
ride from a "gypsy" cab. If a cab
is not yellow and does not have an
official Taxi and Limousine Commission numbered aqua-color plastic medallion riveted to the hood,
you could be putting yourself in
danger by getting into the car.

You can see if a taxi is available
by checking its rooftop light; if the
center panel is lighted and the side
panels are dark, the driver is ready
to take passengers. Once the meter
is engaged (and if it isn't, alert your

driver; you'll seldom benefit from
negotiating an off-the-record ride)
the fare is $2.50 just for entering
the vehicle and 40¢ for each unit
thereafter. A unit is defined as either
.2 mi when the cab's cruising at 6
MPH or faster or as 60 seconds when
the cab is either not moving or
moving at less than 12 MPH. A 50¢
night surcharge is added between
8 PM and 6 AM and a $1 weekday
surcharge is tacked on to rides after
4 PM and before 8 PM.

One taxi can hold a maximum
of four passengers (an additional
passenger under the age of seven
is allowed if the child sits on someone's lap). There is no charge for
extra passengers. You must pay any
bridge or tunnel tolls incurred during your trip (a driver will usually
pay the toll himself to keep moving quickly, but that amount will
be added to the fare when the ride
is over). Taxi drivers expect a 15%
to 20% tip. Most taxis now accept
credit cards and will give you a
printed receipt with tips and sur-
charges included.

To avoid unhappy taxi experiences, try to know where you want
to go and how to get there before
you hail a cab. You should assist
your driver, however, by direct-
ing him to the specific cross streets
of your destination (for instance,
"5th Avenue and 42nd Street"),
rather than the numerical address,
which means little to drivers. Also,
speak simply and clearly to make
sure the driver has heard you cor-
rectly. A quick call to your destination will give you cross-street
information, as will a glance at a
map marked with address num-

bers. When you leave the cab, remember to take your receipt. It includes the cab's medallion number, which can help you track the cabbie down in the event that you lose your possessions in the cab or, if after the fact, you want to report an unpleasant ride.

Taxis can be extremely difficult (if not impossible) to find in many parts of Harlem, Brooklyn, Queens, the Bronx, and Staten Island. As a result, you may have no choice but to call a car service. Always determine the fee beforehand when using a car service sedan; a 10%–15% tip is customary above that.

Note that taxis are exempt from car seat or seat belt requirement for your kids. If you do have a car seat, the driver is required to help you use it. Children seven and up may sit on your lap, and drivers do encourage the use of seat belts whenever possible. Driving in Manhattan can be more perilous than you might imagine, and being safe is always wise. If you feel a driver is going too fast, it is your right to ask him to slow down.

Car Services **Carmel Car Service** (☎212/666–6666 or 800/922–7635 ⊕www.carmelcarservice.com). **Dial 7 Car Service** (☎212/777–7777 or 800/222–9888 ⊕www.telavivlimo. com).

London Towncars (☎212/988–9700 or 800/221–4009 ⊕www.londontowncars.com).

BY TRAIN

Metro-North Commuter Railroad trains take passengers from Grand Central Terminal to points north of New York City, both in New York State and Connecticut. Amtrak trains from across the United States arrive at Penn Station. For trains from New York City to Long Island and New Jersey, take the Long Island Railroad and New Jersey Transit, respectively; both operate from Penn Station. The PATH trains offer service to Newark and Jersey City. All of these trains generally run on schedule, although occasional delays occur. Check the fares when you book or at the ticket windows; some offer free rides for kids under 5.

Information **Amtrak** (☎800/872–7245 ⊕www.amtrak. com). **Long Island Railroad** (☎718/217–5477 ⊕www.mta. info/lirr). **Metro-North Commuter Railroad** (☎212/532–4900 ⊕www. rnta.info/mnr). **New Jersey Transit** (☎800/772–2222 ⊕www.njtransit. com). **PATH** (☎800/234–7284 ⊕www.pathrail.com).

Train Stations **Grand Central Terminal** (✉Park Ave. and E. 42nd St., Midtown East ☎212/340–2210 ⊕www.grandcentralterminal.com). **Penn Station** (✉W. 31st to W. 33rd Sts., between 7th and 8th Aves., Midtown West ☎212/630–6401).

ESSENTIALS

■ USEFUL MAGAZINES, NEWSPAPERS & WEBSITES

ONLINE, PRINT & TV TRAVEL TOOLS

NYCvisit.com is the online site of NYC & Company, the official tourism organization of New York City, and is full of useful information about what's going on in the city. The "Visitors" section of NYC.gov, the official New York City Web site, also has useful information about events around town. If the local morning news channel you've tuned in to turns out to be exasperatingly uninformative, turn on the local all-news cable channel New York 1 (not available in all parts of the city) or log on to their news Web site, which is frequently updated with the city's breaking stories as well as mass transit and weather information. And if our sometimes enigmatic bus or subway maps are causing you to scratch your head too hard, pull up the HopStop Web site for directions. MommyPoppins.com is a well-written site from local moms about daily family-related activities. Two other useful tools are the online version of Big Apple Parent and goCityKids, both designed to give you ideas on how to make the most of your time with your kids.

For print listings of children's events, consult *New York* magazine or the Friday *New York Times* "Weekend" section. Other good sources on happenings for youngsters are the monthly magazines *New York Family* and *Big Apple Parent,* both available free at toy stores, children's museums, and other places where parents and children are found. On cable TV, New York 1 features a segment about noteworthy children's events.

All About New York City **Big Apple Parent** (⊕www.parentsknow. com).**Fodors.com** (⊕www. fodors.com). **goCityKids** (⊕www. gocitykids.com). **HopStop** (⊕www. hopstop.com). **Mommy Poppins** (⊕www.mommypoppins.com). **New York 1** (⊕www.ny1.com). **NYC & Company** (⊕ www.nycvisit.com). **Official New York City Web site** (⊕www.nyc.gov).

■ BABYSITTING

Concierges at most hotels have a list of child-care options for you to consider. Babysitters will come to your hotel room and entertain your little ones with games, toys, and TV. The Baby Sitters' Guild offers babysitters who speak a wide range of languages. Additionally, Barnard College has a full-time staff of trained student babysitters. There is a $20 registration fee for this service. New York City Explorers, while based in Brooklyn, will travel to Manhattan as well. Fees for any babysitter will depend on the number of children to be cared for.

Contacts **The Baby Sitters' Guild** (☎212/682/0227 ⊕www.babysit tersguild.com). **Barnard Babysit-**

ting Agency (☎212/854-2035 ⊕www.eclipse.barnard.columbia. edu/~bbsitter/). **New York City Explorers** (☎718/625/6923 ⊕www. nycityexplorers.com.

▌ PLAYSPACES

Indoor playspaces at Chelsea Piers, the Children's Museum of Manhattan, and the Children's Art Museum of Manhattan are great options for rainy day activities or simply for letting little ones let off steam. At A-ha!, kids ages 9 and under can play and burn off some energy for a $20 day session. Adults must accompany their children. Little Spirits offers a Kids' After Hours Club where kids can climb, play, and create while parents get a few hours to themselves. If you're in Brooklyn, New York City Explorers offers drop-off childcare where kids can enjoy a colorful playspace, have a snack, and create cool arts-and-crafts projects. Rates vary by age. There are plenty of other indoor amusement (or rainy day) options in a city as diverse as Manhattan. Additionally, creative outdoor playgrounds can be found in pretty much every neighborhood. Note that adults are not permitted at city playgrounds unless accompanied by a child. For older kids, interactive exhibits and arcades can be found at museums, at some restaurants, and in the Times Square area.

Contacts Chelsea Piers (☎212/336–6666 ⊕www.chelsea piers.com). **Children's Museum of the Arts** (☎212/941–9198 ⊕www.cmany.org). **A-Ha!** (☎ 212/517–8292 ⊕www.ahalearning.

com). **New York City Explorers** (☎718/625–6923 ⊕www.nycity explorers.com).

▌ RESTROOMS

Public restrooms in New York are few and far between. Plans are in the works to add coin-operated street toilets at several location (at this writing, the first toilet was operating in Madison Square Park with 20 more on the way). In the meantime, when looking for a clean restroom head for Midtown department stores, coffee shops, or the lobbies of large hotels. Public spaces or shopping concourses, such as those at the Citicorp Center, Trump Tower, the AOL Time Warner building and the concourse at Rockefeller Center also provide good public facilities, as do Bryant Park and the many Barnes & Noble bookstores and Starbucks coffee shops in the city. If you're in the area, the Times Square Information Center, on Broadway between 46th and 47th streets, can be a godsend. Riverside Park and Central Park also have public restrooms scattered throughout, many near play areas.

Find a Loo The Bathroom Diaries (⊕www.thebathroomdiaries.com) is flush with unsanitized info on restrooms the world over—each one located, reviewed, and rated.

NYRestroom.com (⊕www.nyrest room.com) will graphically show you the locations of both public and not-so-public restrooms throughout the city with a map and an accompanying address.

▌SPORTS & THE OUTDOORS

BASEBALL

The subway will get you directly to stadiums of both New York–area major-league teams. A fun alternative, the *Yankee Clipper* cruises from Manhattan's East Side and from New Jersey to Yankee Stadium on game nights. The round-trip cost is $22, $18 for kids under 12, and those under 3 are free. The regular baseball season runs from April through September.

The New York Mets play at the new Citi Stadium, at the next-to-last stop on the 7 train, in Queens; the New York Yankees play at Yankee Stadium, also brand new for the 2008–09 season. Founded in 2001, the minor-league Brooklyn Cyclones are named for Coney Island's famous wooden roller coaster. A feeder team for the New York Mets, they play 38 home games at KeySpan Park, next to the boardwalk, with views of the Atlantic over the right-field wall and views of historic Astroland over the left-field wall. Most people make a day of it, with time at the beach and amusement rides before an evening game. Tickets sell out quickly so try to reserve in advance. Take the D, F, or Q subway to the end of the line, and walk one block to the right of the original Nathan's Famous hot dog stand.

For another fun, family-oriented experience, check out the Staten Island Yankees, one of New York's minor-league teams, which warms up many future New York Yankees players. The stadium, a five-minute walk from the Staten Island Ferry terminal, has magnificent panoramic views of Lower Manhattan and the Statue of Liberty.

Contact Information Brooklyn Cyclones (✉1904 Surf Ave., at 19th St., Coney Island ☎718/449–8497 ⊕www.brooklyncyclones.com Ⓜ D, F, Q to Stillwell Ave.). **Citi Stadium** (✉Roosevelt Ave. off Grand Central Pkwy., Flushing ☎718/507–8499 ⊕www.mets.com Ⓜ 7 to Willets Pt./Shea Stadium). **Staten Island Yankees** (✉Richmond County Bank Ballpark at St. George, Staten Island ☎718/720–9265 ⊕www.siyanks.com). **Yankee Clipper** (☎800/533–3779 ⊕www.nywaterway.com). **Yankee Stadium** (✉161st St. and River Ave., Bronx ☎718/293–6000 Ⓜ B, D to 167th St.; 4 to 161st St.–Yankee Stadium).

BASKETBALL

The New York Knicks arouse intense hometown passions, which means tickets for home games at Madison Square Garden are hard to come by. The New Jersey Nets play at the Meadowlands in the Continental Airlines Arena but have plans to relocate and become the Brooklyn Nets. Tickets are generally easy to obtain. The men's basketball season runs from late October through April. The New York Liberty, a member of the Women's NBA, had its first season in 1997; some of the team's more high-profile players are already legendary. The season runs from Memorial Day weekend through August, with home games played at Madison Square Garden. These games are especially fun for kids with giveaways and fun entertainment.

If the professional games are sold out, try to attend a college game where New York stalwarts Fordham, Hofstra, and St. John's compete against national top 25 teams during invitational tournaments.

Contact Information Madison Square Garden (⊕www.thegarden.com). **New Jersey Nets** (☎201/935–3900 box office, 800/765–6387 ⊕www.nba.com/nets). **New York Knicks** (☎212/465–5867 ⊕www.nba.com/knicks). **New York Liberty** (☎877/962–2849 tickets, 212/564–9622 fan hotline ⊕www.wnba.com/liberty).

BICYCLING

Central Park has a 6-mi circular drive with a couple of decent climbs. It's closed to automobile traffic from 10 AM to 3 PM (except the southeast portion between 6th Avenue and East 72nd Street) and 7 PM to 10 PM on weekdays, and from 7 PM Friday to 6 AM Monday. On holidays it's closed to automobile traffic from 7 PM the night before until 6 AM the day after.

The bike lane along the Hudson River Park's esplanade parallels the waterfront from West 59th Street south to the esplanade of Battery Park City and is also busy with rollerbladers, pedestrians, and joggers. The lane also heads north, connecting with the bike path in Riverside Park, the promenade between West 72nd and West 110th streets, and continuing all the way to the George Washington Bridge with some minor street riding around

125th Street. From Battery Park it's a quick ride to the Wall Street area, which is deserted on weekends, and over to South Street and a bike lane along the East River, which, unfortunately, requires some street riding once you get to midtown.

The 3⅓-mi circular drive in Brooklyn's Prospect Park is closed to cars weekends year-round and from 9 AM to 5 PM and 7 PM to 10 PM weekdays. It has a long, gradual uphill that tops off near the Grand Army Plaza entrance. (Biking around Manhattan streets next to the dense traffic is best left to messengers and seasoned cyclists.) Bike rentals with kids' bikes, kids' helmets, tag-alongs for toddlers, and baby seats can be found at several locations in the city. Call to make sure they have the size bike and the types you need.

Bike Rentals Bicycle Rentals at Loeb Boathouse (✉Midpark near E. 74th St., Central Park ☎212/517–2233). **Pedal Pusher** (✉1306 2nd Ave., between E. 68th and E. 69th Sts., Upper East Side ☎212/288–5592 Ⓜ 6 to 68th St./Hunter College). **Bike & Roll** (✉12th Ave. at W. 43rd St., Downtown ☎212/260–0400 ⊕www.downtownny.com/bikearound).

GROUP BIKE RIDES

Time's Up is an environmental organization that also organizes bike-related tours and children's programs. For organized rides with other cyclists, call or e-mail Bike New York, the Five Borough Bicycle Club, or the New York Cycle Club for rides for every level of ability.

Contact Information Bike New York (✉891 Amsterdam Ave., at W. 103rd St., Upper West Side ☎212/932–2453 ⊕www.bikenewyork.org). **Five Borough Bicycle Club** (✉891 Amsterdam Ave., at W. 103rd St., Upper West Side ☎212/932–2300 Ext. 115 ⊕www.5bbc.org). **New York Cycle Club** (✉Box 4541, Grand Central Station, 10163 ☎212/828–5711 ⊕www.nycc.org). **Time's Up!** (☎212/802–8222 ⊕www.times-up.org).

BOATING & KAYAKING

Central Park has rowboats (plus one Venetian gondola) on the 18-acre Central Park Lake. Rent your rowboat at Loeb Boathouse, near East 74th Street, from March through October; gondola rides are available only in summer. Both are great activities for kids 10 and older. In summer at the Downtown Boathouse you can take a sturdy kayak out for a paddle for free on weekends and weekday evenings. Beginners learn to paddle in the calmer embayment area closest to shore until they feel ready to venture farther out into open water. More experienced kayakers can partake in the three-hour trips conducted every weekend and on holiday mornings. Sign-ups for these popular tours end at 8 AM. Due to high demand, names are entered into a lottery to see who gets to go out each morning. No reservations are taken in advance. **Manhattan Kayak Company** runs trips (these are not free) and gives lessons for all levels. Children under 16 require an adult to join them;

for teenagers 16–18, an adult can be in a separate boat.

Contact Information Downtown Boathouse (✉Pier 26, N. Moore St. and Hudson River, TriBeCa ☎646/613–0740 daily status, 646/613–0375 information ⊕www.downtownboathouse.org Ⓜ 1 to Franklin St. or A, C, E to Canal St. for Pier 26). **Loeb Boathouse** (✉Midpark near E. 74th St., Central Park ☎212/517–2233 ⊕www.centralparknyc.org). **Manhattan Kayak Company** (✉Chelsea Piers, Pier 63, W. 23rd St. and Hudson River, Chelsea ☎212/924–1788 ⊕www.manhattankayak.com ⓂC, E to 23rd St.).

FOOTBALL

The football season runs from September through December. The enormously popular New York Giants play at Giants Stadium in the Meadowlands Sports Complex. Most seats for Giants games are sold on a season-ticket basis— and there's a long waiting list for those. However, single tickets are occasionally available at the stadium box office. The New York Jets also play at Giants Stadium. Although Jets tickets are not as scarce as those for the Giants, most are snapped up by fans before the season opener.

Contact Information New York Giants (☎201/935–8222 for tickets ⊕www.giants.com). **New York Jets** (☎516/560–8200 for tickets, 516/560–8288 for fan club ⊕www.newyorkjets.com).

ICE-SKATING

The outdoor rink in Rockefeller Center, open from October through early April, is much smaller in real life than it appears on TV and in movies. It's also busy, so be prepared to wait—there are no advance ticket sales. Although it's beautiful, especially when Rock Center's enormous Christmas tree towers above it, you pay for the privilege: adult rates are $13.50–$17.50, kids under 12 are $12; skate rentals are $9.

The city's outdoor rinks, open from roughly November through March, all have their own character. Central Park's beautifully situated Wollman Rink offers skating until long after dark beneath the lights of the city. Be prepared for daytime crowds on weekends. The Lasker Rink, at the north end of Central Park, is smaller and usually less crowded than Wollman, with less expensive rates of $2.25 for kids. Prospect Park's Kate Wollman Rink charges a mere $3 for kids, borders the lake, and has a picture-postcard setting. Chelsea Piers' Sky Rink is more expensive, charging $10 for children, but has two year-round indoor rinks overlooking the Hudson. Rentals are available at all rinks. The Pond at Bryant Park offers free skating, not including the cost of skate rental, from late October through January, from 8 AM to 10 PM from Sunday through Thursday and from 8 AM to midnight Friday and Saturday.

Contact Information Bryant Park (⊠6th Ave. between 40th and 42nd Sts., Midtown West ☎866/221-5157 ⊕www.bryantpark.org Ⓜ B, D, F, V to 42nd St.). **Kate Wollman Rink** (⊠Ocean Ave. and Parkside Ave., Prospect Park, Brooklyn ☎718/287-6431 Ⓜ 2, 3 to Grand Army Plaza; B, Q to Prospect Park; F to 15th St./Prospect Park). **Lasker Rink** (⊠Midpark near E. 106th St., Central Park ☎917/492-3856 ⊕www.laskerskatingrink.com Ⓜ B, C to 103rd St.). **Rockefeller Center** (⊠50th St. at 5th Ave., lower plaza, Midtown West ☎212/332-7654 ⊕www.therinkatrockcenter.com Ⓜ B, D, F, V to 47th–50th Sts./Rockefeller Center; E, V to 5th Ave.–53rd St.). **Sky Rink** (⊠Pier 61, W. 23rd St. and Hudson River, Chelsea ☎212/336-6100 ⊕www.chelseapiers.com Ⓜ C, E to 23rd St.). **Wollman Rink** (⊠North of 6th Ave., between 62nd and 63rd Sts., north of park entrance ☎212/439-6900 ⊕www.wollmanskatingrink.com).

▌ STUDENTS IN NEW YORK

Wherever you go, especially museums, sightseeing attractions, and performances, identify you kid as a student up front and ask if a discount is available. However, be prepared to show ID as proof of enrollment and/or age.

A great program for those between the ages of 13 and 18 (or anyone in middle or high school) is High 5 for the Arts. Tickets to all sorts of performances are sold for $5 online, and also at Ticketmaster outlets in the city, including at music stores such as HMV. Tickets are either for a single teen (Friday and weekends), or for a teen and his or her guest of any age (Monday–Thursday). Write or call to receive a free catalog of events, check it out online, or pick a catalog up at any New York public library or at High 5's offices. These $5 tickets cannot be bought over the phone or at the venue box offices. With the $5 museum pass or film-screening pass, a teen can bring a guest of any age to participating museums and movie theaters.

IDs & Services **High 5 for the Arts** (⊠1 E. 53rd St., at 5th Ave., Midtown ☎212/445-8587 ⊕www.highfivetix. org). **STA Travel** (☎212/627-3111, 800/781-4040 24-hr service center ⊕www.sta.com). **Travel Cuts** (☎800/592-2887 in U.S. ⊕www. travelcuts.com).

▌ VISITOR INFORMATION

The Times Square Information Center on Broadway between 46th and 47th streets has a wealth of information, ticket and tour services, e-mail stations, and restrooms. It is also the present location of NYC & Company's main information facility.

The Grand Central Partnership has installed a number of information booths in and around Grand Central Terminal (there's one near Vanderbilt Avenue and East 42nd Street). They're loaded with maps and helpful brochures on attractions throughout the city and they're staffed by friendly, knowledgeable, multilingual New Yorkers.

Visit the NYC & Company storefront for brochures, subway and bus maps, discount coupons to theaters and attractions, and multilingual information counsel-

ors. In addition to its main center near Times Square on 7th Avenue between 52nd and 53rd streets, the bureau also runs kiosks in Lower Manhattan at City Hall Park and at Federal Hall National Memorial at 26 Wall Street, in Chinatown at the triangle where Canal, Walker, and Baxter streets meet and in Harlem at the Apollo Theater in Harlem at 253 West 125th Street. The Downtown Alliance has information on the area encompassing City Hall south to Battery Park, and from the East River to West Street. For a free booklet listing New York City attractions and tour packages, contact the New York State Division of Tourism.

Contacts **City Information** **Brooklyn Information & Culture Inc.** ([BRIC] ⊠647 Fulton St., 2nd fl., Brooklyn ☎718/855-7882 ⊕www.brooklynx.org). **Downtown Alliance** (⊠120 Broadway, Suite 3340, between Pine and Thames Sts., Lower Manhattan ☎212/566-6700 ⊕www.downtownny.com). **Grand Central Partnership** (☎212/883-2420 ⊕www. grandcentralpartnership.org). **NYC & Company** (⊠810 7th Ave., between W. 52nd and W. 53rd Sts., 3rd fl., Midtown West ☎212/484-1222 ⊕www.nycvisit.com). **Times Square Information Center** (⊠1560 Broadway, between 46th and 47th Sts., Midtown West ☎212/768-1560 ⊕www.timessquarenyc.org).

Statewide Information **New York State Division of Tourism** (☎518/474-4116 or 800/225-5697 ⊕www.iloveny.com).

INDEX

ABOUT OUR WRITER

To anyone who's ever questioned her desire to raise children in New York City, travel writer and restaurant reviewer Meryl Pearlstein unhesitatingly replies, "Are you kidding?" A Bostonian-turned-New Yorker, Meryl has taken her family to every corner of the city, carefully choosing the right activities for the right age (and the right gender). Meryl lives with her husband Jim and teenaged sons Evan and Elias—all three born in New York City—on the Upper East Side, an area perfect for introducing visitors to the city's arts and leisure scene. A restaurant reviewer for *Gayot.com* and travel columnist for *www.ClubMom.com,* Meryl has also written about New York for the *Boston Herald, Global Traveler Magazine,* and *New York* magazine.